David Brower

*The publisher gratefully acknowledges the generous support
of the General Endowment Fund of the
University of California Press Foundation.*

*The publisher gratefully acknowledges the generous
contribution to this book provided by the
David Brower Center.*

David Brower

THE MAKING OF
THE ENVIRONMENTAL MOVEMENT

Tom Turner

Foreword by Bill McKibben

UNIVERSITY OF CALIFORNIA PRESS

University of California Press, one of the most distinguished university presses in the United States, enriches lives around the world by advancing scholarship in the humanities, social sciences, and natural sciences. Its activities are supported by the UC Press Foundation and by philanthropic contributions from individuals and institutions. For more information, visit www.ucpress.edu.

University of California Press
Oakland, California

Library of Congress Cataloging-in-Publication Data

Turner, Tom, 1942– author.
  David Brower : the making of the environmental movement / Tom Turner ; foreword by Bill McKibben.
    pages cm
  Includes bibliographical references and index.
  ISBN 978-0-520-27836-3 (cloth : alk. paper)
  ISBN 978-0-520-96245-3 (ebook)
    1. Brower, David, 1912–2000.   2. Environmentalists—United States—Biography.   3. Conservationists—United States—Biography   4. Sierra Club—History.   I. McKibben, Bill, writer of supplemental textual content.   II. Title.
  QH31.B859T87   2015
  508.092—dc23

                                        2015007045

Manufactured in the United States of America

24   23   22   21   20   19   18   17   16   15
10   9   8   7   6   5   4   3   2   1

In keeping with a commitment to support environmentally responsible and sustainable printing practices, UC Press has printed this book on Natures Natural, a fiber that contains 30% post-consumer waste and meets the minimum requirements of ANSI/NISO Z39.48–1992 (R 1997) (*Permanence of Paper*).

For my granddaughter, Alice

CONTENTS

FOREWORD

David Brower, for all the reasons this fine book makes clear, was a very great man—along with his Sierra Club predecessor, John Muir, quite likely the most important conservationist in twentieth-century America. And that's because he figured out how to do the hardest thing for any movement leader: capture the attention of a large enough slice of the public to change the American zeitgeist and thus allow a new set of political possibilities.

Muir had invented a new grammar of wildness in his early trips to the Sierra, a brand of stunned sublime that was unlike anything that had come before and that infected people almost immediately—not most people, perhaps, but for the purposes of, say, protecting Yosemite, there were more than enough who could imagine climbing a pine tree in a storm. But there things lingered for more than half a century, with Muir's Sierra Club the perfect example: it never seemed to really get beyond its status as a hiking club for Westerners with some elite conservation work on the side.

Then came Dave Brower, one of those rare lifelong learners. He went from mountaineering ace to wilderness devotee to the heir of Rachel Carson's fears, and as the '60s progressed he managed to keep pace—he understood intuitively that Muir's homely ecological insight about everything in nature being hitched to everything else applied also to politics: that population and pesticides and nuclear bombs were linked with wilderness and species conservation. He'd been in Berkeley since his boyhood, of course, but he was open to the new meaning of "Berkeley" as the '60s wore on; he understood change and was comfortable with it. Excited by it.

Which most people in positions of power and influence are not. It's so sad to read about the lesser men who dominated the Sierra Club in those days, unable to understand that they had as their leader a truly remarkable visionary who was changing the world in front of their eyes. They were happier to stick with the old, and so they did, casting Brower out in what is arguably the worst management decision any nonprofit organization has ever made (and one that the club is only now recovering from, under the inspired leadership of Mike Brune). But if it cost the Sierra Club, it didn't derail Brower, who was fully freed to be John McPhee's archdruid, and to argue and push and prod and provoke and excite with everything he had. And so: Friends of the Earth and Earth Island Institute and a hundred grand battles. I remember seeing him, near the very end of his life, in an eighth-of-an-acre community garden on the Lower East Side of New York, fighting alongside the impoverished local residents to save their vegetable patch from encroaching development. It was a long way from Glen Canyon, and it wasn't.

I remember, too, a lovely week with Dave and Anne in Yosemite Valley. I was conducting a long interview with him for *Rolling Stone;* it was a pleasure for him to reminisce, pointing out all the routes he'd pioneered up the steep granite from the valley floor. But he never looked back for long; he used the occasion to instruct me about what needed to be done in the looming twenty-first century, that it had to be a time when *restoration* and *repair* became the watchwords. At the time I thought of myself solely as a writer, but as I've gone on to be a small-time organizer as well, his words have often echoed in my head.

And more than his words, his great, indomitable spirit. That thatch of hair, that broad smile, that bubbling stream of conversation. It drew you in. A truly great organizer is a person whom others want to be around, who lends energy to everyone he comes in contact with. That was Brower—I remember that he startled me by saying that as far as he could recall, he'd never spent a night outdoors alone, not in all those endless first ascents. He lived for connection, for contact, for gregarious exchange. And if he wore some people out (the Sierra Club board chief among them), he drew far more in to the great fight.

It was in his time that the real contours of that fight became clear. No single mountain range, not even the Range of Light, was terrain enough; the entire planet was at stake. Brower figured that out before almost anyone else. He was a friend of the earth indeed.

Bill McKibben, 2015

A Tense Meeting in the Mountains

It is a crisp, bright, clear Sierra Nevada morning, September 15, 1968. The Sierra Club's board of directors is having one of its quarterly meetings in the meadow behind Clair Tappaan Lodge in the mountains 170 miles or so east of San Francisco.

The air smells of pine, cedar, and fir. The lodge, whose floors creak and are scarred from thirty years of pounding by ski boots, is used mostly for winter skiing parties. The club maintains and operates its own modest ski run, Signal Hill—still served, at this time, by a rope tow—above and behind the lodge. It is a ramshackle affair—half a century later the club's website description uses the word *rustic* twice in one paragraph.[1] Visitors sleep in dorm-style rooms in their own sleeping bags and must do a chore—dishwashing, floor-sweeping, snow-shoveling—each day. Meals are served in a big dining room where diners eat at long tables, sit on benches, and serve themselves from bowls of salad; big, steaming trays of spaghetti; and other such communal fare.

The lodge sits about 7,000 feet above sea level, perched just above U.S. Highway 40, rerouted and rechristened a decade previously as Interstate 80, near Donner Summit. The summit is named for the Donner party, which got caught by blizzards on its way to California in 1846. For several months, about eighty men, women, and children were trapped just below the pass near what is now called Donner Lake. The party ran out of food, and after they ate their livestock, according to some survivors, they began to eat each other as people died of starvation.

The Sierra Club, a hundred twenty years later, is about to imitate the phenomenon.

The thirteen directors (two are absent) are sitting behind two long folding tables, set up in a splayed V shape. They are all men, all white, mostly of middle age.

The board president, Dr. Edgar Wayburn, sits at the apex of the V.

Sitting at the end of one of the tables is a tall, lanky, handsome, white-haired man in a plaid cotton shirt, reviewing the agenda. He is David Brower, fifty-six. He has been a member of the Sierra Club since 1933 and is its first—and so far only—executive director.

Brower has served on the club's rock climbing committee, its publications committee, and its outings committee, among others. He was editor of the *Sierra Club Bulletin* from 1946 to 1953. He has been chairman of the San Francisco Bay chapter. He led club outings for more than a decade. He served on the club's board of directors from 1941 to 1952, when he was named executive director. He is a familiar sight on Capitol Hill, where he has led campaigns to create parks, block dams, and win passage of the Wilderness Act of 1964.

He has designed, edited, written forewords to, and overseen publication and distribution of many books for the club, including the celebrated Exhibit Format series of oversize photo-and-text books (don't say "coffee table books" within earshot), most of which were published to assist one conservation campaign or another. He is a decorated combat war veteran, a celebrated mountaineer, a skilled filmmaker, and an accomplished photographer, and he virtually invented the use of newspaper advertising for conservation.

The club is on a roll. Its membership is growing smartly, with now approximately 77,000 members, up from about 7,000 when Brower took over sixteen years earlier. The club recently defeated plans to build two hydroelectric dams inside the Grand Canyon and led successful efforts to create new national parks in the redwoods in Northern California and the North Cascades in Washington State. Its short documentary on the redwoods has just won an Academy Award.[2]

Brower has been at the center of these efforts and many others and is undeniably the public face of the Sierra Club and the main reason for its fame. He is, simply, the best-known and most influential conservationist in the country.

On the downside, the Internal Revenue Service has just confirmed a provisional decree it had made two years before: it has found that the Sierra

Club violated agency rules by being too active legislatively, specifically with newspaper ads challenging the Grand Canyon dams. The result is that contributions to the Sierra Club will no longer be deductible by contributors for income tax purposes.

President Wayburn gavels the meeting to order.

Upward of one hundred members and staffers have gathered on folding chairs in the meadow or sit on the grass behind the lodge. Two or three microphones are set up on the tables for directors to use. The moment the gavel hits, director Richard Sill, a physics professor at the University of Nevada, leans into the mike closest to him and says: "The Executive Director, in spite of great energy and remarkable ability, is not an able administrator of money." Sill argues that Brower's "very energy is hazardous to the Sierra Club, in that he sees what he thinks should be done and acts rapidly, not infrequently involving the Club in unwise contracts, excessive financial burdens, and other actions which countervene [sic] Board policy or budgets." He pauses for effect, then continues: "This seems to be beyond his own self-control and beyond the control of the Board of Directors. With the greatest reluctance I therefore feel compelled to support the immediate dismissal of David R. Brower from employment by the Sierra Club."[3]

Directors Ansel Adams, the world-renowned photographer, and Richard Leonard, an attorney and onetime close friend and rock-climbing companion of Brower, quickly second the motion. Director Larry Moss, a nuclear engineer and supporter of Brower, then moves that the matter be tabled. Martin Litton, former travel editor of *Sunset* magazine, now operator of Grand Canyon Dories, seconds the motion, which passes on a vote of ten to three. Adams immediately tries again, saying, "Because of repeated financial and administrative irresponsibility, I move that David R. Brower be dismissed as Executive Director of the Sierra Club and as an employee, effective at the end of the fiscal year, December 31, 1968." This motion fails on a vote of ten to three. Brower has dodged a bullet, but Sill, Adams, and Leonard are not about to give up.

This is in part a generational matter. Ansel Adams has served on the board continuously since 1934, Dick Leonard since 1938. Brower's supporters on the board, several of whom he recruited to run for election in the first place, have served for five years or less. The old-timers, who now number somewhat fewer than half the total, are uneasy about Brower's bold, some would say scatter-shot, approach to his job. His supporters admire him for precisely the same reasons the detractors are nervous. Feelings run deep. The cannibalism will be only metaphorical but painful, dramatic, and decisive.

. . .

I was there that day, age twenty-six. David Brower had hired me the previous May to winnow a book from the writings of the legendary Sierra mountaineer Norman Clyde, a task to which I would bring enthusiasm but absolutely no training or experience. Upon completion of that project, I became Brower's administrative assistant. When Adams and Sill moved to fire Brower, I was stunned; I'd had no idea what was brewing, being a callow newcomer.

I had known Dave Brower slightly my whole life. His wife, Anne, and my mother, Beth Turner, had met and become friends on the University of California campus in the 1930s before either was married, and our families lived only a quarter mile from one another in the Berkeley hills starting in the late 1940s. My family had been on a few Sierra Club trips, and I was deeply in love with the mountains. When Dave asked me to come work for the Sierra Club, I didn't have to think twice. I worked with him at the Sierra Club and Friends of the Earth for the next eighteen years. I was in touch periodically over the following fourteen years, until his death in 2000.

So I knew him as a grown-up, a boss, and a colleague. He was a many-sided character, who attracted both fervent admirers and dedicated enemies. He was quick to admit his own shortcomings and to forgive hostilities. He tended to keep his eye on the big picture, sometimes at the expense of immediate and demanding details.

I decided to write his life for several reasons. First, to learn. He threw out stories of his early years now and again, but my knowledge was sketchy and I knew the whole story would be fascinating and instructive. I also sensed that, despite his fame, notoriety, and great influence during the years I saw him in action, his legacy as one of the world's greatest and most effective environmental activists seemed to be slipping to the margins of history. That was confirmed over the course of dozens of interviews for this project, and also by young college graduates in environmental studies or environmental law who, when I said I was working on a biography of David Brower, would say, "Hmm. David Brower. I've heard that name somewhere." To me, that was shocking and needed to be rectified.

So I set out to write a professional biography of David Brower, an attempt to examine his career as an environmental pioneer and leader. This is not meant to be a thorough personal biography, though many features of his personality show through.

Despite—in some ways because of—the conflicts that rose up around him, David Brower was a key figure in the evolution of the environmental movement or, as some would have it, the evolution of the conservation movement *into* the environmental movement. There's much to learn from his story, from his philosophy and his synthesis of various competing themes and concerns. Much to learn also from his mistakes.

Brower was a complicated man—charismatic, impatient with authority, some would say reckless, visionary (a word he probably wouldn't like), driven. Working for him was exhilarating, maddening, frustrating, and inspiring. I wouldn't have missed the opportunity for anything.

———

PART ONE

Climber

_____

ONE

From Berkeley to the Sierra

AN OUTDOORSMAN IS BORN

I'd like to send Moses back up the mountain. He brought back
the tablet with the Ten Commandments telling us how to treat
one another. But he never brought back down a thing that tells
us what to do about the earth.

In 1912, the year David Brower was born, the world was a vastly different
place, and nature still held dominion in most parts of California, including
his hometown of Berkeley. Back then, the town's population was just over
forty thousand. Today, it's more than 110,000.[1] During that same time, the
U.S. population grew from 92 million to something over 300 million.
California's population rose fastest: from 2.3 million to 37 million. Brower
often bemoaned this rapid population rise and argued that it must be slowed
and eventually reversed in order to avoid running out of air, water, and the
other necessities of life—and to leave some space for the other beings that
share the planet with us. "How dense can people be?" was one of his many
quips, this one later turned into a lapel button.

Berkeley stretches from Grizzly Peak and its ridgeline down to the shore
of San Francisco Bay, with the university campus at the base of the hills. The
house David grew up in and lived in until the age of thirty is a handful of
blocks from the university. Ross Brower, David's father, worked there for a
time as an instructor of mechanical drawing, and David would attend classes
there for a little more than a year.

In the earliest days, the Browers lived on Carleton Street in Berkeley.
There were three kids (with a fourth, Joe, to come along a few years later).
Edith, the only girl, was eldest. Ralph was two years younger. Then Dave,
three years younger than Ralph, then Joe, born in 1920, when Dave was eight.

_____

David Brower and goat, circa 1920, Berkeley. Photograph courtesy Brower family.

Ross Brower was born in Bath, Michigan, in 1879. He earned a degree in engineering from the University of California and a master's from the University of Michigan and then taught in a high school in Oakland and at the university in Berkeley. He was a strict Presbyterian, and alcohol was banned in the house. Dave's mother, Grace Barlow, was born in Two Rock Valley, near Petaluma, California, in 1882. She earned degrees in English from Berkeley and Stanford and was a devoted mother, but tragedy would knock her sideways by the time she delivered her last child. Grace and Ross met at the First Presbyterian Church in Berkeley and married in 1906, ages twenty-four and twenty-seven—late by the standards of the day.

When David was about four, after brief stays at two other Berkeley addresses, the family moved to 2232 Haste Street, a half-dozen blocks from the campus of the university. Ross's mother, Susan B. Brower, owned a house on the lot, and Ross had built a second one on it in 1904. The family lived in one of the buildings and rented out apartment space in that building and in the other as well, mainly to students. Monthly rents ran from twenty-five dollars for a single bedroom with kitchenette and bath down the hall to forty dollars for a two-bedroom unit with bath and kitchen.[2] Browers occupied the house until the 1960s, and it became an official Berkeley landmark in 2008.[3]

When the First World War erupted, David took credit for his father's being exempted from military service: "One of my first achievements was keeping my father out of combat. They called him in for various physical tests, which he passed, but they did not want to draft the father of three."[4]

When Joe came along, everything changed. Grace, who had mysteriously lost her sense of smell some years previously, abruptly went blind and lost the hearing in one ear as well. It was a crippling blow. She could no longer keep house or cook meals, and she began to have what the family referred to as fits. Much later, doctors surmised that she had had a brain tumor. To make matters worse, Ross soon was laid off from his job. He found a bit of part-time work here and there, but the family subsisted mainly on the income from the rental properties. And when they had vacancies, which, as Dave later wrote, was often, it was very difficult to make ends meet. Things would only get worse when the Depression hit eight or nine years later.

The kids all attended Berkeley public schools, first McKinley elementary (torn down in the 1960s), then Willard Junior High, then Berkeley High School, from which Dave graduated in December 1928. Traffic was light back then, and David and friends spent hours playing touch football (they called it "passball") in the streets.

DAMS, BUTTERFLIES, AND THE SIERRA NEVADA

Once the winter rainy season ended, and when they weren't in class or playing passball, Dave and Joe would spend hours building mud-and-stick dams across Strawberry Creek on the campus, then breaching them and watching the torrent race downstream. That ended in 1921 or '22, when a new football stadium was built where the Hayward earthquake fault intersected with Strawberry Creek. Dirt was sluiced away from the hillside using a technique that is now illegal. Some of the mud became the floor of the stadium. The rest gushed down the creek.

According to David, "It was no longer any fun to build a dam on it, or even possible. . . . It was a mess."[5] And, perhaps, the beginning of an environmental activist.

Although Mother Grace had lost her eyesight, she had not lost her love of walking. David would take long walks with her in the hills behind the campus, describing the landscape, the animals, birds, and butterflies they encountered, trying to help her enjoy the view based on her memory and his descriptions. There were no buildings up there then, and few roads. Much of the walking was cross-country, so David was his mother's guide dog as well as raconteur. He would later surmise that these walks had been the beginning of his ability to observe and to describe, which he would do with growing command and facility throughout his life.

In 1924 a family named Furer rented one of the units on Haste Street. They were avid butterfly collectors. Albert Furer and his younger brother, Fred, took young David on butterfly-collecting expeditions in the hills above Berkeley, and by the time winter came they had netted about thirty different species, "or at least we thought they were different,"[6] wrote Brower.

This began an interest in butterflies that continued for years. David would look for which plants various species of butterfly preferred to feed on, what preyed on them, and how they looked in flight. Eventually, he became so familiar with local butterfly varieties that he could identify them by flight patterns, even at a distance of several hundred yards.[7] Dave would later observe that this "kind of identification of living things [is] almost automatic in any people not so insulated from nature as city people ordinarily are."[8]

The pinnacle of his lepidopterist career came on April 16, 1928, when he found and netted a previously unknown "tip" or "sport" (a mutation) of the common checkerspot, which he sold to a collector in Pasadena for ten dollars. The collector then named the subspecies *anthotharsis sara Reakerti, transition form Broweri* (Gunder).

The butterflies also taught young Brower hard lessons. He was raising some western swallowtails from eggs he had harvested from a wild anise plant. The eggs became caterpillars; the caterpillars, after careful feeding, wove themselves into chrysalids and began the magical transformation into butterflies.

Eventually the chrysalids began to split open as the butterflies strove to make their way out into the world. The exertion pumps fluid from the abdomen into the wings, which unfold and prepare to get airborne. David decided to help. He carefully widened the split so the butterfly could emerge more easily. They came out all right, and crawled to convenient twigs, but the wings never unfurled, not having had the exertion of fighting out of the chrysalids to pump fluid into them. The butterflies ran around helplessly for a little while, then died. "Freeing them, I had denied them their freedom."[9] A lesson that would echo forever: it is a good idea to understand as much as possible about a situation before trying to help.

When David was six, his family took its first big trip into the Sierra Nevada, driving in their 1916 Maxwell. Ross had built an ingenious wooden box that attached to the running board of the car. It carried the camping gear and folded down to make a table for cooking and eating. The first day they got as far as Sacramento, the second to Colfax, still west of Donner Pass. They made camp and David went exploring and found a spring, "a wonderful thing to find." The next time they visited the spot a year or two later, the spring was gone, buried under debris from a clear-cut. "I was quite upset by that. I've never forgiven the Forest Service. And I don't intend to."[10]

On the third day they reached Donner Lake, and on the fourth the south end of Lake Tahoe. After dabbling in the waters of the lake, chasing squirrels and boulder hopping, the Brower clan headed for Yosemite. They drove down into the Owens Valley, whose thin water supply had not yet been appropriated by the Los Angeles Department of Water and Power, and turned west at the tiny enclave of Lee Vining (named for a nineteenth-century miner named Leroy Vining) on the shore of the mysterious Mono Lake. The road up to Tioga Pass from the east is steep, and Grace and the kids had to get out and push to get the heavy Maxwell over the top. From there they wound down through Tuolumne Meadows, and eventually down into Yosemite Valley itself.

Dave, who would ultimately make first ascents of many Sierra peaks and pioneer routes up Yosemite Valley walls, was a late bloomer as a mountain climber. Although he claims credit for the first ascent of the west face of Founder's Rock (a rock at the northeast corner of the Berkeley campus that towers a good dozen feet high) at the age of about five, he was unenthusiastic about hiking and climbing on his first trip to Yosemite, preferring to chase squirrels or stay in the car while the rest of the family climbed to Vernal Fall and other sites.

The lessons of the temporary destruction of Strawberry Creek in the Berkeley hills, the backfiring of good intentions in his informal study of butterflies, and the needless loss of a beloved spring would stick with Brower forever. The Berkeley experiences certainly were important, but Dave's brother Joe insists it was this Sierra trip and others that followed that started Dave on his life's journey—a crusade to protect and preserve nature, especially wilderness.[11]

UC BERKELEY VERSUS ECHO LAKE CAMP AND JOHN MUIR

After racing through grade school, junior high, and high school—Dave skipped three grades along the way[12]—he enrolled in January 1929 as a freshman at the University of California at Berkeley, where his parents and elder brother and sister had gone. He was seventeen. As a senior in high school, he said he "got quite a charge out of genetics. . . . I dug through library shelves to find out all I could about the evolutionary course of things."[13] With that and his love of butterflies, he expected to major in entomology and signed up for several science classes—pomology, botany, bacteriology, forestry, chemistry. He found them less than challenging, and with the urgent necessity to work to help the family pay the bills, he dropped out in his sophomore year.

He delivered the *Berkeley Daily Gazette* and telegrams for Western Union and worked as a clerk in the Bunte Brothers Candy Company and on an assembly line in the Merco-Nordstrom Valve Company.[14] But his first love by now was the Sierra Nevada, and he escaped there as often as he could, usually with one or two friends.

These were anything but comfortable trips: On one of them, Brower and two friends left Berkeley at 3:45 in the afternoon and reached Merced by

8:00 P.M. They stopped for pie and coffee and pressed on, stopping at Bear Flat for the night. "Fate had destined little sleep for that night, though," recalls Brower. His friend George slept in the backseat. Vernon and Dave, each more than six feet tall, made do in the front seat, sleeping "for 17 1/2 minutes all told." They listened for passing cars, heard all of four, and spent the rest of the time listening to frogs and "wondering why the moon didn't move a bit faster."[15]

In his diary, Dave admitted to a minor larceny the next day: "I herewith confess that I took a little sign off the trail [to Bridalveil Fall] for my room: 'Horses have the right of way. Avoid any act that will startle them.' It was weather stained and dirty, anyway." A few pages later, he wrote of a surprise: "Sunday dawned fairly fair. We found we had been sleeping next to the sewage disposal system, and decided that we would not breakfast there, but a little way down the river. . . . A dozen eggs, 2 quarts of chocolate, and a half pound of bacon furnished our meager breakfast."[16]

An important break came when Brower landed a job at a family camp run by the city of Berkeley at Echo Lake in the Sierra several miles west of and a thousand feet higher than Lake Tahoe. He did various chores around camp and, despite his inherent shyness, led campers on hikes into Desolation Valley and up surrounding peaks. He kept meticulous records of his climbs and hikes and wrote letters home, many on a typewriter; he kept carbons.

He wrote of a "gala hike," leaving camp in the dark of 3:00 A.M. with two friends and walking around Echo Lakes,[17] up the Tamarack Trail, and along the entire eastern side of Desolation Valley, where they headed east around Heather, Suzy, and Gilmore Lakes up to the summit of Mt. Tallac at 9,785 feet elevation. "I don't think I ever climbed the Tamarack trail under more beautiful conditions, and I have gone over it 53 times." They ascended three more peaks (Dick's, elevation 10,015 feet; Jack's, 9,910; and Pyramid, 10,020) before returning to camp, having logged forty-two miles.[18] His brother Joe says that David knew the elevation of every major peak in the Sierra and kept track of all his hikes and climbs.[19]

The following May, Brower got welcome news: he would be hired for another summer at Echo Lake Camp. In his second summer at the camp, Brower became acquainted with a camper who suggested that, since he so loved the mountains, he investigate the Sierra Club and consider joining it. As part of the investigation Brower visited the club's headquarters in San Francisco and began collecting and devouring back issues of the *Sierra Club Bulletin,* then published annually; it had been started in 1893, a year after the club's founding in 1892. He wouldn't get around to joining the club for another two years.

He also began reading the works of John Muir, the Scotsman who arrived in San Francisco in 1868 and wrote volumes about his travels in the Sierra, Alaska, and many other places. Muir's favorite spot was Yosemite Valley and surroundings, and he and the publisher of *Century Magazine,* Robert Underwood Johnson, for whom Muir frequently wrote articles, hatched the idea of expanding the Yosemite Reserve—the valley and the Mariposa Grove of giant redwoods set aside by Congress and President Lincoln in 1864—to include nearly a million acres, temporarily leaving responsibility for the valley and the Mariposa Grove to California. There was little resistance, and the park was created in 1890. Yosemite National Park was born.[20] This seemed to have caught some commercial interests by surprise, and shortly loggers, miners, and sheep-ranchers, who sought to whittle the park down by a considerable fraction, mounted an attack. To counter this assault, Muir and several friends and acquaintances from the Bay Area founded the Sierra Club to defend the new park. A major battle ensued, in which the Sierra Club largely prevailed. Minor boundary adjustments were made, and in 1906, the state conveyed the valley and the grove to the federal government.

One of Muir's better-known essays concerns his penchant for climbing high in tall trees during storms to enjoy the full power of the wind and rain.[21] Brower, during his first summer at Echo Lake Camp, decided to try this stunt himself, with somewhat disappointing results. "I was rather disillusioned in my tree-climb. . . . The most fun was had in talking about it afterwards. In the tree I found plenty of pitch and on the descent very prettily scratched my arm. However, if I find another easy tree I'll do it again."[22]

Brower worked at Echo Lake for three summers, 1930–32, and became thoroughly addicted to high country. He also became addicted to climbing mountains, but the technical climbs he would become well-known for would wait a while. Tallac, Dick's, Jack's, Pyramid, and the others require no ropes or pitons. But here was the thing: David Brower was scared of heights. Just as he would overcome his shyness by teaching himself to be comfortable speaking to audiences from one to ten thousand or more, he overcame his fear of heights by learning to climb mountains.[23] It was a character trait that led him to confront challenges head on.

In 1933 the shy boy from Berkeley turned twenty-one. He was still living at home (except for the years to come in Yosemite and frequent Sierra outings, he would live with his parents until he reached the age of thirty). Upon reaching his majority he was able to vote—he was a staunch Republican in those days and a harsh critic of President Roosevelt. He would remain a Republican for another decade and a half and then begin a rapid shift leftward. On turning twenty-one he also was now able to drink alcohol, as soon as Congress repealed Prohibition, which would happen on December 5 of that year.

LEARNING TO CLIMB

In the summer of 1933, Brower and George Rockwood, a friend from Berkeley, took a seven-week backpacking trip in the Sierra that would cement his love of the mountains and rock climbing, a trip that he would refer to frequently in subsequent years. He wrote of preparing food for the first leg of the journey: "Today I baked six cake tins of eggless, milkless and butterless cake, cornbread, or what have you, using with variation flour, cornmeal, cocoa, sugar, salt, baking powder, bacon grease, and dried fruit, assorted. It is all rather indigestible to the ear, I suppose, but we enjoy it." They also prepared "big batches of beans, cooked for five hours, flavored with salt, bacon, onions, and pepper, delectable. Oatmeal for breakfast, with raisins, cornbread, and coffee. Lunch dried fruit, bacon or cheese, and cornbread."

Then he and Rockwood set out to conquer some mountains. Brower very nearly didn't survive it. They camped at the first lake on the South Fork of Big Pine Creek and found all the peaks too formidable except for the Thumb. "I went up the couloir a short distance, then started swarming up its east wall. One block on the wall was just waiting for me. I grabbed the top of it with both hands, which didn't faze it, but when I put my knee against it and drew myself up, it came free."[24] He was just able to grab a narrow ledge above where the rock had been—"with two fingers"—and save himself from a seventy-five-foot fall.

Two nights later he and Rockwood happened to meet Norman Clyde at Glacier Lodge over dinner. Clyde was a legend, the first-ascender of more than one hundred Sierra peaks, generally on solo climbs. He listened to Brower's near-calamity and explained the theory of the three-point suspension: "in a tough place, you move only one limb at a time, first making sure that the other three are secure."[25]

Days later, near Evolution Basin, the two happened to meet Hervey Voge, a young mountaineer from the Bay Area, with whom they shared stories and information on trails and climbing routes and the like. Voge strongly suggested that Brower join the Sierra Club, which he had not yet done, and get some expert training in mountaineering and, in particular, rock climbing. At the conclusion of the trip Brower did just that, and threw himself into learning climbing techniques involving ropes and pitons and carabiners.

But this trip had one more fateful meeting. The next day, descending from Pilot Knob, they spotted "this bearded type, camera and tripod over his shoulder, coming up through the timberline forest. 'You must be Ansel Adams,' I said. He agreed. Neither of us knew who I was. The conversation was brief. I spoke of my admiration for his work. He complained of the early morning cumulous clouds; they were still too fuzzy to photograph." These two events—meeting Ansel Adams and joining the Sierra Club—would prove to be pivotal in the young man's life. Adams would become a close friend and would teach Brower much about photography—composition, darkroom techniques, and the like. The Sierra Club would become the center of Brower's life and the focus of his energies for the next thirty-five years.

But he originally joined the Sierra Club to learn rock climbing, which he would pursue with vigor in the Sierra and in Berkeley as well, where climbers would hone their skills and invent techniques to make the sport safer. In an undated bit of whimsy, Brower wrote of the climbing fraternity in Berkeley that "there was ample opportunity . . . to learn how to manage a rope at Cragmont Rock in Berkeley. Here one handles the rope properly, or he ventures into the luxurious poison oak that the city allows to grow in this public park."[26] He went on to point out that skills and balance learned climbing rocks would stand one in good stead throughout life, even if one didn't take up the sport seriously: "They would be sounder hill scramblers, safer fishermen, and would be less apt to enter into actuarial totals on household accidents—bathtub falls, misjudgment of handholds when climbing to a top shelf, or slips down the basement steps."[27] The joy of risk-taking, years later, would become an apt characterization of Brower's style in publishing books and running a long string of organizations.

The following summer, 1934, Brower and Voge backpacked for ten weeks in the Sierra, bagging more peaks and seeing very few other people. There were a few hardy mountaineers like Norman Clyde and occasional large parties—"High Trips"—organized by the Sierra Club, plus fishermen taken into the backcountry by packers, but it was possible to spend days on end seeing nobody but yourself and your companion.

. . .

These early backpacking trips clearly had great influence on the young Dave Brower in his growing reverence for wilderness and evolution, his budding skill as a mountaineer, and, a little later, his increasing concern for unwelcome intrusions into his beloved Sierra and appreciation for those who would defend the range. These forays and climbing excursions into the Sierra would also cement lifelong friendships—with Ansel Adams, Dick Leonard, and others—that would be severely tested later.

TWO

Yosemite

A new fact has recently become clear to me: It is not variety that
is the spice of life. Variety is the meat and potatoes. Risk is the
spice of life. Those who climb mountains or raft rivers understand this.

Dave Brower, who would become one of the celebrated mountaineers and
rock climbers of his day, first had to overcome severe acrophobia. He reports
being frightened of heights and of cliffs, even when he wasn't looking down
from one. When he was fourteen, he took the eleven-mile trail from Glacier
Point down to Yosemite Valley. "I was aware of this horrible cliff to one side.
Even though it was out of sight and some two hundred yards away, I felt
uncomfortable because there was so horrible a cliff so close."[1] He confronted
this fear, as he confronted his shyness, head-on. He forced himself to climb
mountains and sheer faces partly *because* he was afraid, and in so doing overcame the fear. Similarly, he forced himself to lead hikes at Echo Lake Camp
and to speak before groups on Yosemite buses and later on Sierra Club trips
partly because it was difficult.

As mentioned in chapter 1, Brower had been urged by Hervey Voge to join
the Sierra Club and take advantage of the expert training available through
the RCS   the Rock Climbing Section of the club's San Francisco Bay chapter. He did so, joining the club in 1933. Dick Leonard, who had invited
Brower into the club's RCS and would figure prominently in Brower's Sierra
Club career, sponsored his membership application. Back in the thirties,
forties, and fifties, the Sierra Club was a rather exclusive society, numbering
just a few thousand, and its leaders wanted to keep close control of who was
allowed to join. Until the 1950s the Sierra Club required applicants for
membership to present signatures of two club members who would vouch

David Brower with accordion and an unidentified companion, Sierra Nevada, late 1930s or early
1940s. Photograph by Cedric Wright, courtesy Brower family.

for them (in the thirties only one sponsor had been required), a far cry from today's membership solicitations sent to millions of anonymous people.

SIERRA CLUB CLIMBERS

The climbers—whose ranks were mostly but not exclusively male—were close friends, relying as they did on each other for safety, and they loved to conduct spirited debates about, for example, whether it is ethical to use pitons and expansion bolts to aid climbers or reserve them for situations requiring enhanced safety. Climbing was central to the lives of Brower and other young men such as Dick Leonard, Raffi Bedayan, John Dyer, and Bestor Robinson. It taught them about conquering fear, about safety, about watching out for each other, and about respect for mountains. They loved to face new challenges and to bag peaks.

One famous climb in 1939 would etch the Sierra Club men into the nation's pantheon. It was a successful attempt to reach the summit of Shiprock on the Navajo Reservation in New Mexico. Shiprock is an ancient volcanic neck, made up mostly of fairly rotten rock, which had defeated a dozen previous attempts. But Brower, along with Sierra Club colleagues Dyer, Robinson, and Bedayan, found a route that involved climbing a bit, then going down and traversing in search of climbable rock. They sank pitons and expansion bolts to tie ropes to, then retreated to the ground for dinner and the night. The climbers took turns leading, and after most of a week, they reached the summit. Brower's account of the climb was published in the *Saturday Evening Post*,[2] and Robinson wrote it up for the *Sierra Club Bulletin*.[3] In his later years, Brower regretted violating the mountain, which the Navajos consider sacred.

Brower was a natural—tall, skinny (six feet one and a half inches and 170 pounds in those days), with strong arms, hands, and legs, great balance, and a natural feeling for the rock. He and others in the RCS spent as much time as they could in Yosemite Valley exploring myriad routes up various cliffs and monoliths. As Brower wrote years later, "I found about thirty ways out of Yosemite Valley that were unusual—not the usual trails."[4]

In 1935 Brower was among those invited to join an elite group of climbers in an attempt on Mount Waddington in the Coast Range of British Columbia. The mountain had defeated previous attempts by several groups, and it posed a new challenge to the Yosemite-trained group of Sierra Clubbers: much of the climb was over ice and snow, therefore requiring not only ropes and pitons, but also ice axes and crampons. Brower wrote a long, exciting account of the three-week battle the party of eight waged against the mountain and, mostly, the weather.[5] In the end they conceded defeat, though the attempt left strong impressions on all the participants.

LANDING A JOB AT YOSEMITE

When the party returned from Canada, Brower found that his job at Bunte Brothers Candy Company was no longer his—the company had finally wearied of his frequent absences. But he soon landed a job with the Yosemite Park & Curry Company in Yosemite Valley, running an adding machine—a Moon Hopkins model similar to the one he had worked on at Bunte Brothers.[6] This was 1935, and it must have been a dream come true for the budding outdoorsman and climber.

His principal climbing companion was Morgan Harris, another Berkeley boy working in the valley. Whenever they could get time off, he and Brower would look around for an unclimbed challenge. When he wasn't looking for a rock to climb, Brower was looking for a piano to play. He reported on this quest in letters home, especially on his desire to play the piano in the Ahwahnee Hotel: "Still haven't been able to play the Steinway grand in the Ahwahnee, been restricted to four uprights and two lesser grands."[7]

The letters include wry reports of various adventures as Brower played with his writing. In a letter dated October 30, 1936, to Jack Tarr, a San Francisco friend, he wrote about an impromptu camping trip with Sterling and Helen Cramer and their young son, Stuart:

> Immediately upon your departure I resigned myself to a life of sorrow and remorse; wailing and gnashing of teeth. Platitudinous gyrations of rhetoric and allegory notwithstanding, a certain Mr. Sterling Cramer strode to my rescue. Little man, why are you crying. I'll hike with you. I'll even bring my wife. And Stuart will stand on his head for you.
>
> So I dried my eyes and we went up to Bridal Veil Creek by the notch between the two lowest Cathedral Rocks. Three fourths of the party used the rope extensively for direct aid. We ate, Helen and I discussed. Sterling fished. Stuart waded and stood on his head in the creek.[8]

The party then took a circuitous route up and around the higher Cathedral Rock, cross-country, and got caught by darkness.

The sun sinks slowly in the west it is dark what no flashlight what the hell. So we built a big fire, slept the night out, ate carefully rationed food remains, and were two hours late to work which was getting to be a habit. I was sick. Envisioned headlines: Noted Alpinist Lost in Dark. Love Tryst on Yosemite Walls Starts Probe. Fiend Lures Family to Mountain Hideout. Rangers Rescue Quartet. Handwriting on the wall. My reputation gone.

Fortunately there were not enough people in the Valley to tell the rangers they had seen a fire anywhere. The rangers were in bed anyway.

During his first winter in Yosemite, Brower came up with an idea that would seem preposterous today and was fortunately deemed preposterous soon after it was mooted: a funicular, or "téléphérique," to carry skiers from Mirror Lake in the valley to the summit of Mount Hoffman at 11,000 feet before a miles-long slide back down. Sierra Club directors considered the idea, and one of them, Bestor Robinson, a lawyer, climber, and good friend of Brower, said that, as long as the machinery was not visible from the valley, the club might go along. Brower credits a man named Arthur Blake, an active Sierra Clubber, with talking him out of the idea, which died a quiet death. His sophisticated conservation conscience clearly had a ways to go.

AND THEN PUBLICITY MANAGER

After a year running the adding machine and doing other administrative duties, in May 1936 Brower was promoted to publicity manager on a trial basis. He was twenty-three. "Yosemite still seems as nice as ever," he wrote to his parents. "There were times when it was not too enjoyable as seen thru the barred window of the Accounting Dept., but the Publicity Dept. window is a floor higher, just across the hall from the President's office, and Yosemite Falls are in full view."[9] His main job was to photograph visitors, especially celebrities, and provide the photographs to hometown papers with pithy stories about what a wonderful time the visitors had had in Yosemite, hoping to attract more business.

Yosemite was then attracting just short of a half-million visitors a year; in comparison, the number for 2012 was just a hair under four million and had been higher.[10] Back in the thirties, visitors could hike, climb, play golf, and catch fish in the summer, and ski and ice-skate in the winter. During the summers from 1872 to 1968, a big fire was built on the lip of Glacier Point, three thousand feet above the valley floor, and pushed over the lip at

9:00 P.M. sharp, the fire fall resembling a glowing waterfall. The fire fall was eventually discontinued and the golf course removed, both being deemed inappropriate to a national park.

At this time, Ansel Adams was a consulting photographer for the YP&CC. Brower had met Adams on his long 1933 backpacking trip and had admired his images in the *Sierra Club Bulletin* starting a year or two earlier. In addition to other duties, Brower put together pamphlets and brochures for the company, and he used Adams photographs in many of them. This required poring endlessly over Adams prints, and he began to understand how the master worked.

They became fast friends and took endless trips around the valley and into the high country, Adams to make photographs, Brower to observe and learn. Dave found himself spending many an hour on many a day in Adams's dark-room, watching him print and listening to his advice. He absorbed Ansel's ideas about the purpose of national parks and how they were an American invention. And "what stone, space, and sky were doing for us, and simple growing things."[11] Brower learned from Adams what was behind and within a photograph, "and what could happen when words and photographs worked their magic together."[12] Here we see the harbinger of the oversize word-and-picture books that Adams and Brower, along with Nancy Newhall, would create and Brower would refine and perfect over three decades.

Brower also ran and wrote a newsletter for visitors, with gossip and announcements and news bits of various sorts, some light and breezy, some more serious. "Resplendent in a shining new coat of silver armor—or as cynics would have it, aluminum paint—the Queen Mary is back at Badger Pass again." The Queen Mary was an "upski." By means of a rope or cable that went around a pulley attached to a tree or rock at the top of a slope, this metal-bottomed rowboat-like vessel hauled skiers up the slope.[13] Continuous rope tows would be invented a few years later.

Another sample of news with a humorous slant is this: "Returning Tuesday evening from a fishing trip at Merced Lake, Gabe Goldsworthy and Bill Hubbard report mild weather and good fishing, the smallest trout taken being 10 inches. Three more days and the trout are safe until spring."[14]

On the more serious side were articles such as the one reporting a visit by Dr. François Matthes, senior geologist at the U.S. Geological Survey: "Dr. Matthes has behind him a record of brilliant geological achievement, and is greatly responsible for the modern conception of Yosemite's prehistoric past. At the time he took up the Yosemite problem there were thirteen conflicting theories concerning the origin of the Valley. His is the only theory that has survived."[15]

In addition to occasional parties, where he would play the piano and sing, Brower was introduced to alcohol during this time, all liquor having been verboten in his Berkeley home. In a letter on YP&CC stationery dated August 21, 1935, Dave told his parents, "After 21 years of complete abstinence I have chosen moderation as a more enjoyable course." He wrote that he preferred tokay to gin and that at a few parties he had accepted "a rather heavily ginned cocktail but set it on the first convenient mantle." He claimed he had yet to become even slightly drunk and had promised himself to get drunk sometime just to see what would happen, but might wait until he reached the age of seventy.[16] He didn't. Brower overcame his distaste for gin, probably after the war. In his years at the Sierra Club and Friends of the Earth he was famous for two-martini lunches: "Tanqueray martini, straight up, with no distractions." No olive or onion.

Despite all the joys of climbing and hiking in and around the valley, homesickness weighed heavy. "It's a blank old stairway up to this communal room. Four walls and a roof. There's a letter now and then, and it cheers, but how little does ink and paper convey!" But, he hastened to add, "I am not sick of this place. I never could be."[17]

For the most part, these years in Yosemite were idyllic. At the beginning of one September there was an unusual trip down through the Grand Canyon of the Tuolumne River and the Muir Gorge, a trek that took sixteen hours, "down into a canyon in many respects grander than Yosemite itself." At one place in the Muir Gorge, he reported that the steep canyon walls plunged unbroken into the stream, and for three hours he and his companions devoted themselves to the task of negotiating their way through the river, often having to swim.

They then made their way back to the car on the road far above, paying special attention to plants and wildlife: "We watched the flowers hastily going to seed, preparing for the inevitable winter, and doing likewise were the little Chickarees—prettiest of all the Squirrel family, as they scampered about with acorn-filled cheeks, burying the treasure in every likely place." But squirrels are famous for forgetting where they bury acorns and other seeds. Brower called them "unpaid employees of the C.C.C., aiding the reforestation program."[18]

He then wrote a flowery appreciation of the canyon wren, "perhaps the prettiest of the Sierra, an apt student of chromatics." And, as the squirrels prepare for winter, so do bears. "The bears are getting ravenous, and even wander up here around the dorms and cabins to upset garbage cans, not being content with the quantities of garbage they get at the pits."

Back to acorns briefly: "It is interesting to observe how many creatures derive sustenance from the acorns, of which there are probably tons. A partial list: Bears, deer, two kinds of squirrels, woodpeckers, flickers, jays, (17 birds altogether, I'm told) and Indians. Oh yes. We have our Indians. Got to have 'em to show the tourists. Don't forget this is way out West."[19] This use of Indians as tourist attractions would no doubt have made Brower wince later in life.

Laced through his letters home are constant references to money and his worries over his family's well-being back in Berkeley. On August 21, 1935, he wrote, "I hope you have gotten rid of some of those vacancies since the last letter.... P.O. money order for $15.00 enc." And on October 29 he wrote, "Still in regard to finance, I should like to send more, oftener; but the cost of living is high.... Will continue to do what I can."[20] And the following January this, to his mother: "Your last letter is justifiably impatient for an answering letter and for a promised remittance. I have now paid Dad, which makes a fairly good hole in today's check. Next time I'll pay you, Mother."[21] His mother, incidentally, continued writing letters to young David even though she was blind. They are in longhand and all but impossible to decipher, but Dave kept them as he kept everything—and no doubt appreciated them a great deal.

The job as publicity manager ended after the 1937 season. The following year Brower was hired by the concessionaire's transportation department to ride around the valley in tour buses, describing the scene to visitors through a megaphone, which, he reported, helped him lose his diffidence about speaking before crowds of strangers and served him well a few years later in the army and in his conservation career.

. . .

Through it all, he continued scaling sheer walls and bagging peaks, eventually amassing more than seventy first ascents in the Sierra Nevada and elsewhere. The importance of mountaineering in the evolution of David Brower is difficult to overstate. He came to love taking risks—it made the rewards of success that much sweeter, and he usually succeeded. It also made him willing to take risks in publishing and other organizational activities later in life. His success rate there was not as high as his success rate in climbing, but his approach to both was more "Is it worth trying?" than "Am I likely to succeed?"

THREE

Into the Sierra Club

Don't expect politicians, even the good ones, to do your job for
you. Politicians are like weather vanes. Our job is to make the
wind blow.

After finally leaving his on-again, off-again jobs with the Yosemite Park &
Curry Company, Brower returned to his parents' house on Haste Street in
Berkeley in 1937 and began to get seriously involved with the Sierra Club. By
this time, not only was Brower an active member of the Rock Climbing
Section, but he also served on the editorial committee for the *Sierra Club
Bulletin*. His relationship with the *Bulletin* had started much earlier, how-
ever: he had submitted an article almost immediately upon joining the Sierra
Club in September 1933. It was an account of the backpacking trip he'd taken
the previous summer with his friend George Rockwood.

The editor of the *Bulletin* was Francis Farquhar, an accountant by profession and an active Sierra Clubber, mountaineer, and Sierra historian.[1] The
submission, praised but not published, resulted in an invitation to the
Farquhar house in San Francisco with Dick Leonard and a few others to get
acquainted and to look over proofs of the forthcoming *Starr's Guide to the
John Muir Trail*,[2] which the Sierra Club was preparing for publication under
the direction of Farquhar.

FROM VOLUNTEER TO PART-TIME EMPLOYEE

Undeterred, Brower tried again, submitting another article in 1935, in which
he recounted the ten-week trip he had taken into the Sierra with friend and
fellow Sierra Club member Hervey Voge. This resulted in his first Sierra Club

David Brower dozing on a coil of rope on a minaret near Yosemite, 1937. Photograph by Morgan
Harris, courtesy Brower family.

publication, "Far from the Madding Mules," which was heavily edited and greatly improved by Farquhar. This, in turn, resulted in an invitation to serve on the *Bulletin*'s editorial board, which he did, starting in 1935.

The next two years he spent mostly in Yosemite, and his contributions to the *Bulletin* were modest—a book review here, a news snippet there.[3] But after he returned to the Bay Area, he took on more and more work, as a volunteer, for the *Bulletin*, becoming associate editor in 1940.

In the course of his *Bulletin* activities, Brower learned much about photography and photographic reproduction from Farquhar and, particularly, from Ansel Adams, whose tutelage had begun in Yosemite. He also learned about writing, editing, and typography from Farquhar. The combination of fine photography, fine type, and elegant prose would become his hallmark and a major reason for the growth in his stature and that of the Sierra Club in later years.

But Brower's ambitions reached beyond the pages of the *Bulletin*, and the club's directors, impressed by his energy, intelligence, and commitment to the club's ideals, also had their sights set on giving him more responsibility. As early as 1937 several club directors, including Dick Leonard and Ansel Adams, had suggested hiring him full-time as executive director or executive secretary. In Brower's papers there is a handwritten note outlining his qualifications. He considers that he has sufficient experience to handle correspondence, keep the books, organize the library, and produce agendas for various meetings. He also has "an interest in mountains," making him "fundamentally useful in representing them." He professes an interest in the Sierra Club's ideals, which, at the time, were largely focused on preservation of the Sierra Nevada and providing members ways to enjoy and help protect the range. He also mentions his experience with promotional activities, publicity, motion pictures, and writing—gained during his years in Yosemite. The note concludes, a little ego showing through: "My importance will increase as the Club's increases. Contacts, prestige will increase in proportion to the time and effort applied."[4] The idea of a full-time executive director foundered, however, partly because there was concern that having a professional staff might discourage volunteers from committing as much time to club affairs as they were then doing.

In 1938, the San Francisco Bay chapter of the club began to publish a newsletter called the *Yodeler* ("All the News that Won't Fit . . . in the *Sierra Club Bulletin*"). Brower was its first editor. By 1941 he had been elected to the board of the club and to the chair of the Bay chapter, both volunteer positions.

In 1938 Brower was hired half-time, for seventy-five dollars per month, to write a new member handbook for the Sierra Club. The club paid for half his time, but he worked full-time and then some on club projects. Brower would later write in his memoir, *For Earth's Sake*, "Whatever else I was supposed to do in the Sierra Club office there was a battle going on and I concentrated on it. It was the campaign to establish Kings Canyon National Park."[5]

THE KINGS CANYON CAMPAIGN

In the early part of the century, the Sierra Club had fought—and lost—a major battle to block construction of a dam in Hetch Hetchy Valley in Yosemite National Park. For the next two decades, the club's conservation activities had taken a backseat to its outings. The effort to establish Kings Canyon National Park marked the beginning of the Sierra Club's reemergence as a conservation power, and it was also the first flowering of David Brower's conservation conscience and his emergence as an activist. It sparked early efforts to turn what he had learned in Yosemite to the conservation cause.

Back in 1890, Congress had created Yosemite and Sequoia National Parks, but much vital land had been left out of Sequoia. That park had been expanded in 1926, but still the high country around Mount Whitney and the major, Yosemite-class valleys of the Kings River—Tehipite Valley and Cedar Grove—had been omitted. The federal Forest Service had always been loath to turn over land to the National Park Service, and it was interested in the two valleys as possible future reservoir sites. The agency likely had its eye on some merchantable timber there as well.

The pro-park partisans found a major champion in Harold L. Ickes, President Franklin D. Roosevelt's secretary of the interior. Ickes fought valiantly for the park, doing battle with chambers of commerce, local water districts, and the Forest Service on the one hand and cajoling skeptical conservation groups, including the Sierra Club, on the other. One proposal was to name the new creation John Muir National Park.

To get a handle on the situation, Ickes sent Irving Brant, a trusted lieutenant recently involved in the creation of the Olympic National Park in Washington State, into the Kings Canyon high country with Joel Hildebrand, then the president of the Sierra Club. Brant wrote the secretary to report that one could draw boundaries almost anywhere and encompass "a park of superb beauty." The political problem, he said, was double: the tussle between the Park Service and the Forest Service and the contest between the conservationists and the irrigationists over the two valleys.[6]

As T. H. Watkins writes in his splendid biography of Ickes, "Brant also returned convinced that the active support of the Sierra Club was going to be necessary for the success of any kind of legislation affecting its native state of California." So Ickes went to California and hauled the directors of the Sierra Club to the Bohemian Club in San Francisco for dinner. After a simple meal, Ickes spoke for an hour, insisting that the department was passionately in favor of a wilderness national park. Hildebrand responded with a letter to Ickes: "The whole thing was a grand triumph, on both sides."[7]

Many squabbles ensued, however, with more hearings and speeches and the stripping of John Muir's name from the proposed national park, but finally a compromise was struck. The bill presented to Congress in the late 1930s to create Kings Canyon National Park still omitted Tehipite and Cedar Grove. The Sierra Club supported the bill since it did include the high country, reasoning that it would be prudent to seize what was then on offer and come back for the rest later. The young Wilderness Society, created in 1935, and the National Parks Association, created in 1919, opposed the bill because of these omissions, but it passed anyway in March 1940; the two valleys were added to the park in 1965. No reservoirs had been built, no trees logged.

Part of the backstory over the creation of the new park, as Brant suggested, had been the reluctance of the Forest Service to relinquish land for national parks. Its spokespeople had argued that the land might be needed later for development or, in the case of exquisite wilderness, that the agency would protect it as what it called a primitive area.

Brower, as a matter of policy, generally sided with the Park Service in this and many struggles to come. The whole purpose of the Park Service, he argued, was to preserve wilderness. The National Park Act, which created the agency in 1915, declared this as its primary purpose and suggested that the only development that should be undertaken or allowed was that which was necessary to permit areas to be enjoyed forever as wilderness.

But Brower had criticism for the Park Service as well, pointing out that it read its founding law as a dilemma, saying that wilderness preservation and providing public access were at odds. He said in an oral history interview conducted in 1974, "They misread the act and still do, so there's still need to do battle."[8] The extent to which the Park Service emphasized wilderness as it considered a new park at Kings Canyon shaped that battle.

Brower had neglected his obligation to update the club's member handbook in order to devote himself to the Kings Canyon campaign. It was his first political campaign in a career that would see him engaged in little else for the next sixty years. He also used his position on the *Bulletin*'s editorial board to increase the number of articles devoted to conservation, although still keeping plenty of coverage of outings and scientific discoveries and observations. No doubt increasing the frequency of the publication was in the back of his mind, but that would wait until after the war.

HIGH TRIPS STAFFER

Earning only seventy-five dollars a month, Brower was still badly in need of money, so he joined the staff of the Sierra Club's High Trip, large outings into the Sierra backcountry then led by Dick Leonard. In the summer of 1938, he was assistant cook, pot-washer, and occasional climbing guide. By 1939 Brower was assistant leader, and in 1940 he became a full-fledged trip leader, a position he would continue to fill (with time out for the war) until 1956. He once calculated that he had led about four thousand campers over a million person-miles on seventeen High Trips.

It was around High Trip campfires that Brower began to discover his voice. He would explain the importance of wilderness and encourage his listeners to become active in its defense. His eldest son, Ken, wrote decades later, "At High Sierra campfires, as I watched the circle of fire-reddened faces listening raptly to the Sermon [a moniker Dave Brower would use later to describe his stump speech], I realized that this was not just your normal father; that he had a gift, that there was something very large in him."[9]

The High Trips in 1938 and '39 were taken into the Kings Canyon high country with the dual purpose of providing enjoyment for the club members who attended and showing them the country and recruiting them to fight for its preservation, the purpose of the High Trip since club secretary William Colby organized the first one in 1901.

Brower and George Rockwood had happened on a Sierra Club High Trip in 1933 and were rather put off, as small groups of backpackers often were. The High Trip would take two hundred or more people into the high country for two or four weeks, moving the camp about every third day. Great strings of mules would carry literally tons of food and tents and sleeping bags and heavy iron cookstoves from place to place. Guests would carry their cameras and lunches and binoculars and jackets and ponchos and fishing gear between camps and on day hikes and climbs. Hikers like Brower and Rockwood who came upon High Trip encampments would be invited to dinner and given the reasons the club would take such large parties into the backcountry.

High Trip camps were anywhere from three to eighteen miles apart, but generally six to eight. There was, in fact, some uncertainty about distances. Some people thought Brower underestimated distances and coined the expression "Brower miles," the idea being that when Brower announced that the next day's hike would cover six miles, one should prepare for eight or ten. Phil Berry, who worked on and later led many High Trips—and served on the Sierra Club board, on and off, for decades—said that Brower insisted his estimates were accurate and that he had a pedometer to prove it.[10]

Brower became a staunch supporter of the High Trip idea for a couple of reasons. He was coming to understand that the bigger a wilderness is, the better. But big wilderness is prone to being carved up for roads, dams, and timber extraction and is difficult to defend, so it needs many defenders. A wilderness able to accommodate a party of over two hundred campers who move camp every two or three days must be a big wilderness. As Brower observed in a *Bulletin* account of the 1939 High Trip, once camp is broken and the hikers hit the trail, it is quite easy for two hundred people to all but vanish in a big wilderness: "The High Trip was the best source of the conservation warrior."[11]

Conversely, missed opportunities could be costly. The failure to use the High Trip to its best advantage prompted this observation from Brower: "We lost [the chance to create a national park in the Oregon Cascades] because we didn't run a High Trip operation there. . . . We settled for trying to save little pieces and now have barely saved those. We needed the string for those beads. We lost it, and so lost the beads."[12]

The High Trips ended in 1972, when club leaders decided that they were simply too big and caused too much impact on meadows and streams. Brower didn't agree and continued to push for their resumption. He argued that the High Trip used wood that small parties were not equipped to handle. Also, there were enough experienced leaders and followers to keep the impact low, to cover tracks, even to cover spoor and keep it away from streams. Pack stock impact, he conceded, had been heavy, but careful studies of high meadow ecology and meticulous management had controlled and reduced the impact. High Trip participants were indeed welded into an effective force for protecting big wilderness.[13] In addition,

Brower had started Sierra Club–sponsored knapsack trips in 1938 (we'd call them backpacking trips today). He had also instituted club river trips in the early 1950s.

On the two Kings Canyon High Trips, Brower brought along a 16mm Bell & Howell movie camera and shot remarkably skilled moving pictures of the Kings high country and people enjoying it. After the 1939 trip ended, he edited the footage down to an hour-long silent movie that he carted all around California to sing the praises of, and drum up public support for, a new national park in the watershed of the Kings River. He showed it to 125 audiences, including one in the Longworth House Office Building in Washington, DC. Brower would introduce the film from the front of the audience, then withdraw to the projector "and sell Kings Canyon National Park for the next hour."[14] It was called *Sky-Land Trails of the Kings* and may have been the first conservation propaganda film ever made. It would not be Brower's last. From then on, he was rarely seen in the backcountry without a moving-picture camera of some sort, taking film that would later be turned to a conservation purpose.[15]

. . .

As his conservation conscience grew, Brower began to push the Sierra Club to get more active. He urged that the frequency and the size of the *Bulletin* be increased. He served on countless committees, often as chairman: outings, mountain records, rock climbing, visual education, publications, winter camping, and others. He would not become executive director for a decade, but already the Sierra Club was his life, his second family. In recognition of his contributions, he was elected to the board of directors in the spring of 1941, as war bore down on the country.

FOUR

Love and War

Long-range education is fine, but to say that long-range education will do the job is a little like telling a front-line soldier that
he doesn't need a rifle or artillery or an air umbrella, but should
rely instead on the League of Nations.

As war heated up in Europe in 1939 and '40 and it seemed likely that the
United States might eventually get involved, some climbers and skiers—
members of the National Ski Patrol, the Appalachian Mountain Club, and
the Sierra Club—thought they would offer their services to the military for
possible combat in the mountains of Europe or Japan. To that end, David
Brower and about twenty experienced skiers made a trip into Little Lakes
Valley (10,500-foot elevation) on the east side of the Sierra Nevada to test
equipment. This was in April 1941. Peter Shelton describes the expedition in
his wonderful history of the Tenth Mountain Division: "They carried with
them every piece of mountain gear they believed might work for the Army,
all of it from civilian suppliers," including skis from Northland and Anderson
& Thompson, boots by the Bass Company and L. L. Bean, sleeping bags and
tents from Abercrombie & Fitch, winter clothing from Montgomery Ward
and Marshall Field. They tested gasoline stoves and different ski waxes as well
as snowshoes, repair kits, rucksacks, packboards, pitons, snap rings, climbing
ropes, knit caps, knives, sunscreens, mess kits, mittens, goggles, gaiters, wool
pants, poplin pants, poplin parkas, and caribou-hide parkas.[1]

Bestor Robinson, a Sierra Club director, was on the trip to Little Lakes
Valley, and he shortly enlisted in the army and was sent to the office of the
quartermaster general in Washington armed with the results of the winter
testing by members of the Sierra Club and the other organizations.
Meanwhile, Charles Minot ("Minnie") Dole, founder and president of the

Anne and David Brower soon after their wedding, Claremont Hotel, Berkeley, 1943. Photograph
courtesy Brower family.

National Ski Patrol System, was engaged in a furious campaign to persuade the army, particularly General George C. Marshall, to establish a specialized mountain division within the army to train soldiers to fight in snowy, mountainous country. As Shelton put it, "The United States had no troops trained and equipped for either vertical landscapes or cold weather. Our most recent conflicts abroad had been in Cuba and the Philippines, and almost all of our training facilities were in the Deep South, Hawaii, and Panama. The U.S. Army, small and underequipped as it was, was a tropical army."[2] Nevertheless, the army resisted for months, but finally it decided to create what became the Tenth Mountain Division.

On October 30, 1941, the secretary of war formally announced activation of an infantry mountain regiment, at Fort Lewis, Washington, which would be transferred to a permanent station to be announced later. This was the first unit ever set up in the U.S. Army for the specific purpose of conducting winter and mountain warfare training.[3]

Shortly thereafter, a bulletin appeared from Minnie Dole:

IMPORTANT NOTICE
U.S. ARMY FORMS WINTER AND MOUNTAIN WARFARE TRAINING UNIT

The bulletin contained a description of the planned service and a questionnaire asking how the volunteer wished to apply—local draft board, recruiting office, or transfer for those already serving. Letters of recommendation required. And it wanted to know if the applicant was married or single, with or without dependents, native born, and what sort of skiing and mountaineering experience he had. (Clearly, women need not apply.)

David Brower hastened to apply. Although he was single and without dependents, he'd recently become smitten with the woman who would become his wife two years later.

UC PRESS AND ANNE

Six months before Minnie Dole's bulletin, Brower had landed a new job. It happened that Francis Farquhar's brother, Sam, was the manager of the University of California Press in Berkeley, and when an editorial assistant position opened up in the spring of 1941, Francis urged Brower to apply for it. Brower got the job in May 1941.

He was assigned to an office outside that of the press's editor, Harold Small, whom Brower credits with much of his advanced editorial education. The office he was assigned to was not private, however. There was another editor already working there, a young Piedmont native named Anne Hus, a student at the university, who had been working at the press for four years.

Their son Ken described his parents' meeting:

> My parents met in 1941 as editors at the University of California Press. To my mother's annoyance, the press manager assigned my father a desk in her small office. The new hire—a *mountain climber*, tall, unpolished—irritated her not just by his personality and his invasion of her space, but by his salary. . . . My mother had seniority, yet from his first day my father . . . drew a paycheck nearly equal to hers. In time she relented. Their conversations grew warmer. My father could make her laugh, if he avoided puns—not an easy thing for him.[4]

After their somewhat frosty start (Anne said and Dave concurred that he was a little full of himself at the outset), they became friends, though a thirtieth birthday lunch at Spenger's Fish Grotto and sherry at Anne's parents' house in Piedmont would be their only social engagements before Dave joined the army.

THE CAMPAIGN TO JOIN THE ARMY

But first he had to get in. One of his letters of recommendation came from Joel Hildebrand, a noted mountaineer, onetime Sierra Club president active in the Kings Canyon effort, and professor at the University of California. He pointed out that Brower was a mountaineer "of unusual ability and experience" and that he was a director of the Sierra Club, a leader of the High Trips, and editor of *The Manual of Ski Mountaineering*. "He is a man of fine character and vast energy. He would be a brilliant addition to the ski troops."[5]

Dave Brower was by then in the highest ranks of climbers and ski mountaineers in the country. But there was a problem. With no college degree, bad teeth, and having nearly reached the age of thirty, he would not find it easy to be accepted into officer candidate school (OCS) without pulling a string or two. Bestor Robinson and Dick Leonard, climbing pals who were with the quartermaster general in Washington, did much of the pulling, and Brower helped his cause with heartfelt and persuasive letters to army brass. One dated May 27, 1942, was typical: He wrote that his "extraordinary technical training" should be of special use "to compete with enemy mountain troops" and urged that the new American troops be taught the fundamentals of rock climbing "this summer and fall" and the fundamentals of ski mountaineering beginning with "the first snow of next winter, sooner if possible."[6] Brower then went on to enumerate his qualifications: he was one of only five first-class ski mountaineers in the country as measured by the National Ski Association, and he claimed to have trained more ski mountaineers than anyone else in California the previous winter. He also pointed out that he had edited and contributed to the only book on the subject of ski mountaineering.[7]

Eschewing unnecessary modesty, he wrote in another letter, "The extraordinary technical training volunteered is unique because mountaineering has not matured in this country. Experts are rare. The General Staff, realizing the military importance of mountaineering, is expanding the mountain divisions. It is urgent that experts be put to full use if we are to compete on even basis with enemy mountain forces. German, Italian, and Japanese mountain units have a long head start. Formalities, precedent, and red tape will be fatal."[8] To this letter he attached a two-page chart with three columns of information including his positions in the Sierra Club (member, board of directors, acting chairman, outing committee, associate editor of the *Bulletin*, and chairman of Visual Education, Mountain Records, and Winter Camping committees) and as vice-chairman of the Defense Committee of the California Ski Association, among others.[9]

PRIVATE BROWER

The army's first response was to turn him down, owing to his age and his teeth. But he pursued his campaign and prevailed. He was assigned to the mountain troops. The matter of whether he would be deemed officer material, however, was left open. He enlisted on October 12, 1942, and was sent immediately to Camp Carson, Colorado, for basic training. His orders were from the adjutant general of the army, acting upon the recommendation of Dick Leonard.[10]

Brower wrote to a skiing buddy named Alan Hedden, "I rather dreaded getting into the Army with no more than a 'private' handle and still don't like it, but your guess on how long I'm carried by that handle is as good as mine."[11]

He spoke of men who were promoted to private first class two days after arriving at boot camp, to corporal after ten days, and sergeant after six months: "Promotion seems to be haphazard."

Brower's potential was recognized right away, in fact, and he was put to work writing part of a new climbing manual and editing the rest. And the chance to get into OCS looked promising as well, string-pulling and all. His letter to Hedden continued, "Personally, I still think men make the most progress in the Army when they know the most people. . . . If I don't get somewhere, I'll have to change my mind. For to date I have a Lt. Col., a major, two captains, a lt., and a sergeant looking out for me."[12] The major was Paul Lafferty, who had been at Little Lakes Valley and would prove important to Brower's campaign to become an officer.

Still, army life took some adjustment. "Taking orders, as you well know, isn't something that your middle son David relishes," he wrote to his father. "I don't know from whom I got my independence, but I got it." He added that he nevertheless had made up his mind to lay low and obey orders: "I'm lucky enough to be working with men I can reason with most of the time, rank or no rank."[13] This seems to predict pretty well Brower's later experiences in his various organizations. He was not comfortable taking orders, especially from people in positions of power over him. Sometimes he did not have the patience to reason with people with whom he disagreed; at other times, he was simply too busy to reason with them.

Camp Carson, elevation about 6,300 feet, was a challenging place to be. Pollution from coal-fired furnaces in the camp buildings and from coal-burning trains ferrying troops and cargo to and from the base was acrid, thick, and stubborn, and the weather was harsh. In a letter to Dick and Doris Leonard he wrote, "This business of gaining weight in the army doesn't refer to the Mountain Troops. I weighed 183 when I joined up, and weigh 174 now. At the rate of 9 lb. per month I won't last long." He said he'd never heard so many coughs before in his life, a combination, perhaps, of alkaline Colorado dust and the heavy pall of coal smoke that hung over the place whenever, if ever, the wind stopped blowing.[14]

But his connections were serving him well. As he wrote to his father on November 24, "When I got to Camp Carson I almost immediately ran into Charles Hanks, who I had known in the Sierra Club, in Yosemite. . . . Charlie became my press agent, and it wasn't more than a day or two before I was spending half of my daytimes in the office working with the Captain."[15] This was all well and good, but there was a bit of a drawback: He didn't have enough time to get the basic training he'd been sent to Carson to learn, which he would need if ever he was to attend officer candidate school.

And there was the weather to contend with. In a letter home dated November 30 he wrote, "Saturday night they tell me that in our barracks they didn't get the heat going and it dropped to 20 below in the building. The boys were cold. I was a bit on the cool side myself, since I was camping out on the snow 2500 feet higher with Charlie, Captain Woodward, and Lt. Lafferty. What a trip."[16]

The stay at Camp Carson was only temporary, for soon a new base opened at Camp Hale near Pando, Colorado, at an elevation of 9,300 feet, where conditions were even tougher. But the point of the exercise was to toughen the soldiers, and Camp Hale was up to that challenge. Brower reported that he was happy to have his father's borrowed typewriter because on at least one occasion, the ink other soldiers used to write letters home had frozen on the shelves overnight.

WOOING ANNE

After Dave left for the army, he wrote frequent letters to Anne, who answered sporadically. By all accounts, they were drawn to each other, but there was a problem: Anne was "spoken for," as Dave put it, engaged to a man named Paul, who was married or recently divorced. So Dave enlisted the help of a mutual friend, Doris Leonard, the wife of Dick Leonard, to be his agent in the arms-length courtship of young Miss Hus.

One letter from Doris to Dave dated December 4, 1942, reports that Paul had "released" Anne from their engagement and, what's more, had taken up with a twenty-one-year-old girl, being of the advanced age of thirty-five himself. Doris expressed relief that Dave was far away and didn't have to watch this up close. Despite the younger woman, Paul said he was still in love with Anne. This must have been agony for Dave to receive, off in the wilds of Colorado in the army. Doris went on to say that Paul was still seeing Anne, and that she was still in love with him, or said so, but believed that he had changed in the past six months. Anne told Doris that if she and Dave had had a chance to get to know each other outside the office, "she would know more about how she felt about you." Doris continued quoting Anne, saying that "she and Paul thought more alike than you and she" and that "Paul was more aware of the arts and more educated in the finer things." Doris had risen to Dave's defense: "I bridled at this and pointed out your love of the mountains, your marvelous ability to make music." She said that Anne was mostly confused, and ended with the advice to let things stand as they were: "If you and Anne are in love with each other, you can make sure of it after the war when you can get to know each other better."[17]

Dave dug in and refocused on his army career. It was time to become an officer. He had been so busy working on the training manual that he was woefully unprepared for the officer's exam: "I did not know the answers to many questions," he wrote. But fate, in the person of Major Paul Lafferty, intervened. Lafferty told the other examining officers that Private Brower had been assisting in headquarters on the training manual. He proceeded to answer the first question himself and all the others Brower didn't know the answers to. Brower later said, "It was a relief to have a friend in a high place. And why was he a friend? For one reason: because the president of the board was Major Paul Lafferty, who had snow-camped with us when he was a captain and we were testing army equipment in Little Lakes Valley."[18]

Around this time, as basic training was ending and Brower was gearing up to move on to officer candidate school at Fort Benning, Georgia, he received a postcard from Anne with a hand-drawn traffic light on a pole: the green light was blazing. Dave could take the hint and wrote a letter back proposing marriage, a letter he began on the train to Georgia and completed on his bunk at Fort Benning. Anne accepted, also by mail. They had never kissed, never been to a movie together, never had a proper date.

They were evidently rather secretive about their plans. Barbara Bedayn, the wife of Raffi Bedayn (who had changed the spelling of his surname from Bedayan to Bedayn), one of Dave's main climbing buddies, wrote to Dave, on April 8, 1943, just three weeks before the wedding, "I can't say that I was overcome with astonishment when Raffi wrote that you 'were thinking about being married the 24th' and 'the gal might be the Ann [sic] in his office.'" She then twitted Dave for being secretive: "Now for heaven's sake why can't you fellows go into this matter a little more fully and add a few details? Men!" And she added congratulations: "I was pleased, Dave, that you are making definite plans to relieve yourself of single bliss. . . . I haven't met Ann, but I want to, and if I ever get over to Berkeley again, I think I shall."[19]

Once at Fort Benning, Brower was assigned to OCS for infantry, learning how to operate rifles, machine guns, and other implements of war. He was also learning combat strategy and tactics as well as history—everything necessary to produce a worthy officer, into whose care many soldiers' lives would soon be entrusted.

He described his life in a letter to his parents and siblings. Training was to last thirteen weeks. "Three weeks are now behind me, but they seem to have been months, at least.... If I remember half the things they're teaching me, I'll be a military expert in no time, and ready to shoot the first person who refers to OCS graduates derisively as '90-day wonders.' The only wonder about it is how they survive and come out normal, rather than addled idiots."[20]

He was a little less complimentary about his surroundings: "Except for the fact that there are no mountains here, and all the trees are skinny, anemic-looking pines of no size whatever, and all the soil is sandy, and the weather is too cold or too muggy, and there's no snow—except for those these things, Ft. Benning is really quite all right. Well, maybe not the Fort, but the OCS course."[21]

The latest ninety-day wonder, Second Lieutenant David R. Brower, graduated from OCS and received his commission April 19, 1943, with orders to report back to Camp Hale and the Tenth Mountain Division, a relief, since he had feared being assigned to an infantry unit. He secured a short leave and hopped a train for Berkeley for his hastily planned wedding to Anne. The two were married at Anne's parents' house on May 1, 1943, in front of around fifty friends and family. Anne was twenty-nine, Dave thirty. The ceremony had to be delayed owing to Dave's attending a morning meeting of the Sierra Club board that ran overtime, a stark omen of things to come. Dave gave Anne a present for their wedding: a membership in the Sierra Club.

Almost immediately the couple left for Colorado by automobile, via King City, California, through Arizona to a rainy night in a tent at the base of Shiprock. Then to Mesa Verde, though the condition of the road made the last few miles to the ruins impassible. Finally to Denver, where they spent a frantic few days looking for accommodation for Anne. Dave reported being turned away by seven realtors: the area was crawling with military people, and housing was all but impossible to find. Finally, they found a room in a private home; not ideal, but they were grateful nonetheless. Dave then returned to army life and an every-other-week trek to spend time with his bride. Later, Anne would say, "I married a complete stranger."[22] Stranger or not, the marriage lasted fifty-seven years.

LIEUTENANT BROWER

Teaching, manual-writing, and filmmaking continued at Camp Hale for Lieutenant Brower until the following October, when he and several fellow

Mountain Troop officers were sent to the Seneca Rock Assault Climbing School near Elkins, West Virginia. Anne pulled up stakes in Denver and moved to Washington, DC, where she found a job editing for the War Department in the Pentagon. As her son Ken recounts, "My mother departed for the Pentagon and the Historical Division of G-2, where her manuscripts now were blood-flecked, bug-squashed combat journals—gritty primary sources from which she and her colleagues recorded the history of the war as it happened. . . . The message of the bloody combat journals did not elude my mother, and she gave me, her firstborn, my middle name, David, in the event her husband did not come back."[23]

The Seneca assignment lasted until June 1944, when the school was closed. The instructors, officers and enlisted men alike, were to be scattered to the winds, and they didn't like it. Brower and his friends got busy. At maneuver headquarters in Elkins, West Virginia, near the Seneca camp, they assembled around the pay telephone, got their coins together, and Brower went to work calling everyone he knew who might conceivably see how foolish it was to dismember what they had put together. He talked to Dick Leonard, Bestor Robinson, and others for about two hours altogether, wondering if they would overstuff the phone. He kept at it, and was still at it when one of the men, who had gone inside, came out beaming. "The orders have been changed. We're all going to Camp Swift."[24]

Camp Swift, Texas, that is—"and mountainous it wasn't." They were being sent there to get a taste of what flatland combat might be like, without "a bit of mountain defilade to hide in or height to observe from."

Before reporting to Camp Swift, Dave escorted Anne, now four months pregnant with Kenneth David, back to Berkeley. She would live with her parents until Dave could come back permanently, assuming he survived combat, which was coming soon.

His unit spent the next few months at Camp Swift, where they sweltered in heat and humidity. Then in early December, they boarded a train for Newport News, Virginia, and embarkation across the Atlantic. William Hosking, a sergeant in Brower's unit remembered, "Dave taught our section how to play bridge. Which we did in Italy. One rule was NO WEAPONS IN THE BRIDGE ROOM."[25]

Brower's unit, the 86th Mountain Infantry Regiment, Third Battalion, Tenth Mountain Division, set sail in a converted luxury liner, the SS *Argentina*, from Newport News on December 10, 1944. It was a rough crossing, especially for landlubbers: "We were told that we would be fed two meals a day on the trip across. For most of us, in the first few days," Brower recalled, "that was two too many."[26]

Sergeant Hosking further reported that in addition to rough seas, "the biggest problem and morale lowerer was we got salt water showers, officers got fresh water. Morale was boosted by Dave Brower coming down to the lounge area to play the piano while we sang. I am sure any rats on the ship jumped off preferring to drown than to listen to our singing."[27] This is one of several references in letters and elsewhere indicating that Brower was quite happy to fraternize with enlisted men, while most of the other officers were not, and in fact were discouraged from doing so. Some speculate that this may be because he hadn't finished college, and most of his fellow officers had. In any event, his men report great loyalty to him. Sergeant Hosking wrote, "Dave looked out for us. We did the best we could for him."[28]

They traveled in convoy with other troopships, and Hosking recalled, "We watched the ships in our convoy as they changed speed and direction to complicate any submarine's attempt to line up its sights on us. Our ship led the convoy."[29] They didn't know their destination until the entered the Mediterranean at Gibraltar.

They landed in Naples on December 23, "and for the first time, for most of us," said Brower, "we were now foreigners."[30] Two days later they took a small Italian freighter to Livorno, even more war-damaged than Naples, then rode twenty miles in trucks and pitched their pup tents just outside Pisa.

THE TENTH MOUNTAIN DIVISION SEES BATTLE

The objective was to dislodge a part of the German army from its well-dug-in and heavily fortified positions in the Apennine Mountains near Verona. The prime objective was to capture Mount Belvedere, but first they had to take Riva Ridge, which soared two thousand feet above the valley of the Silla and Reno Rivers. German snipers on Riva Ridge had a perfect vantage point to thwart any attack on Belvedere. So starting at 7:30 P.M. on a dark, foggy night, eight hundred men—not including Dave Brower, who was one of many held in reserve—clothed all in white, climbed silently up the face of the ridge. They carried grenades and rifles with bayonets but no bullets. The Germans had thought no one could possibly climb the ridge, let alone without sound and with weapons, in the dark, and they were utterly surprised. The Americans lobbed grenades into bunkers, and the battle was over without a single American casualty. The Riva attack was mounted over the night of February 18–19, 1945. (February 19 is also the date when American Marines stormed the beaches of Iwo Jima in the Pacific.)

Next, the Tenth mounted an attack on Mount Belvedere. Here the going was much harder, but eventually they dislodged the Germans and took many prisoners, some of whom were captured and others of whom had deserted.[31]

From the mountains, the soldiers moved into and across the vast valley of the Po River, home to much of Italy's agriculture and the cities of Milan, Turin, and Bologna. They traveled so quickly that the Germans were caught by surprise. They eventually reached Lake Garda, Italy's largest lake, nestled at the foot of the Italian Alps. They proceeded along the road, which, as the cliffs around the lake became ever more precipitous, soon became a series of seven tunnels. Here the fighting was protracted and bloody, with artillery rounds ricocheting inside the tunnels. Brower's company took heavy casualties before eventually clearing the tunnels of enemy troops.

A horrible irony of this battle was that the Germans had signed an agreement suspending hostilities in Italy and southern Austria four days before, but neither the American soldiers nor their German adversaries near Lake Garda knew it, so thoroughly disrupted were their communications.[32] Eventually the news reached the American commanders, and the troops relaxed. A little. They didn't know whether the Germans had been informed that they were all now about to become prisoners of war.

Brower may have had a hand in heading off further bloodshed. His unit was near the end of a column of vehicles four miles long. Lieutenant Colonel John Hay was at the head of it. Brower was a good three miles behind, but in radio contact. They wound slowly up the Alpine road, passing the German troops, who needed to retreat no longer and who were still armed. They wound slowly up the grade, the pace governed by the slowest vehicle. Out of habit they turned on their blackout lights, which provide enough illumination for driving but are invisible to the enemy.

They were about to travel the final miles to Passo di Resia on a road that meandered several miles up a broad meadow. Brower called the commander on the radio. "Jack, the war is over. Why the hell are we driving with blackout lights?" he asked. Colonel Hay granted that he had a point and gave the order to turn on the normal headlights. The four-mile-long meandering task force lit up. The Germans in the pass had noted the approach of the convoy and were preparing to blow it up. When the lights came on they inferred that something big must have happened and withheld fire.

In the end, the Tenth Mountain Division spent just 130 days in combat. Of its 14,000 men, just under 1,000 were killed and about 4,000 were wounded. It is not known how many Sierra Club members perished, but of the club's 4,000 members at the start of hostilities, 1,000 served in the military, many in the Tenth Mountain Division.

Following the end of hostilities, Brower and his mates were able to spend about three months in the Alps of Switzerland, France, Italy, and Austria, partly to keep an eye on Tito's troops across the border in Yugoslavia to make sure they didn't try to carve out a bit of defeated Italy to add to their real estate holdings. The mountain troops were delighted to be able to explore the magnificent peaks and glaciers of the Alps, but Brower came away disillusioned. He wrote about it in a piece for the *Sierra Club Bulletin* titled "How to Kill a Wilderness": "In such parts of the mountains of Italy, Austria, Switzerland, and Jugoslavia as I have been able to observe are the shattered remains of what must have been beautiful wildernesses. These wild places had their one-time inaccessibility to defend them—their precipices, mountain torrents, their glaciers and forests. But they lost their immunity; they felt the ravages of a conqueror. And now they're dead."[33]

He went on to describe what had killed the wild places in a postmortem of sorts. The killers were trails, which often became roads; power plants ("from quaint old mills to lusty powerhouses"); buildings (from stone farmhouses and huts for hikers to villages and hotels); mines, mostly by then abandoned; and fortifications: "Forts are everywhere, on canyon bottoms, high on the canyon walls, built into commanding peaks." Finally, a tongue-in-cheek manual on how to kill a wilderness: "(1) Improve it and exploit it. Keep adding the comforts that each preceding addition has brought people to demand. (2) Rely always on the apparently democratic argument that you must produce the greatest good for the greatest number.[34] Chances are that no one will call to your attention that irreplaceable treasures are destroyed if they are divided or trampled." Of this piece, Peter Shelton, in *Climb to Conquer*, wrote, "David Brower's fifty-five-year run as point man and conscience of the conservation movement had begun."[35]

As the troops were sailing for home on August 6, 1945, the *Enola Gay* dropped an atom bomb on Hiroshima. Three days later, as the weary fighters rested at Fort Patrick Henry, a second exploded over Nagasaki. Japan surrendered a week later. The Tenth had had orders to go to the Pacific to wage war against the Japanese. As Shelton tells it, "The War Department estimated hundreds of thousands of U.S. casualties and as many as two million Japanese dead. And the Tenth was slated to lead the attack."[36] Though he would later deplore the carnage visited upon those cities, Brower and his comrades were only too happy to avoid further combat and go home.

For his service, Brower was awarded a Bronze Star and a Combat Infantryman Badge. His son Kenneth said that the latter meant more to his father than the former: "The badge identified you as one of the guys in the mud and bullets. The Bronze Star is for heroism or merit in the combat zone. But I'm not sure you had to be an infantryman in combat to get it. And some units dispensed the star freely, and for some it meant much more. The infantryman's badge, it was clear what it meant."[37]

. . .

The war experience had a profound impact on Brower, as it did on the many who lost friends and were sometimes grievously wounded. Brower learned about leadership and managing people, and his experience just after the fighting ended in the Alps would influence his attitude about "improvements" in wild country.

PART TWO

Campaigner

FIVE

A Sierra Club Leader Emerges

Too often in what we do we fail to consider the two most important things: the cost to the future and the cost to the earth. We can be very clever, we humans, but sometimes not so smart.

First Lieutenant David Brower was mustered out of active duty on January 14, 1946, and immediately returned to Berkeley, to his young family, to his Sierra Club activities, and to his job at the University of California Press. First son, Kenneth David, had been born on November 10, 1944, while his father was on active duty. Second son, Robert Irish, was born on June 6, 1946. Two more children would follow: Barbara Anne on May 8, 1949, and John Stewart on December 7, 1952.

In 1947, Dave and Anne, with help from the GI Bill, were able to scrape together a down payment on a lot near the top of the ridge that separates Berkeley from points east and began building a modest home with a sweeping view of the bay and San Francisco. The house was built of redwood, which became a little awkward in subsequent years as Brower led Sierra Club and Friends of the Earth campaigns to preserve the fast-disappearing redwood forests in Northern California. At least the house was built to last. Dave and Anne would live out their lives there after adding a room for their growing family in the early fifties and eventually converting the garage into an office in the late nineties.

Even before the house was built, the Browers started a tradition that would continue for more than fifty years: the weekend waffle breakfast with guests. Nearly every weekend when Dave was in town, the Browers would invite friends, colleagues, and out-of-town visitors to drop by for homemade waffles with strawberries and whipped cream. The recipe—based on

Anne, David, Ken, and Bob Brower watching Phil Berry cook pancakes, Sierra Nevada High Trip, 1952. Photograph courtesy Earth Island Institute.

Bisquick—evolved, eventually including a dash of Worcestershire sauce and a bit of grated zucchini and carrot. The idea was conviviality and stimulating conversation, and the breakfasts provided just that, becoming quite an institution.

AT THE PRESS ONCE MORE

Back at UC Press, Brower plunged into an eclectic variety of editorial projects. At one point, in the midst of a protracted correspondence with a professor of vertebrate zoology who evidently was not thrilled with some of Brower's editorial suggestions Brower wrote, "*Taxonomy.*—I fear my queries will never be those of an expert. An editor here can only be a sciolist. I am sure you know what an editor is up against when manuscripts on so great a variety of subjects pass over his desk. (On my desk right now: skinks, *Gigantomonas*, Hawaiian species of *Caulerpa*, Cultivated Primulas, Yosemite History, Wartime Shipyards, Moenkopi vertebrates, Florida history, variation in music, and ski mountaineering!)"

And later in the same letter, a revealing note: "I have moved on in the discussion [of the manuscript] farther than I had intended. . . . I somehow want to prove to you that even though my editing may be too evangelical, it is not meant to be malicious, overbearing or ill-advised. I am sincerely trying to help the author express himself clearly."[1] He was, in fact, a very skilled editor, able to clarify, to ask the right questions, and improve others' writing with minimal intervention.

By the time Brower returned to the press, August Frugé was pretty much running the publishing side of the operation. (The printing operation was then four or five times bigger in budget and staff than the editorial side; the press printed UC Press books and many others as well).

Frugé had joined the Sierra Club in Sacramento, where he worked for the state library, before he came to Berkeley in 1944 to work for UC Press. He became active in the club's publications committee and would go on to serve briefly as editor of the *Sierra Club Bulletin* in the early '50s.

Tension had been building between the press and the university's publications committee over long delays in getting manuscripts edited and printed, and Frugé assigned Brower to be his expediter, to make schedules and ride editors and printers. Though they would clash later, Frugé acknowledged that Brower did a good job, another brick in Brower's education and training as a publisher that eventually would stand him in good stead. He became in fact, though not in title, UC Press's first production manager.[2]

Brower's second full-time job, though as a volunteer, was with the Sierra Club. Francis Farquhar retired as editor of the *Bulletin* in 1946 and passed the mantle to Brower when Brower returned from the war. Farquhar had served as editor for a record twenty-one years and the magazine had flourished, becoming highly respected, mainly as a mountaineering journal.

The guts of the *Bulletin* was its annual issue, with beautifully reproduced black-and-white photographs by Ansel Adams, Cedric Wright, and many other photographers. Since the twenties, a short "circular" was also sent to members every other month carrying information on High Trips and other outings, intramural news, and so forth. When Brower took over the magazine, things started to change.

For one thing, the circular adopted the *Bulletin* name and began to be published monthly, except for the month the annual appeared. It started small, often only eight pages, longer as content merited. And the contents began to change rather dramatically. Though news of mountain trips and mountaineering accomplishments continued to be included, there were more frequent articles about conservation battles the club was involved in, urging members to learn about them and participate by bringing pressure to bear on legislators and bureaucrats.

Brower also began to bring in other voices about what was going on in the out-of-doors nationally, with stirring essays often reprinted from other journals, including "The West against Itself" by Bernard De Voto, "How Much Wilderness Can We Afford to Lose?" by the Wilderness Society's Howard Zahniser, and "The Problems of the Wilderness" by Bob Marshall, also of the Wilderness Society.[3]

Brower introduced the De Voto piece with an appreciation of *Harper's*, where the article had first appeared: "In presenting the De Voto articles, *Harper's* has demonstrated editorial leadership that brings happily to mind the alliance of John Muir with Robert Underwood Johnson of the old *Century Magazine*—an alliance which contributed immeasurably to wise use of the public lands in general, and specifically to the creation in 1890 of Yosemite National Park."

De Voto, a columnist for *Harper's* and an honorary life member of the Sierra Club, was at his fiery best as he railed against the plundering of the West: "The first wealth produced in the West was furs, mainly beaver furs. It made a good many Easterners rich. Partnerships and corporations sent technical specialists—trappers and Indian traders—into the West to bring out the furs. . . . They cleaned up and by 1840 they had cleaned the West out. A century later, beaver has not yet come back." He excoriated cattle ranchers for running too many livestock on fragile lands, causing erosion and befouling streams, then turned his guns on loggers. Lumbering, he said, "perpetrated greater frauds against the people of the United States than any other Western business—and that is a superlative of cosmic size. It was a business of total liquidation: when a tree is cut, a century or two centuries may be required to grow another one and perhaps another one cannot be grown at all."

Zahniser's piece asked how much wilderness we can afford to lose. His answer was none: "As I see it, we can no longer afford to lose wilderness. We have already used up and lost so much that any further loss is a sacrifice, a sacrifice to be made only under the most extreme compulsion. The tenseness of our present situation as civilized, cultured human beings is that so many of us do not sense what sacrifice." Zahniser and Brower were in the early stages of a long and productive working relationship of vast mutual respect, whose most tangible product would be the Wilderness Act of 1964.

Marshall's piece had been originally published twenty years before in the *Scientific Monthly*. It is a passionate, erudite plea for wilderness preservation and a vigorous debunking of the argument that wilderness preservation would serve only the pleasures of the elite few at the expense of the resource-hungry masses. Marshall, incidentally, was a former chief of the Forest Service, who led the agency to preserve many wilderness acres before his untimely death in 1939 at the age of thirty-nine.

Another major *Bulletin* piece was "Yosemite: The Story of an Idea" by Sierra Club member Hans Huth.[4] This article expounded on the national park idea—that the parks were set aside primarily to protect wilderness, with recreation a welcome but secondary benefit. Huth, Brower, and others in the Sierra Club insisted that the national park idea was born with Congress and President Lincoln's setting aside of the Yosemite Reserve (the valley and the Mariposa Grove of giant sequoias) and that Yosemite was in fact the world's first national park. This goes against the common story that the national park idea was born around a campfire in Yellowstone about 1870. Yosemite was set aside in 1864, Yellowstone in 1872. Yosemite was managed by the state of California until the early 1900s, when it was conveyed back to the federal government. Yellowstone was the first place to be named a national park, but Huth's argument is that Yosemite was really the first national park. This is important because Yosemite was set aside for its wilderness, and Yellowstone mainly for its exotic features—mud pots, geysers, travertine terraces—and its formidable collection of bison, elk, wolves, and grizzlies.

THE SAN GORGONIO SKIRMISH

Meanwhile, there were plenty of conservation battles to write about. The first big one after the war ended involved San Gorgonio Mountain in Southern California, and it unfortunately pitted some Tenth Mountain Division veterans against each other.

Many veterans of the Tenth were, of course, enthusiastic skiers, and many went into the skiing business, helping to establish new ski resorts in the Rockies and the Sierra Nevada. A major tussle broke out in the late '40s with a proposal to install a resort on San Gorgonio Mountain east of Palm Springs to serve the rapidly growing cadre of skiers in Southern California. Brower—who had pioneered the sport of ski mountaineering, produced a book about the sport,[5] and made several first winter ascents of Sierra peaks—was all for skiing, but not necessarily mechanized skiing and all the roads, lifts, and buildings that necessarily accompany it.

At San Gorgonio, a key factor was that the resort was planned on national forest land in a "primitive area," which had been so designated in 1931. Such areas were de facto wilderness areas established by the Forest Service but with no formal, permanent legal protection, so they were subject to losing what protection they did have at the whim of the agency. (This, in fact, is what led to the campaign to pass the Wilderness Act the following decade.)

The San Gorgonio proposal split not only the Tenth vets; it also split the Sierra Club. Dave Brower opposed the plan, not surprisingly; Bestor Robinson, who was both a veteran and a club board member just elected president, supported it, as did many members who resided in Southern California.

In the *Bulletin* for January 1947, Brower issued a ringing call to arms: "The San Gorgonio Wild Area, unique in Southern California, is up for sacrifice. It is important—it is urgent—that all persons interested in conservation study this threat carefully, and act as soon as possible." He urged readers to turn out at a public hearing scheduled for February 19 in San Bernardino and let the Forest Service know what a lousy idea it was pushing. He concluded, "The wilderness concept is on trial, is up for sacrifice under the guise of compromise. . . . Where wilderness is concerned, there can be no compromise. Wilderness, like life itself, is absolute. A man cannot literally be half dead or half alive. He is dead or he is alive. A developed area cannot be wild."[6]

Given the controversy, Brower decided to give space to a differing opinion. He printed "San Gorgonio: Another Viewpoint."[7] It was written by Robinson, though published anonymously. Why the anonymity is not clear. Brower never explained why Robinson asked to remain anonymous. Perhaps he thought signing his name as president of the board would give him an unfair advantage. Maybe he didn't want to take the flak that his position would predictably provoke. We may never know. We do know that Brower was willing to go up against the president of the Sierra Club, something he would make a habit of.

Robinson wrote, "The value of wilderness areas does not lie in their being set aside in splendid isolation as museum pieces, but in their use by human beings for inspiration, invigoration, and escape from a mechanized civilization." He acknowledged that wilderness areas "should be considered a sacred trust," but he argued that "a proposed extension or retraction of a boundary line should be decided on the basis of whether it will increase or decrease the overall value of the wilderness for the human use it is designed to serve."

The two articles clearly define an important divide in the club's thinking about wilderness and development and recreation, a divide that would remain an important theme in the development of the club and the conservation movement as a whole, with Brower playing John Muir to Robinson's utilitarian Gifford Pinchot.

Brower summed up, "Can a conservation organization place the construction of ski facilities, or any development, above wilderness?" He went on to poke fun at the proponents of the resort, chiding the "enthusiastic and sometimes even evangelical skiers," reminding them that "the sole value of a mountain is not just that it tips a snow slope downhill."

Robinson, the lawyer, finished dryly, "It may well be that human intelligence is not capable of evolving a plan which will provide reasonable winter use without destroying the wilderness." Until the making of such a plan is earnestly attempted, he went on, "it cannot be said that it is hopelessly objectionable. The result is too important to pre-determine its impossibility."

In the end, after frenzied lobbying of his fellow directors a week or less before the Forest Service hearing, Brower was just able to turn a scant majority against the project.[8]

The Forest Service hearing in San Bernardino on February 19, 1947, was packed. Dick Leonard, the Sierra Club board secretary and a meticulous attorney, listened intently and took careful notes. Leonard reported in the March *Bulletin* that testifying in favor of the ski development were "the California Chamber of Commerce and three other chambers, the National Ski Association, and 18 small ski clubs." Opposing the scheme were "7 chambers of commerce and civic clubs, 7 water-users' organizations, 7 sportsmen's clubs, 6 youth organizations, 4 natural science groups, 5 hiking clubs" and ten organizations including the Sierra Club, the Wilderness Society, and the National Audubon Society. He also noted that, surprisingly, the American Forestry Association opposed the plan.[9]

Five months later, in July 1947, the *Bulletin* could gleefully carry excerpts from a Forest Service press release announcing that the Forest Service would not allow the project to go forward: "Following intensive study of the proposal, Mr. Watts [chief of the Forest Service] had come to the conclusion that the San Gorgonio primitive area has higher public value as a wilderness and a watershed than as a downhill skiing area."[10]

But what of the skiers who still wanted new playgrounds? Many of them, after all, were Sierra Club members. As a way out of the San Gorgonio dilemma, the club sought to find a compromise solution and, in so doing, fell into a trap that would come back to haunt the organization, and not just at San Gorgonio but also at the Grand Canyon, at Diablo Canyon on the California coast, and elsewhere. Dave Brower, who would be known in later years as an uncompromising hard-liner, was then only too willing to seek a compromise to save San Gorgonio Primitive Area.

To that end, he and Richard Felter, another Sierra Club skier, undertook an aerial survey of possible alternative sites within reasonable driving distance of Los Angeles. They argued that it would behoove the defenders of San Gorgonio "to point out that there was in California much ski terrain not in wilderness and not yet developed for skiing," and that the best way to secure protection for San Gorgonio "would be to point out to skiers where, outside the wilderness areas, they could have their ski lifts."[11]

Brower and Felter examined several possibilities and concluded that the most promising was Mineral King, an old mining district in Sequoia National Forest, surrounded on three sides by Sequoia National Park. They described it as "probably the most spectacular site for commercial development on the west side of the Sierra."[12] The mines had been abandoned in the 1880s but had left enough damage behind—including a primitive road into the valley, mine shafts, cabins, and rusting machinery—to cause it to be left out of the park when it was created in 1890 and expanded in 1926. The Sierra Club board, somewhat grudgingly, passed the following cramped motion: "Although the Sierra Club does not advocate the development of any particular area for skiing, the Club cannot, as a matter of principle, oppose the development of Mineral King or any other non-wilderness area."[13]

Nearly twenty years later, a gigantic resort was proposed for Mineral King, to be built by the Walt Disney Corporation. The Sierra Club, after fiery internal debates, eventually opposed the Disney plan as being out of scale with the relatively small valley and a violation of the national park, provoking charges that the word of the club would never be trusted again. This was not the last time we would hear such accusations.

ROADS VERSUS WILDERNESS

A festering problem related to all this was buried in the Sierra Club's bylaws, adopted in 1892, at the birth of the organization. The purposes of the club were, formally, "to explore, enjoy, and render accessible the mountain regions of the Pacific Coast." This reflected the thinking of John Muir and Will Colby, who believed that to save mountain wilderness, people must be introduced to it and be allowed to fall in love with it, then work in its defense, and that meant not only High Trips but also more roads.

Indeed, in the 1920s the Sierra Club had supported the building of roads across many wild Sierra passes. However, by the late thirties, there was a serious difference of opinion within the club over how far to push a road into the new Kings Canyon National Park, with the pro-road contingent successful over Brower's objections. A decade later, roads had fallen out of favor, and the club changed its bylaws so that its purposes were now "to explore, enjoy, and protect the Sierra Nevada and other scenic resources of the United States." The preservationists, led by Brower, Ansel Adams, and Dick Leonard, were inching forward in influence within the club.

But the going was anything but smooth. When the Park Service suggested blasting a new road across a glacier-polished granite apron adjacent to Tenaya Lake in the Yosemite high country, the club split again. It had approved the realignment of the road in principle in the 1930s, then later suggested modifications that would spare the magnificent granite slopes that are at the fringe of the lake. Brower and board member Harold Bradley argued against the new road, to no avail.[14] Debate raged within the club until Ansel Adams, frustrated at the club's vacillation, offered his resignation from the board. The resignation was rejected, and the board eventually took a stand against the road project, but it was too late. Tenaya was permanently scarred. The ugly result of dynamiting the road across the polished granite stands to this day, and will forever. Still, Brower saw this as a turning point for the club, a clear stiffening of the spine for battles yet to come.

Another big battle that Brower waged against development in designated parkland soon after World War II involved Olympic National Park on the Olympic Peninsula in Washington State. Like most of his conservation campaigns, this one aired in the pages of the *Bulletin*.[15] The National Park Service, under pressure from the Forest Service, which had always seen providing timber as its first mission, proposed to "relinquish" a large amount of timber for logging under the guise of "sanitation" logging. Such logging is generally justified in cases where fire suppression has led to the buildup of undergrowth that can make new fires more destructive. Clearing undergrowth is often a good idea, but it is also often a front for logging mature trees, just as "salvage" logging, often proposed after a fire, disguises logging of live trees.

For Brower, the essential point was this: "When any particular resource of the nation becomes so scarce as to be found only in national parks, then it is high time to find a substitute, rather than to deplete or extinguish it in the parks."[16] Lowell Sumner, the Park Service regional biologist, made aerial photographs of the stands to be logged and provided them to the Sierra Club. Brower published them in the *Bulletin*,[17] and the scheme was stopped cold.

In 1949 the Sierra Club hosted the first in a series of biennial wilderness conferences in San Francisco. Conservationists and scientists from across the country attended, listened to speeches and presentations of papers, and watched films and slide shows. Brower credited the Wilderness Society's Benton MacKaye with conceiving of the conferences and suggesting that the club play host. The club, after all, was far older and larger, though by no means large. It was also headquartered in the West, where most of the remaining wilderness was.

Wilderness was by this time Brower's first concern, as it would remain forever. He could be eloquent on the subject: "The most important source of the vital organic forms constituting the chain of life is the gene bank that exists in wilderness, where the life force has gone on since the beginning uninterrupted by man and his technology. For this reason alone, it is important that the remnants of wilderness which we still have on our public lands be preserved by the best methods our form of government can find."[18] It is a theme he would elaborate and return to again and again. His favorite line on the subject is from Nancy Newhall: "The wilderness holds answers to more questions than we yet know how to ask."[19]

The conferences brought together wilderness stalwarts including Brower, Howard Zahniser, Starker Leopold, Luna Leopold, Ian McTaggert Cowan, Frank Fraser Darling, and Roderick Nash, and politicians including California congressman Jeffrey Cohelan, who then represented Berkeley; Washington State senator Henry M. 'Scoop" Jackson; California governor Edmund G. "Pat" Brown; Arizona congressman and future interior secretary Stewart Udall; Pennsylvania congressman John Saylor; and many more. Others attended from the land-managing agencies of the government: the National Park Service, the Bureau of Land Management, and the Forest Service. Still others came with economic interests in wilderness, such as packers, loggers, and fishing guides. Brower compiled speeches and panel discussions into books, wrote forewords to them, and published them under the Sierra Club imprint.[20]

There were discussions about the meaning of wilderness to science, wildlands in our civilization, and other wilderness-related matters, all aimed, at least informally, toward building the rationale and support for an eventual national law to protect wilderness permanently.

. . .

And what did the wilderness conferences accomplish? Brower suggests that they led President Eisenhower to set aside the Arctic National Wildlife Range (later reclassified a national wildlife refuge) in Alaska in 1960, just before leaving office.[21] Michael Cohen, in his history of the club, suggests that they provided grist for the Rod Nash classic *Wilderness and the American Mind*.[22] They most certainly helped build momentum leading to the passage of the Wilderness Act of 1964. The conferences also persuaded Brower of the utility of such gatherings, of face-to-face exchange of ideas and opinions. He would be a conference addict his whole career, attending hundreds if not thousands, often with a featured speaking role.

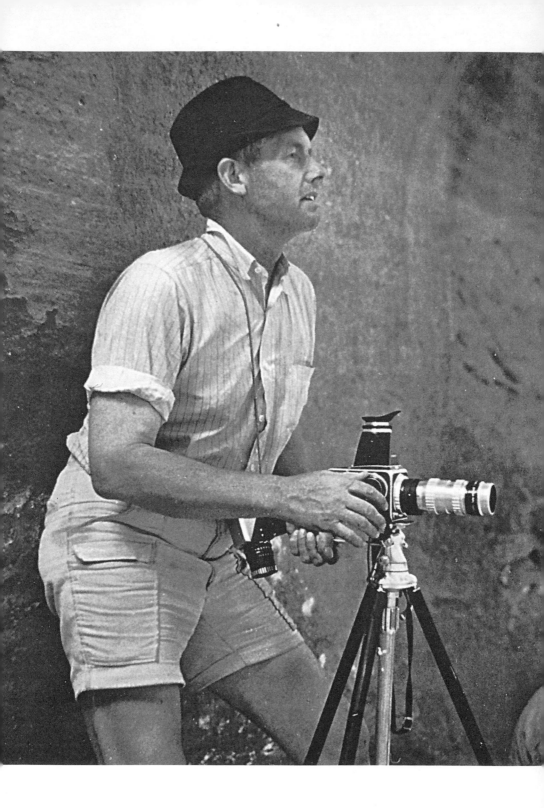

SIX

The Battle against Dams in Dinosaur

Science creates two problems for every one it solves.

The *Sierra Club Bulletin* for January 1953 begins with this announcement: "On December 15, following action taken by the Directors ten days previously, David R. Brower became [the first] Executive Director of the Sierra Club."[1]

The club was sixty years old; Brower, forty.

The author of the announcement pointed out that this move had been considered for at least fifteen years, but "not until late this year did it become both necessary and practicable." As to his duties, "The new Executive Director will be responsible to the . . . Board of Directors. He will prepare recommendations . . . pertaining to establishing club policy and will exercise general supervision over the carrying out of Board directives."

The move had become "practicable" when the Sierra Club could afford a full-time, if modest, salary and Brower could be persuaded to leave UC Press. It had become necessary because of a federal government plan to build two dams within the boundaries of a unit of the national park system. It was the first step in making the Sierra Club a professionally run, national organization. The Wilderness Society, the National Parks Association, and the Izaak Walton League already had professional employees; it was high time the Sierra Club joined the party.

One early task for the new executive director was to help the board think about whether the club should consider expanding beyond California. A chapter had been formed in Southern California as early as 1911, and a San Francisco Bay chapter followed in 1924. In 1950 some self-styled "temporary

David Brower photographing the drowning of Glen Canyon, 1963. Photograph courtesy Earth Island Institute.

exiles" in New York had persuaded the board to establish an Atlantic chapter, which encompassed the entire East Coast. This made some directors nervous, including Francis Farquhar and Bestor Robinson. When members in Seattle started talking about forming a Northwest chapter, the issue of expansion found itself before the board, with a background paper prepared by David Brower.

Farquhar, in his oral history, looking back on the decision, said, "I think that the Sierra Club would have been better if we had just concentrated on California." He noted that the membership passed the hundred thousand mark by 1974, which "[changed] the character of the club entirely." People didn't know each other as they once had: "At one time, back in the 1920s and 1930s we all knew each other very well."[2]

Brower's talking paper for the board had raised several questions: "Should our conservation scope have national, regional, or state limits? . . . Should our roster be limited to the state? . . . Should our activities have a border too? . . . How many chapters? Where? . . . Should we actively try to increase the membership? . . . Should we set a ceiling on numbers?"[3] His presentation was utterly neutral in contrast to his open, forceful, and public opinions about most other matters.

At the end of a two-hour discussion, the board approved the following: "No arbitrary geographic limitations shall be placed on the organization of chapters of the Sierra Club with respect to location. The Sierra Club has no policy objection to the formation of a chapter in the Pacific Northwest."[4] Sixty years later, the club has chapters that cover the entire United States and Canada.

A discernible division was opening in the club between a majority who were happy to see the club grow and expand geographically and a minority who pined for the old days when everybody knew everybody. Diehards in the latter group would become more and more nervous about the activities of their new chief of staff as years went by.

The principal reason Brower's hiring became necessary, however, was a proposal to build two hydroelectric dams near the confluence of the Green and Yampa Rivers within the boundaries of Dinosaur National Monument in northeastern Utah, near the town of Vernal. The resulting reservoirs would drown thousands of acres of little-known and little-visited sandstone wilderness and the rivers that had carved the canyons.

This would be a national campaign, impossible to entrust to volunteers. It needed a vigorous, full-time leader. Brower had cut his teeth on Kings Canyon, was familiar with publishing books and periodicals, and had seemingly limitless energy, which would be needed for frequent cross-country trips. That he had a wife and four small children at home didn't faze him. Anne would later say that she naively thought that, as a full-time Sierra Club employee, Dave might take off a weekend now and then instead of devoting all his free time to the club. It didn't work that way. He traveled a great deal and spent long hours on club work whether he was at home or not. The rearing of the children fell to Anne, who bore up remarkably well but would certainly have appreciated more help from her peripatetic husband.

DINOSAUR NATIONAL MONUMENT

Dinosaur National Monument, all of eighty acres, had been established by President Woodrow Wilson in 1915 to preserve a trove of fossilized dinosaur bones embedded in sandstone near the Green River. Franklin Roosevelt expanded the monument by 200,000 acres in 1938 to preserve the river canyons of the Green and the Yampa. By this time, ironically, most of the dinosaur fossils had been shipped to museums in the East.[5] The expansion of the monument came at the behest of Roosevelt's secretary of the interior, Harold L. Ickes, who argued that all the canyons of the Colorado Plateau should be protected within the national park system. He envisioned a dozen or more parks from Flaming Gorge to Grand Wash Cliffs; this was not to be.

The heart of Dinosaur National Monument was Echo Park, just downstream from the confluence of the Yampa and the Green. Here the government proposed to erect a dam 525 feet tall that would create a reservoir extending sixty-three miles up the Green and forty-four miles up the Yampa. A second dam, at Split Mountain downstream, would be a smaller installation, more to regulate the river flow than to generate electricity. But electricity was the main objective. Irrigation was almost an afterthought, and a tough sell in those days of food surpluses. President Truman would nonetheless say, "It has always been my opinion that food for coming generations is much more important than bones from the Mesozoic period."[6] Truman presumably enjoyed his quip, but it was irrelevant: the dams and their irrigation canals and power plants would have been far from the fossil beds; neither would have interfered with the other in any respect.

The dams had first been proposed in the 1940s, and the director of the National Park Service at the time, Newton Drury, had signed a secret agreement with the head of the Bureau of Reclamation (both agencies within the Department of the Interior) pledging not to oppose such dams. The memo was signed on November 4, 1941.[7] This secret agreement would be a principal justification cited by the dams' proponents as they argued in favor of the dams. As the dam battle heated up, Brower was fond of quoting Drury as saying, "Dinosaur is a dead duck."[8]

The Truman administration approved the two hydro projects in mid-1950, just days after the first American troops were sent to join the fighting in Korea, and sent a bill to Congress that would authorize construction and provide the necessary funds. By this time Drury and the National Park Service had come to oppose the dams as a violation of protected land, but the far larger and more powerful sibling within the Interior Department, the Bureau of Reclamation, prevailed and persuaded Interior Secretary Oscar Chapman to approve the project.

One compromise that Drury floated as a way around the invasion of the park system was simply to redraw the monument's boundaries to leave out the dam sites.[9] That was a nonstarter. Drury was forced to resign about this time, some thought for opposing the dams.

THE CONSERVATION COALITION

The conservation community, such as it was, rallied to the defense of Dinosaur. David Brower was already active and known to insiders on the national scene. Other principal conservation leaders were Howard Zahniser of the Wilderness Society; Ira Gabrielson, a former official of the Fish and Wildlife Service; Fred Packard of the National Parks Association; and Arthur Carhart and Joe Penfold of the Izaak Walton League. They met regularly at the Cosmos Club in Washington, DC, to plot strategy over drinks and meals. The leaders were all men, all white, mostly well educated—"male, pale, and Yale," as some would ruefully observe. Brower didn't fit into the Yale part of the slogan but was certainly male and pale.

Zahniser and Brower were great mutual admirers. Zahnie had worked as a publicist in the government and coached Brower as the younger man learned the ropes. Zahnie was in fact an informal representative for the Sierra Club in Washington, DC, in the early 1950s: "Dear Dave, I am continuing to represent myself at meetings of the Emergency Committee on Natural Resources as speaking for the Sierra Club and trust that that is in accordance with your wishes. . . . My, it was encouraging and inspiring, as well as pleasant, to have you among our ranks here. I cannot tell you how much you strengthen our wilderness-preservation influence among the conservation leaders when you come into our councils."[10]

Brower replied, "Dear Zahnie, It is my devout wish that you will continue to be representative of the Sierra Club. With you there to represent it, the Sierra Club can feel well endowed indeed." He went on to propose "a weekly telephone call from you, paid for by us, initiated from your home after you have settled down comfortably with your demi-tasse and while we are still working like beavers in the office out here."[11] This call became routine, though the timing and frequency varied. According to Zahniser's son Ed, then fourteen or fifteen years old, "Dave would lose track of the time in California and often call during our dinner in Maryland. I was the one to answer the phone to see if it was Dave. My job was to put Dad's plate in the oven. This was nearly every day. We'd be eating dinner at six-thirty when Dave would call."[12]

There were two principal issues involved with the Dinosaur matter, one concrete, the other abstract. First was the desire to preserve Echo Park and the rest of the monument as wilderness, for recreation and for its own sake and the well-being of the wildlife that lived there. The other was a matter of principle: Hetch Hetchy Valley in California, within the boundaries of Yosemite National Park, had been dammed and flooded in the early part of the twentieth century despite the Sierra Club's best efforts to preserve it. Conservationists were determined never to see such a loss repeated. Allowing dam construction in Dinosaur would set a dreadful precedent. No park or monument would be safe.[13] Indeed, as the Dinosaur battle was heating up, the Sierra Club's president, Dick Leonard, told the *San Francisco Chronicle* that no fewer than sixteen dams were being proposed in eight different units of the national park system.[14]

THE DEVELOPMENT PROPOSAL

Dinosaur and its proposed reservoirs were only one part of a larger plan for development of the upper basin of the Colorado River. In 1922 the states adjoining the river system (Wyoming, Utah, Colorado, Arizona, New Mexico, Nevada, and California) had formed the Colorado River Compact as a way to divvy up precious river water for irrigation, hydroelectricity production, and domestic purposes. The system was arbitrarily divided into an upper basin and a lower basin. The line was drawn near the Arizona-Utah border.

The Dinosaur proposal was part of a development plan for the upper basin that included Glen Canyon Dam just north of the line dividing the lower and upper basins in Arizona; Flaming Gorge Reservoir in Wyoming on the Green, the Colorado's largest tributary; and several smaller edifices. The dam proposals were accompanied by hundreds of pages of technical information on geology and hydraulics and—this proved to be pivotal—evaporation. The Colorado Plateau is essentially desert with a big river running down the center of it. The air tends to be very dry and the summer very hot. As anyone knows who has hiked there in the summer, perspiration dries instantly, so hikers get the impression that they are not perspiring. It's a dangerous illusion and can lead to debilitating dehydration.

Brower, the college dropout, began to dig into the numbers in the dam proposals, and he began to find mistakes. He consulted with experts. Luna Leopold, son of Aldo Leopold, the great naturalist and writer, cautioned him not to challenge the calculations of bureau engineers. Richard Bradley, a professor at Princeton University and member of a large and active Sierra Club family, said he'd help Brower check the numbers. Anne Brower thought he was crazy to consider going up against the mighty Bureau of Reclamation. "David," she would say, "don't embarrass yourself: they have *slide rules!*"[15]

Still, as he hauled out what he would later call his "ninth-grade arithmetic," Brower became firmly convinced that the bureau, either deliberately or inadvertently, had miscalculated relative evaporation rates for various configurations of the various dam projects.

The matter boiled down to an argument over whether building the Glen Canyon Dam some thirty-five feet taller than planned, therefore increasing storage capacity and surface area, would make the Dinosaur dams unnecessary. The bureau said that the three-reservoir solution with a lower Glen Canyon dam plus the two dams in Dinosaur would save the most water. Brower's calculations said the opposite: that building a higher Glen Canyon dam would make the Dinosaur dams unnecessary and conserve water.[16] This approach made some in the conservation bloc uneasy. Penfold, Carhart, and Gabrielson were afraid that getting into technical arguments would weaken their case and thought they ought to stick to conservation arguments: the value of Echo Park and the rest of the monument and the sanctity of the park system.

The House Interior Committee's subcommittee on irrigation and reclamation called a hearing, to begin January 18, 1954. It would be Brower's first time testifying before Congress, so he decided to attend the entire hearing, which would last eight days. He booked into the Cosmos Club as a guest of Howard Zahniser.

Ralph Tudor, undersecretary of the interior and chief engineer of the Bureau of Reclamation, led off. Tudor was an engineer and had played a major role in the design and construction of the Golden Gate Bridge. He described the Echo Park dam as the "piston" that would drive the whole system. Tudor was followed by a string of other pro-dam witnesses from the federal government and from Utah and other basin states. Finally, on the seventh day of the hearings, the conservationists got their chance.

Retired general Ulysses S. Grant III led off. He decried the invasion of a national monument and argued that there must be other sites that would provide necessary storage and power-generating capacity. Joe Penfold and Howard Zahniser followed with similar arguments. The economics of the project came in for mild criticism, but no one mentioned the bureau's evaporation calculations until Brower took the witness chair. What followed was a confrontation that would become famous in the annals of conservation history.

Brower began with a prepared statement introducing himself and the Sierra Club to the committee members. He pointed out that the club's membership included "the past president of the American Society of Civil Engineers, the current president of the American Society of Radio Engineers [engineers being one of the keys to the dispute], the next president of the American Chemical Society, the president of a major pharmaceutical house, of a major railroad, of a major mining firm, and an assistant U.S. attorney general."[17]

He then listed three questions "which we feel haven't been answered properly yet. 1. What are the important park values in Dinosaur? 2. Would they be destroyed by Echo Park and Split Mountain dams? 3. Can Dinosaur's scenery be made accessible without dams?" The answers: "This area has superlative park values. They would indeed be destroyed by the proposed dams. And the dams are not needed to make this area accessible." After a few paragraphs of elaboration, he tossed a hand grenade into the proceedings: "My point is to demonstrate to this committee that they would be making a great mistake to rely upon the figures presented by the Bureau of Reclamation when they cannot add, subtract, multiply, or divide. I am not trying to sound smart, but it is an important thing."

Congressman William Dawson of Utah couldn't contain himself: "I would just like to make one comment. If Mr. Tudor is such a poor engineer as you seem to claim he is, I'm surprised he ever got that Golden Gate Bridge down in your town to meet in the middle."

Brower responded, "Mr. Tudor made a great contribution on the San Francisco bridge."[18]

Wayne Aspinall, a Colorado Democrat and chairman of the committee, was incensed. "And you are a layman and you are making that charge against the engineers at the Bureau of Reclamation?"

"I am a man who has gone through ninth grade and learned his arithmetic," Brower replied. "I do not know engineering. I have only taken Mr. Tudor's own figures which he used and calculated in error to justify invading Dinosaur National Monument."

Aspinall wondered if the evaporation calculations might be overblown. Brower answered, quoting Tudor: "In conclusion, in the final analysis, the increased loss of water by evaporation for the ultimate site is the fundamental issue upon which the department has felt it necessary to give any consideration to the Echo Park Dam and the reservoir." In other words, unless the two Dinosaur dams would save a large amount of water that would otherwise be lost to evaporation, they should not be considered. At this point, the hearing was abruptly halted, to be resumed the following morning.

The next day several bureau engineers had been summoned to do battle with Brower; a blackboard and chalk were provided. One of the engineers, Cecil B. Jacobson, hastened to confess that he had indeed found a "slight error" in the figures in Tudor's statement. Tudor had reported that not building the dams at Echo Park and Split Mountain would cause the loss of between 100,000 and 200,000 acre-feet of water to evaporation, but the number was really closer to 70,000. Upon further examination, following the hearing, the number dropped to 25,000 acre-feet.

The hearing proceeded. Congressman Leslie Miller of Wyoming barked at Brower, "Are you an engineer?"

"No sir," Brower replied. "I am an editor."

"You do not propose to know the engineering techniques that go into the building of a dam or the estimate of storage?"

"All I can apply, Dr. Miller," Brower answered, "is just an editor's natural suspicion when he is working over a manuscript. I have worked for the University of California Press for many years, and I have had a lot of scientific monographs to go over. I know nothing about some subjects, but you can be suspicious, and it is amazing what you can turn up."

The Bureau of Reclamation, in short, came out of the hearing with dinosaur egg on its face. It was going to be difficult to justify invading a national monument with two dams and reservoirs in order to save a paltry 25,000 acre-feet of water a year—and Brower calculated that the real number was closer to 20,000. It was a huge setback for the dams' promoters.

THE CAMPAIGN TO SAVE DINOSAUR

Meanwhile, Brower and allies brought everything they could think of to bear on the battle. The Sierra Club started organizing float trips through the monument; nearly two hundred people—including Brower and his two older sons, Ken and Bob—floated the canyon in the summer of 1953, the mountaineer's first float trip. The following summer the number reached nine hundred.

Float Trips and the Press

The trips were for the public and, in a fine stroke of public-relations savvy, for journalists as well. One of those was Ernest Linford, editor of the editorial page of the *Salt Lake Tribune*, which was a vocal supporter of the dams. The trip changed Linford's mind and the stance of his paper. Another rider was David Perlman of the *San Francisco Chronicle*, who had been introduced to Brower by the editor of the paper, Scott Newhall, who lived not far from Brower in the Berkeley hills. Perlman floated the river and came back to write long articles that were highly favorable to the anti-dam position. He also contributed articles to the *Sierra Club Bulletin*.[19]

Yet another journalist on one of these trips was John Oakes, the editorial page editor of the *New York Times*. Oakes had been invited to visit Dinosaur by the Department of the Interior, which hoped to enlist his support for the dams. Brower caught wind of the Interior Department trip and invited himself along, met Oakes at the Denver airport, and drove with him to the put-in on the Yampa. This provided several uninterrupted hours for Brower to pitch his views to Oakes.

Oakes later reported that "Dave probably didn't realize it, but it was not really necessary for him to work on me to counter the department's propaganda in favor of the dam." The *Times* correspondent in San Francisco, Larry Davies, had written stories about the Dinosaur controversy that had caught Oakes's attention. Oakes, who wrote a monthly conservation column for the paper, had already come to the same conclusion as the Sierra Club. Oakes went on, "But it was characteristic of Dave that he would leave no stone unturned, take no chances of missing an opportunity to expound his views, which he invariably did with brilliance."[20] Brower also cultivated allies: he persuaded Oakes to run for a seat on the Sierra Club's board of directors several years later, a race he won.

A journalist who had already discovered Dinosaur on his own and would figure prominently in this battle and many more to come was Martin Litton. Litton worked as a general gofer at the *Los Angeles Times* but found time to venture into the wilderness and occasionally to fly over it, having been a glider pilot in World War II. He visited Dinosaur on his own and then wrote passionate stories about the plot to drown it. The *Times* splashed them across several Saturday-edition pages with giant photographs, also by Litton. The stories found their way to Brower, who telephoned Litton and asked him to help the campaign. After some cajoling—Litton didn't think very highly of the Sierra Club at the time—he agreed. He would go on to serve on the board and be one of Brower's staunchest allies—and, occasionally, Brower's conscience in the battles over Mineral King and Diablo Canyon to name but two.[21] In an interesting twist, shortly after Brower assumed the executive directorship of the Sierra Club, he was approached by *Sunset* magazine, which was looking for a travel editor. Brower was not interested but suggested Martin Litton. Litton took the job and remained there for a decade, writing frequently about conservation.

Films

Charles Eggert, a filmmaker, floated the river with his camera on one of the Sierra Club trips in 1953. Brower hired him to produce *Wilderness River Trail*, a twenty-eight-minute documentary arguing in favor of the river and against the dams.[22] Dam proponents had claimed that the Green and Yampa were too dangerous to float. The film put the lie to that argument, and it was later acknowledged by people in the Bureau of Reclamation to have been the dam-fighters' most potent weapon.

Brower himself made a second film that didn't mention Dinosaur but drove its point home with a force that still resonates. *Two Yosemites* took on the dam-boosters' argument that the reservoirs created by the Dinosaur dams would be beautiful. In a single day, after the level of the reservoir had dropped temporarily, Brower shot the twelve-minute, handheld film showing the wasteland that Hetch Hetchy became after the valley was dammed, acres of ugly mudflats and stumps, contrasted with scenes of the glorious, undammed Yosemite Valley. He edited the footage, wrote and performed the narration himself, added music and titling, and made a handful of copies. His total expenditure was around $500.[23] Toward the end of the film he laments, "The day of atomic power could have arrived with Hetch Hetchy still beautiful," a theme he would repeat for more than a decade before he turned against nuclear power. At the height of the Dinosaur battle, Howard Zahniser rolled a projector on a dolly through congressional office buildings, pigeonholing anyone he came across and showing the film. Several ended up in tears.

"This Is Dinosaur"

Brower also launched a book, something he would do with great frequency in battles to come. This time he persuaded Alfred Knopf to publish a volume on the controversy, gathered contributions from knowledgeable and persuasive people, and recruited Wallace Stegner to edit it. The result was *This Is Dinosaur: Echo Park Country and Its Magic Rivers*, published in 1955. Among the seven essays was one by Knopf himself, "The National Park Idea." Stegner writes in the 1985 edition, "*This Is Dinosaur* was originally published in 1955, at the height of a bitter controversy. David Brower and the Sierra Club originated the idea. Lovers of the national parks contributed their skill and knowledge as text and pictures. I edited their contributions. Alfred Knopf published the result in an astonishingly short time and with little regard for profit."[24] Brower sent a copy of the book to every member of Congress. Many expressed thanks for being informed about the controversy in such an elegant manner.

New Tactics

The Supreme Court in 1954 issued an opinion that nonprofit organizations that received tax-deductible contributions were not permitted to devote a "substantial" fraction of their budgets to trying to influence pending legislation.[25] *Substantial* was not defined, but this was a shot across the bow of the good ship Conservation, one that would be used by the Internal Revenue Service a decade later to hamstring the Sierra Club and other conservation organizations. The IRS's limits on how much of a nonprofit organization's budget can be used to influence legislation remains a major factor in determining the scope of a nonprofit's lobbying budget.

In response to the 1954 Supreme Court ruling, various group leaders scrambled to form new coalition organizations to which contributions would not be tax-deductible and therefore not hampered by the limitation on lobbying. These coalitions included the Council of Conservationists in New York, the Citizens Committee on Natural Resources in Washington, DC, and Trustees for Conservation in San Francisco. Brower served on the boards of all three.

As matters concerning the Dinosaur dams were coming to a head, the Council of Conservationists invented a tactic that would be used by the Sierra Club to great effect a decade later: the full-page newspaper cause ad. Conservationists had caught wind of a secret meeting pro-dam forces were going to hold in Denver to find a strategy for achieving their objective. The dam opponents wrote an ad that ran in the *Denver Post* on October 31, 1955, aimed directly at the members of the Upper Basin Strategy Committee. The ad—couched as an open letter—said that unless the Echo Park and Split Mountain dams were dropped from the Upper Colorado reclamation plan, the ads' sponsors—leaders of the Sierra Club, the Izaak Walton League, the Wilderness Society, and the National Parks Association, acting through the Council of Conservationists—would block the whole project. From the three preceding years of battles in Congress, it appeared that those making the threat could probably carry it out.

WINNING DINOSAUR, LOSING GLEN CANYON

The committee caved and pulled Echo Park and Split Mountain out of the package so the Upper Colorado project could proceed. Dams would go in at Flaming Gorge, at Glen Canyon, at the Navajo site on the San Juan in Utah, and at the Curecanti site on the Gunnison in western Colorado, but not at Echo Park and Split Mountain.

At least one further concession was offered to the conservationists. On a small tributary of the Colorado River in the area that would be inundated by the reservoir behind Glen Canyon Dam was Rainbow Bridge National Monument. Rainbow Bridge—the largest known natural bridge in the world, tall enough to straddle the Capitol building in Washington, DC, with room to spare—stood several miles upstream from the big river, but unless protective measures were taken, water from the reservoir would enter the monument and eventually pool around the bridge's ankles. The agreement allowing construction of Glen Canyon and the other dams, later adopted by Congress in the legislation approving the project, promised that "no dam or reservoir constructed under the authorization of this act shall be within any national park or monument," and specifically ordered the secretary of the interior to take "adequate protective measures to preclude impairment of the Rainbow Bridge National Monument."[26] It turned out that these were promises just waiting to be broken.

Toward the end of the Dinosaur campaign, some people began telling Brower that Glen Canyon, which he and his allies had sacrificed quite willingly, was spectacular, far more so than even Dinosaur, and bigger—a promising site for one or more national parks. One of these people was Wallace Stegner. Another was the filmmaker Charles Eggert. There was a small Utah group organized to push for an Escalante National Park—the Escalante being a major Colorado tributary that joins the big river in Glen Canyon just above the Utah-Arizona border. Eggert waxed passionate in a letter to Brower dated September 8, 1955, arguing that one could move Glen Canyon Dam sixty miles upstream and save most of the extraordinary features that were about to be lost: "To destroy Music Temple [a magnificent sandstone grotto] would be a first rate crime against the God Almighty."[27]

Eggert's suggestion, moving the dam upstream, reasonable as it appears, was never taken seriously. In fact, there was something of a movement within the movement to oppose the entire Upper Colorado reclamation project. With Brower in DC, the Sierra Club's executive committee debated its position and then wired Brower, telling him to announce that the club would not oppose the project if the Dinosaur dams were removed. Immediately, as Brower writes, the two hundred votes the conservation lobby had amassed to oppose the Dinosaur dams were released, and the authorizing legislation sailed through almost without opposition.

Glen Canyon, named by John Wesley Powell in the mid-nineteenth century, was nearly two hundred miles long with spectacular side canyons—Powell's "glens." The water was gentle here: none of the fierce rapids as in Grand Canyon, not even the medium-fierce rapids as in Dinosaur, Cataract, or Gray upstream. The canyon walls were mainly Navajo sandstone decorated with magnificent tapestries of desert varnish and lined with fern gardens along seeps of clear, sweet water. Its largest tributary is the Escalante River. A side canyon off that river held what may well have been the most awe-inspiring sandstone grotto in the world: the Cathedral in the Desert. All that is now gone under the still waters of Lake Powell—though, as of the early twenty-first century, following years of below-normal rainfall, the reservoir level has dropped and revealed places once covered with water and silt, including the cathedral's floor, and thousands of miles of hideous bathtub ring all along the edge of the lake.

It was six years before Brower visited Glen Canyon himself, and he was shocked, stunned, and horrified. How could the conservation community have given away this sublime place without ever seeing it? How could *he* have? He believed that the conservation groups could have blocked the Glen Canyon dam, and he blamed himself for allowing the dam to go forward. It was probably the single most wrenching experience of his life—a lesson he vowed to learn and never repeat. It undeniably made him more rigid and less willing to look for compromises. "Militant" is how many have described him following the Glen Canyon debacle.

He berated himself for the loss of Glen and was utterly convinced that he could have stopped the desecration of the canyon had he but tried hard enough. The bitterness and regret lingered the rest of his life, and occasionally boiled over. He said, "The magic of Glen Canyon is dead. It has been vulgarized. Putting water in the Cathedral in the Desert was like urinating in the crypt of St. Peter's."[28]

Mark Harvey, the historian and author of *A Symbol of Wilderness: Echo Park and the American Conservation Movement*, the authoritative book on Echo Park and the battle to spare it, is of another opinion. He insists that there was no way Brower and the conservation community could have blocked the Glen Canyon dam no matter what they did, no matter how hard they tried. Dinosaur was in a national monument, part of the national park system. Glen Canyon was federal land, but without an iota of protection. It later became a national recreation area, but in the 1950s it had no formal designation. Brower, one would suspect, would argue that he might have been able to persuade President Eisenhower to declare a Glen Canyon National Monument (unlikely, since the Eisenhower administration favored the Dinosaur dams and the whole Colorado River Storage Project). He might have been able to persuade Congress to set the area apart, but the odds would have been long indeed. Still, Brower regretted the loss of Glen whether it was through ignorance, foolish compromise, or something else.

One gets a sense of how pivotal the Glen Canyon experience was from the frequency with which Brower referred to it throughout his life. Mike McCloskey, who succeeded Brower as Sierra Club executive director, says that that experience, and other compromises that went wrong, marked a turning point in the arc of Brower's life, which he charts as going from mountaineer to administrator to visionary to evangelist.[29]

Brower made his first visit to Glen Canyon in 1962, when he and his youngest son, Johnny, joined a Sierra Club trip led by Dick Norgaard, then an undergraduate economics student at the University of California at Berkeley. Ironically, Stewart Udall had visited Glen with his family two years before and was stunned by its beauty, wondering if the dam should have been built after all, but it was too late. Norgaard says that Brower was likewise bowled over by Glen and desperately sad at what was about to happen.

He also reports a small oddity: While Brower loved the canyon and the river, he was not altogether comfortable on the water. "He liked to keep his feet under him. He'd wear his life jacket even hiking in the side canyons."[30] John McPhee reports a similar instance in the Grand Canyon when Brower chose to walk around Upset Rapid—one of the big rapids—while the other passengers rode in the rafts. Asked why, Brower said, "Because I'm chicken."[31] The great mountaineer was nervous when it came to getting intimate with the roiling waters he so admired.

This began a whirlwind of trips through Glen. Long-time Sierra Club photographer Philip Hyde and his wife, Ardis, joined several, cameras in hand. Eliot Porter made three trips also, taking photos. Toppy Edwards of *National Geographic* came once. Norgaard says they managed to get approximately 160 people in 1962 and 1963 to see what was being lost.

. . .

Brower took at least two lessons from the Glen Canyon experience. The first was never to decide the fate of a place you've never seen. The conservationists were fighting for Dinosaur as a place and also for the proposition that such a development should never be allowed in a unit of the national park system, having learned a painful lesson at Hetch Hetchy. Brower had heard stories of the beauty of Glen from people who had been there, but that wasn't enough to sway him in time.

The second lesson was to be wary of accepting with little questioning the need for a given project and then offering almost glib alternatives in order to achieve immediate objectives—coal and nuclear plants as alternatives to dams, for example. Eventually, Brower came to question the beneficence of economic growth itself, which he later would describe as "a sophisticated device for stealing from our children."[32]

Meanwhile, the Dinosaur battle had launched Brower and the conservation movement onto the national stage. Jon Cosco says it well: "The Echo Park controversy marked the moment at which [the conservation movement] emerged into the light of national politics." He praises its political acumen, its solidarity, and its mastery of technical and economic arguments. "If, with the benefit of hindsight, we can claim that the modern environmental movement had some clearly recognizable beginning, we might start to look for it in a scenic canyon called Echo Park."[33]

SEVEN

The Battle for Wilderness

The people who are destroying the life-support system are radicals. People who use all the resources they possibly can in the name of national security—that is radical. The people trying to correct that are the conservatives. Someone got the names mixed up.

The battle over Dinosaur had preoccupied the conservation movement nationally; the drive to pass a law to protect wilderness was put on hold. But with the passage of the reclamation plan that saved Dinosaur (and doomed Glen Canyon), the attention of wilderness mavens returned to the legislative campaign. The leaders were Howard Zahniser of the Wilderness Society and Brower. Zahniser minded the store in Washington, hatched legislative strategy, wooed lawmakers, and drafted and revised more than sixty times what would eventually become the Wilderness Act. Brower ranged about the country representing the Sierra Club, giving speeches, testifying at hearings, and rallying the troops via articles in the *Sierra Club Bulletin* and elsewhere. To enhance the *Bulletin*'s impact, Brower soon increased its size to 8½″ × 11″ and added color plates. Zahniser kept up a steady drumbeat of pro–Wilderness Act propaganda in *The Living Wilderness* as well.

Brower led a breakneck schedule, leaving Anne at home to watch over four young children when he was away, which was literally more than half the time. And even when he was at home in Berkeley, he would spend most of his waking hours on Sierra Club business, though he did make a point of taking the family up to Tilden Park—just over the ridge from their house—for occasional picnic lunches. Anne carried the major load of child rearing and, according to people who knew her, wasn't altogether satisfied with the division of labor. Dave continued to lead High Trips until 1956, but had given up serious rock climbing by this time.

David Brower on the phone in his Sierra Club office, probably in the mid-1960s. Photograph courtesy Earth Island Institute.

The Forest Service had been designating wilderness areas and primitive areas since the 1930s under the leadership of Aldo Leopold and Robert Marshall, but without a national law that defined wilderness and set up a legal mechanism to protect it permanently, wilderness areas could lose their status at the whim of the agency as the political mood changed.

ALLIES AND OPPONENTS

The conservation community, largely via the biennial Wilderness Conferences that the Sierra Club organized starting in 1949, built a solid rationale for a wilderness act and worked on strategies for achieving it. The conferences also served as recruiting tools for the movement that would be needed to achieve a wilderness protection law. Scientists, politicians, everyday activists, and others backed by solid science and reasoning were published between hard covers by Brower and the Sierra Club so that the messages could spread. The conferences and their published proceedings were the intellectual underpinning that made possible enactment of the Wilderness Act. In fact, it would be useful if some modern-day pundits who hold that there really isn't any wilderness, that the whole concept is outmoded and needs to be rethought, examined the thinking that emerged from the Wilderness Conferences.[1]

Brower and Zahniser, whom Brower considered "my principal coach in the conservation business,"[2] were a kind of tag team, along with Fred Packard of the National Parks Association,[3] Ira Gabrielson of the Wildlife Management Institute, and the other leaders who had knocked off the Dinosaur dams proposal. The coalition they had fashioned for the Dinosaur battle served them well in the push for wilderness legislation, though they faced a long slog.

A principal impediment was the very nature of Congress, especially the Senate. There, the lightly populated Rocky Mountain states—largely the Colorado Basin states—hold power far beyond what their population numbers might suggest. Wyoming, for example, has two senators as do all states, but only one member of the House of Representatives. (Alaska also falls into this elite club but hadn't joined the Union by this time.) Most wilderness areas were in the West, but Western legislators were far more likely than their Eastern counterparts to side with resource-extraction interests, with the result that the pro-wilderness-act legislative leaders came from Minnesota (Senator Hubert Humphrey) and Pennsylvania (Representative John Saylor).

There was much horse trading before the law finally was enacted, and the Western senators extracted several painful compromises, the most damaging of which allowed continued mineral exploration in designated wilderness for nineteen years.

To the surprise of some, the Forest Service staunchly opposed the idea of a wilderness act, even though the agency already had several such areas within its domain and the earliest wilderness leaders, especially Bob Marshall, founder of the Wilderness Society, had worked for the agency. Still, the Forest Service in the 1950s opposed the proposal, since such a law would take away the agency's discretion to manage its land—or portions of its land anyway—as it saw fit. It argued that it needed flexibility to cope with changing times. Indeed, the agency tended to view the wilderness areas and primitive areas it had designated as temporary, awaiting a day when their trees would be needed for lumber and their minerals for commerce. The mission or duty of the Forest Service, founded in 1905, was to protect streams, wildlife habitat, and soils and to provide timber and wood pulp for the use of the growing nation. Conservationists had always felt that the agency put much too much emphasis on logging to the detriment of the other purposes, one of the reasons they felt the need for a federal law to protect designated wilderness areas in perpetuity. Some said that wilderness had been defined as a place "where the hand of man has not set foot."[4] Brower, for his part, would argue that the United States had never had a Forest Service, but instead an agency that should be called the Timber Service.

More surprising was the opposition of the National Park Service, whose mission, after all, was to protect wilderness in addition to providing opportunities for recreation. Again, here the agency was reluctant to cede its authority to grant permission for development of various sorts within its borders—roads, hotels, golf courses, parking lots, chapels, marinas, and tramways among other things. The Park Service tended to view wilderness within the parks as a series of islands surrounded by these kinds of development. The conservationists saw it the other way round: development was a set of islands surrounded by wilderness. It took a long time to sort that out—and it remains an issue to this day in some parks.

WILDLANDS INVENTORY

In the mid-fifties, Brower proposed a massive inventory of wildlands in the United States, arguing that a systematic review was necessary to determine what was there and how it should be managed. This would include federal, state, and local government parks and other holdings. It was patterned after the periodic reviews conducted by the Forest Service. He suggested a Scenic Resources Review, and the Sierra Club board enthusiastically endorsed the idea. This sparked another round of conflict with the Forest Service and the Park Service, which opposed the idea. There was much tussling, but eventually an Outdoor Recreation Review Commission (Brower pointed out that the change of name missed the whole point of the exercise) was established and set out to write a report. Brower was pointedly left off the commission even though the idea had originated with him. He had made too many enemies in Washington. The commission eventually produced a report that was not what Brower and the Sierra Club had hoped for, though it did recommend wilderness designation for more land and paved the way for passage of the Land and Water Conservation Fund in 1965, which would provide money for the federal government to acquire land. The report also proposed creating a Bureau of Outdoor Recreation, which existed for fifteen years.

One profoundly important consequence of the exercise was almost accidental. David Pesonen, a young forestry student at the University of California, Berkeley, was helping one of the commissioners put together the wilderness section of the report. He was concerned that wilderness would get short shrift, so he asked the novelist Wallace Stegner, a professor at Stanford, to write what became known as the "Wilderness Letter," a ringing celebration of wilderness as part of what Stegner called "the geography of hope." Pesonen outlined what he thought such a letter should cover but deemed himself unqualified to write a polished letter. He had read and admired Stegner's *Beyond the Hundredth Meridian* and bravely approached Stegner, who agreed.[5] Stegner sent a copy of his letter to Brower, who printed it in the book that carried the proceedings of the next Wilderness Conference.[6] The letter has been reprinted countless times and is an important part of environmental history and literature.

TAKING ON THE PARK SERVICE

After the commission's report was issued Dave became embroiled in two additional conflicts, which illustrated his growing mistrust of the Forest Service and the Park Service. The clash with the Park Service centered on Mission 66, a plan put forward by Park Service director Conrad Wirth to "improve" the national parks, which had fallen into disrepair during the war. The name came from the fact that the Park Service would celebrate its fiftieth anniversary in 1966, and Wirth proposed roads, hotels, and all kinds of spiffy new developments to make the parks more convenient for visitors.

To boost Mission 66, the Park Service produced a forty-page booklet that had its first distribution at the Wilderness Conference of 1957. It argued that wilderness could be big or small, remote or adjacent to a road. Fred Packard, head of the National Parks Association, took a sniff and smelled a questionable odor. He asked Dave Brower to take a look.

Brower responded with a lengthy article in the association's publication, *National Parks Magazine*, excoriating the Park Service for forgetting its primary mission of protecting wilderness and suggesting that there be launched Mission 65, to celebrate the centennial of Yosemite, the world's first national wilderness park. Brower took pains to lay out the pertinent part of the law that had established the National Park Service in 1916, which was to "promote and regulate" use of national parks, monuments, and other holdings in a way that would serve their primary purpose: "to conserve the scenery and the natural and historic objects and the wildlife therein and to provide for the enjoyment of the same in such manner and by such means as will leave them unimpaired for the enjoyment of future generations."[7]

Brower then quoted passages that seemed to suggest that the Park Service didn't share the conservationists' wilderness-first attitude toward the parks, such as "facilities geared to modern means of transportation and recreation" and "greater dispersion of visitors throughout the parks." He continued, still quoting the booklet: "Comparatively few park visitors experience true wilderness. By contrast, millions profit from those qualities of wilderness which are available to them in the near vicinity of park roads and developed areas. But who may say that the latter gain less than the former?" And finally: "There is no wilderness left" in the United States today.

Brower then commented on these passages: "Add all these up. The Park Service publication is saying that wilderness is large and natural. There isn't any left. Anyway, millions enjoy roadside wilderness. Was the purpose of the publication thus to demonstrate that the Wilderness Bill was superfluous?" He went on to ridicule more passages, especially photo captions, saving his major scorn for this one: "The laws of the Nation require preservation of wilderness in National Parks and Monuments." Brower's comment: "The selection of photograph to accompany this caption is amazing—Echo Park, in Dinosaur National Monument, the subject of one of the greatest of all park-area controversies, but one from which the Park Service was constrained to retire at the very time when the threat became most intense. Volunteers came to the rescue and persuaded the Congress against this threat. Apparently the Service still feels constrained, in this brochure, not to mention it."

Brower's article did not sit well with the Park Service. The director, Wirth, wrote to the magazine's editor, Bruce Kilgore,[8] characterizing the piece as an "unfortunate outburst coming at an unfortunate time." Wirth stood by the booklet and regretted that it should be so criticized by "an evidently bitter and impatient man."[9] Horace Albright, a former Park Service head, wrote to Fred Packard, saying, "The last issue of the *National Parks Magazine* has some pretty bad things in it. Some are unfair, some unkind, some misleading and some untrue. I refer particularly to articles by Brower and [Joseph] Carithers."[10]

Lingering resentment over Dinosaur, fueled by the flap over Mission 66 and other matters, actually led Albright and Wirth to try to persuade the Sierra Club to discharge Brower for intemperate and ad hominem attacks. Brower denied the charges and kept his job, but the board did adopt a resolution, which read, in part: "In the opinion of the Board, objectivity and constructiveness of criticism are to be fostered as follows: No statement should be used that expressly, impliedly, or by reasonable inference criticizes the motives, integrity, or competence of an official or bureau. In publications, objectivity can best be achieved by presentation of both sides of a controversy. If any doubt exists as to compliance with the policies set forth in the resolution, review should be secured from an appropriate Sierra Club official."[11] Brower immediately dubbed this a "gag order" and argued that it made his job all but impossible.

TAKING ON THE FOREST SERVICE

As the movement did battle with the Park Service over Mission 66, the Sierra Club was also engaged in a tussle with the Forest Service over a fine, rare stand of Jeffrey pines at a place called Deadman Summit on the east side of the Sierra Nevada south of Mono Lake near Mammoth Hot Springs. This was a relatively low-elevation stand of big, old, widely spaced trees, ideal for recreation, sometimes called a cathedral grove—the last of its kind, the rest, mostly in Oregon, having been cut. A local fellow named John Haddaway, who had suggested creating a new national monument to protect the Mono Craters and the Inyo Craters plus the Jeffrey pine forest, had alerted Sierra Club headquarters that the Forest Service had begun cutting the healthy old Jeffreys when it had promised to cut only beetle-damaged trees under the guise of "salvage" or "sanitation" logging.

Brower decided to pay a visit, and the Forest Service offered to show him around. He went a day early and got a tour of the area from Haddaway, seeing fallen trees and piles of slash. The next day the Forest Service took him on a very different tour, avoiding the most devastated areas and accusing Haddaway of exaggeration. Brower cites that show-and-tell as cementing his distrust of the Forest Service: "My disillusionment with the Forest Service— which had begun in the Kings Canyon battle, when I saw what they had tried to do but was not aware of all their techniques—my disillusionment did not come until the Deadman Summit controversy in the Mammoth Lakes area."[12]

Brower then received an unsigned article written for the *Bulletin* by a Sierra Club member familiar with the situation that accused the Forest Service of dishonesty in the Deadman Summit matter. Brower had the story set in type and made into page proofs. He circulated it to what he thought were sympathetic organizations, and a copy instantly made its way to the Forest Service and the American Forestry Association. The article did not appear in the *Bulletin*—Brower says he never intended to publish it—but it made some club directors uncomfortable and added impetus to the effort to pass the resolution—or gag order.

Mike McCloskey, who would succeed Brower as executive director of the club a decade later, recalled, "I never saw him attack motives or integrity."[13] McCloskey's comment deals only with years subsequent to the gag order, and he suggests that perhaps Brower changed his behavior after the Mission 66 and Deadman Summit matters. Some of Brower's critics continued to argue that Brower should be a little more polite toward those who disagreed with Sierra Club policies.

THE WILDERNESS BILL, 1964

The Wilderness Bill finally became law in 1964 after a campaign that had lasted a decade. Proponents had had to accept some compromises—to leave wilderness areas open to new mining claims for twenty years and to lose an advisory council they hoped would ensure that the Park Service, the Forest Service, the Fish and Wildlife Service, and the Bureau of Land Management would be diligent about surveying their holdings and recommending lots of new wilderness areas. But it was a historic victory nonetheless. Tragically, Howard Zahniser, the principal architect of the law, would not live to see the signing ceremony. He died of a massive heart attack several months before it took place, at the age of fifty-eight.

Newton Drury, the Park Service director who had agreed not to oppose the dams in Dinosaur but changed his mind and eventually got fired, had gone on to lead the California State Park system and the Save the Redwoods League. He sent Brower a handwritten note on league stationery, dated September 3, 1964: "Dear Dave, Congratulations on the Wilderness Bill. I remember when you and Zahnie sat in the Cosmos Club hatching the original program. There are some provisions we could have done without. But as the Irishman said, 'It didn't come out as I expected, and I never expected it would.' As ever, Newton."[14]

. . .

The growing nervousness among the old guard over Brower's style that resulted in the gag order would build slowly in the coming years. It would lead Brower to encourage allies to run for positions on the board of directors and to seek outside voices in Sierra Club publications.

PART THREE

Visionary

EIGHT

Big Books for a Cause

The book is something well worth getting addicted to.

While Brower was enmeshed in battles with federal agencies to keep public lands untrammeled by development, he was also on the verge of starting what would become a groundbreaking series of oversize word-and-picture books that would profoundly change how the Sierra Club spread its conservation message. But like all Brower's endeavors, this one would not be without significant controversy.

It begins with Ansel Adams and Yosemite Valley.

In 1903 Sierra Club volunteers started building a small, rough-hewn, granite and timber building in the valley to honor the geologist Joseph LeConte, a professor at the University of California at Berkeley and a cofounder of the organization. They finished the LeConte Lodge the following year and began using it as a library and a place for lectures and other public education activities. By the mid-1950s enthusiasm had sagged a bit, and the National Park Service encouraged the club to revitalize the public functions of the lodge or risk losing its toehold on the place.

Ansel Adams was well ensconced in the park and had been for decades. Nancy Newhall was a friend, and he had worked with her; she was a writer from the East Coast who had worked in the Museum of Modern Art in Manhattan and the George Eastman House in Rochester, New York, where Beaumont Newhall, her husband, was director. Dave Brower, fresh off the exhilaration of beating the Dinosaur dams, was looking for new challenges.

David Brower presenting a copy of *In Wildness Is the Preservation of the World* to President Lyndon Johnson, 1964. Photograph by Abbie Rowe, the White House, courtesy Earth Island Institute.

Nancy and Ansel cooked up the idea of a photographic exhibit for the lodge, a celebration of the "American Earth." Forty of the photographs would be Adams's trademark black-and-white landscapes and close-ups. Another forty would be work by around two dozen other photographers, including photographs of urban scenes, farms, pollution, sprawl—even a few scenes from abroad, despite the name. Newhall wrote a long, linked tone poem that stitched together the themes of the exhibit, a ringing call to take care of the earth. The Sierra Club board approved the idea in principle in mid-1956.

Brower confirmed the news of the board's approval in a letter to Adams in September.[1] He also wrote that his wife, Anne, "was especially moved by the LeConte exhibit. . . . She said, 'I guess Ansel is just the greatest photographer there ever has been.' She added that she was moved by Nancy's words, too, and by the way they so superbly complimented what your photographs were saying." Dave thanked Ansel for "the doors you have opened to Appreciation" and the recognition and promotion the exhibit was providing the Sierra Club.

The exhibit drew enthusiastic crowds, and the Smithsonian financed the creation of several copies of the entire exhibition and sent them across the country and around the world in several languages. This enabled thousands of people to view the photographs and absorb the message conveyed by pictures and text, but Adams, Newhall, and Brower thought there should be more. Brower, with his background at the University of California Press, thought it could be bottled, as his son Ken says, and made into a fine book.

THE SIERRA CLUB'S EXHIBIT FORMAT BOOKS

As Brower wrote later, "This is the American Earth needed to be rescued from its exhibit mode, where people might wander in at the beginning of it, or the middle, or the end, and not comprehend its context. It needed to become a book." The text was moving, and the photographs stunning and moving in their own way, but together "something new sprang off the page."[2] This was the important new feature of the "Exhibit Format" books, a synthesis between photograph and text that was more than the sum of its parts. It would be a big challenge—and a major gamble. No such project had been undertaken before. There were big, lavish art books to be sure, but nothing that combined fine photography and stirring words with a conservation message.

To do the photographs justice, the trim size of the book would have to be big. "The eye must be required to move about within the boundaries of the image, not encompass it all in one glance," Brower explained.[3] The printing must be the highest quality obtainable. This meant that the book would not come cheap. The best estimate was that the book would have to cost fifteen dollars at a time when paperbacks cost a quarter and hardback novels sold for a few dollars. The three commercial publishers Brower approached were polite but firm in their refusal to take the project on.

Adams, fortunately, had a photographer friend, Dick McGraw, whose father, Max, of McGraw-Edison, donated $10,000 to the book project and lent a further $15,000. Ansel, Nancy, and Dave repaired to Ansel's studio in San Francisco—where the original exhibit had been organized—to create the book. Ken Brower, then a lad not yet in his teens, remembers watching the three debating and discussing which photos should go where and with which parts of the text, with his father trying diplomatically to tone down the somewhat florid parts of the text, working into the evenings until the martinis they had been drinking took over and it was time to quit.

One challenge was to figure out how to start the book. Rather than begin with a half-title followed by a title page (on whose verso the copyright information must appear), Brower hit on the idea of an extended introduction. "What the book needed was a prelude—a long statement to precede the foreword. But could this be done?"[4] He telephoned the Washington office of the United States Register of Copyrights. There was no official objection to having several pages of material preceding the title page, he was told, but the copyright notice must still appear on the following verso. This extended prelude would become a common feature of the Exhibit Format series and would be copied in other books and, Brower wrote perhaps somewhat immodestly, in films as well. "The audience now has the excitement of trying to determine when the show starts. I had not intended it that way—not for the movies anyway. But there was purpose for it in the book."[5]

Creation of the final illustrated manuscript took many months. The finished book—ten thousand copies at fifteen dollars each—was published in early 1960 by the Sierra Club, by miles the most ambitious publishing project the organization had ever undertaken, especially considering that it had fewer than fifteen thousand members. The Sierra Club had taken a big risk—no other conservation organization was doing anything remotely like this. Brower's training at the

University of California Press and on the *Sierra Club Bulletin* had convinced him of the power that words and pictures could exert. It would become his main preoccupation over the next quarter century.

The book, *This Is the American Earth*, was a sensation. The *New York Times* reviewed it three times. Supreme Court Justice William O. Douglas called it "one of the greatest statements in the history of conservation." A Kansas City paper devoted its entire editorial page to the book. The first printing sold out quickly, allowing the McGraw loan to be repaid promptly, and more printings were ordered. *This Is the American Earth* was quickly followed by two more titles—*Words of the Earth*, later in 1960, words and photos by Cedric Wright, a longtime Sierra Club stalwart; then *These We Inherit: The Parklands of America*, by Ansel Adams, in 1962, both in black and white.[6] Both were modest successes, nothing like *American Earth*, but they sold enough copies to pay for themselves and add to the Sierra Club's backlist, a necessity for a successful publishing program.

ONE OF THE "MOST BEAUTIFUL" BOOKS

Then the Exhibit Format series reached another milestone. Eliot Porter, a New Englander who had graduated from medical school but turned to photography without ever practicing medicine, had spent twenty years making intimate color photographs of New England nature, abstract studies of trees and meadows and streams, and pairing them with passages from *Walden* and the journals of Henry David Thoreau. Porter's work had been exhibited at the Smithsonian and titled *The Seasons*. A half-dozen publishers had expressed interest in the exhibit's book possibilities, but all shied away when they considered the cost of a big color book.

Porter was a friend of Nancy Newhall, who encouraged him to send a mock-up of the book to David Brower. He did so. Brower was immediately captivated. He sought and received a grant and loan from Kenneth Bechtel's Belvedere Scientific Fund to create a book ($20,000 and $30,000 this time), and they were off. The book would have to sell for $25, and no one knew if it would work. Brower titled the book *"In Wildness Is the Preservation of the World,"* a line from Thoreau that Howard Zahniser had used on Wilderness Society stationery for years.

"When you price a book at twenty-five dollars (1963 dollars) . . . you take a deep breath, cross your fingers, pray, hope, and prepare yourself to be considered insane." Brower reports he did all those things, not necessarily in that order, and was stunned that the first printing of thirteen thousand copies was sold before the book was off press.[7] The Leipzig Book Fair called *In Wildness* one of the ten most beautiful books of 1962.

Shortly after that, Brower made a deal with Ian Ballantine of Ballantine Books, whereby Ballantine would publish small paperback editions of the Exhibit Format books. Some in the Sierra Club feared that this would slow down sales of the full-size editions. It did the opposite. *In Wildness*, by Brower's estimate, eventually sold close to a million copies in various editions.[8] Ballantine went on to publish many of the big books in small paperback editions and to use some of the images in wall and engagement calendars, which sold extremely well and spread the club's name ever further.

Brower and his publications program were flying high. If some is good, more is better, and his experience in publishing had taught him that to sustain a major publishing operation, you need a steady stream of new titles and a substantial backlist so that many titles share overhead expenses. Statistics are made to be argued over, but there's no question that the publications program, the Exhibit Format series in particular, attracted thousands of members to the Sierra Club. Before the series launched, the club had seen slow, steady growth and membership hovered in the low five figures. Afterward, it accelerated, though nowhere near as fast as it would a few years later. It was startling to hear over and over, during interviews conducted for this book, from people who were drawn to the club by the books in store windows, in libraries, or on coffee tables around the country. Many of the people who would make important contributions to the Sierra Club as staff members or as active volunteers (several of whom we will meet presently) first learned of the club and its work via the books.

In Wildness appeared in 1962. Over the next six years a further sixteen titles appeared in Exhibit Format, five with photographs by Eliot Porter; two by Philip Hyde; one more by Ansel Adams, his third in the series; and the rest by a variety of photographers, some solo, some with contributions from many photographers. Subjects ranged from conservation battlegrounds—the Grand Canyon, Glen Canyon, the redwoods, the North Cascades in Washington State—to meditations on nature and the human experience. The Glen Canyon book, *The Place No One Knew*, was an elegy, published in the hope that it might help ensure that the Grand Canyon would not suffer the same fate Glen Canyon had. Some members of the publications committee opposed its publication since the place was already lost, but it was published and seemed to have the desired effect.

Some of the books, it goes without saying, sold better than others. Some didn't sell well at all, but most turned a profit, which was plowed straight back into the effort. The least successful was *The Last Redwoods*, which called for creation of a Redwood National Park. The book included photographs of cutover land, ugly scenes meant to spur outrage but instead persuading people to keep their wallets closed. It was the first and last in the series to include shots like that. Lesson learned.

NOT MAN APART AND ON TO THE GALÁPAGOS

One surprise hit in the series was *Not Man Apart*, which paired photographs by several photographers of the Big Sur coast in California with lines from the poems of Robinson Jeffers. Ken Brower, then a sophomore at the University of California, took a semester off school to put the book together at his father's request. It eventually sold more hardback copies (in excess of one hundred thousand) than any other title in the series. As Ken was about to return to school, his father asked him if he'd like to join Eliot Porter on an extended trip to the Galápagos Islands to put together a two-volume book on Darwin, the islands, and evolution. Ken jumped at the chance. He never returned to the university but went on to a distinguished career as writer and editor, eventually editing or writing more than half of his father's thirty Exhibit Format titles plus many other books and scores of magazine articles of his own.

Meanwhile, the disparity between the number of Porter books and the number of Adams books was an irritant to Adams, who was never a big fan of color photography, though he dabbled in it. He felt that black-and-white photographs could be better controlled and manipulated in the darkroom. At one point, Brower remembers, he got up a head of steam at a board meeting and said, "Eliot Porter is the Sierra Club's most valuable property," which miffed both Adams, who had been contributing photographs to Sierra Club publications for decades, and Porter, who resented being called a property. Martin Litton, who served on the publications committee, said that since Porter was working in color, it "kind of eclipsed Ansel Adams."[9] He recalled that Adams was "consumed by jealousy" of Porter,[10] and Brower included two of Adams's color images in the Grand Canyon book to mollify him.

Litton explained that Adams would oppose publishing more books by Porter because "they weren't by him."

BOOK PROGRAM CONTROVERSIES

The speed with which the publishing program grew troubled some members of the board of directors and some on the publications committee. Some worried that Brower was spreading himself too thin (he said that that's how he kept his weight in check); some worried that he was emphasizing publications to the detriment of other club efforts; and some worried that the heavy investment required to publish so many titles was endangering the club's future. Nearly every book Brower proposed for publication met with resistance and required a major push to gain approval.[11] This led him to get projects well under way before telling the committee or the board, so they'd be harder to derail, a technique that angered some on the board who felt that Brower was defying their authority.

And there was at least one other concern—namely, that four of the volumes (the two Galápagos volumes, a single volume on Baja California, and another on the American Everest expedition) discussed places outside the borders of the United States. Some directors had argued that *In Wildness* was well outside the club's Western purview; going international might be going too far. Dick Leonard, a three-decade member of the board and a careful lawyer, wondered if the international publications program might be *ultra vires*, or beyond the power or scope of the organization. If that objection weren't enough, the contracts with the authors and photographers were written by Brower, when there were contracts at all. At one point, he tried to include a small royalty for himself, to be used at his discretion to develop more books. That ran into a storm of opposition among some of the directors, and he dropped the idea.

As early as 1962 a proposal was floated before the board to divide the executive director position into five departments—one to oversee publications, one conservation, one outings, one lodges, and one administration. Brower would get the publications portfolio and be moved to New York. Brower saw this as a move to sideline him. In a letter to Ansel Adams, he wrote, "I shall not willingly go on the shelf and will fight to the last ditch any attempt to fragment the organization because I think it is wrong, wholly wrong. Perhaps you can persuade me into thinking otherwise, but it will be hard work."[12] He went on, "Put a good hard-headed, pure-business-oriented, successful executive-type man in that over-all supervisory spot if you will, but at the same time you had better provide a suitable obituary to intone over my bones—bones bared too early." Adams wrote back, saying that he had no intention of pushing Dave into a box. "It was never my intention that you would ever assume any other position but Executive Director," he wrote, "but that you would concentrate most of your activities in the direction of publishing—because I think that is probably your most potentially important field. The club has gotten to a point where you simply cannot, as a human organism, properly carry the whole burden."[13]

In 1962, the Exhibit Format experiment was barely begun, the gigantic success of *In Wildness, Not Man Apart*, and several other titles not yet realized. But cautious members of the board and the publications committee were getting uneasy. By 1963, one of the publications committee members who worried that Brower might be going too far, too fast, was its chairman, August Frugé, who was then the director of the University of California Press, where he had been Brower's boss a decade before. It was a slightly odd situation, because although vastly different in size and scope, the two publishing operations would occasionally seem to be in competition for a given manuscript—at least that's how Brower, his family, and his staff saw the matter.[14]

In any event, Frugé became sufficiently concerned to write a memo to the members of the publications committee and to Edgar Wayburn, then the president of the board of directors. It said, in part, "We are uncertain about the nature of our publishing program and about where it is leading us. A few years ago publishing was clearly the servant of conservation and of other Club purposes. Since then it has grown enormously to the point where it takes up a major share of our energies and resources. Some of us wonder whether the tail is beginning to wag the dog."[15] Frugé went on to say that if indeed the Sierra Club was to become a publishing house first and a conservation and outings organization second, it should do so explicitly and deliberately, after open and wide-ranging discussion. It was clear that he did not approve of the direction Brower was taking the organization. Brower, of course, argued mightily against this line of thinking, and the memo faded away. In some cases, however, it faded into various file cabinets, to be retrieved and circulated several years later as the water around Brower got hotter.

Controversial as it may have been within the club, the publications program was widely admired outside the institution. In 1965, the Exhibit Format series won the Carey-Thomas award as the year's most distinguished project in American book publishing. The award is sponsored by *Publishers Weekly* "to provide an opportunity to honor book publishing at its best." It was the first time the award had been given to a Western publisher. The *San Francisco Chronicle* noted in its story about the award, "While publication of these books is a Club project, Brower is the spark and drive behind the total excellence of the Series. With this top national honor, the San Francisco-based Sierra Club, Brower and Western publishing are shown to have achieved the highest standard in purpose and execution of producing good books. Congratulations all around."[16]

As mentioned in the last chapter, Brower accelerated and expanded the publications program of the Sierra Club partly in response to the "gag order" the board of directors had adopted forbidding criticism of public officials. Brower explained: "That 1959 resolution . . . was such a severe restriction that that was the main thing that drove me to the publications program. I couldn't do what I was doing in speeches and articles, and I tried to get this general attitude out in books."[17] Mike McCloskey, who would succeed Brower as executive director of the Sierra Club in 1969, echoed the sentiment. He wrote, "[Brower] found a new voice in having the Club publish books by others that were designed to express his vision. Even if he were censored, he felt that no one in the Club would want to censor the words of outside authors."[18]

It is instructive to look at the authors Brower chose to feature, especially at first: writers he admired and whose words he used to advance his notions about nature and conservation and the human condition. Thoreau was the voice of *In Wildness*. Although the selections had been chosen by Eliot Porter, Brower would use Thoreau copiously in subsequent books. Brower chose quotes from John Muir for the Exhibit Format volume on the Sierra Nevada titled *Gentle Wilderness*. Robinson Jeffers's poetry was the backbone of *Not Man Apart*. Other favorites who turned up again and again in later books were the anthropologist Loren Eiseley, the essayist Joseph Wood Krutch, and the conservationist and author Rachel Carson. He would skim quotes from all over, sentiments that said what he wanted to preach—from Adlai Stevenson, Walt Whitman, and dozens of others.

Whatever Brower's motive in publishing them, the books put Brower and the Sierra Club on the map. They appeared at a time when people in America were waking up to the deterioration of their environment—Rachel Carson and her book *Silent Spring* had a great deal to do with that—and beginning to notice that rivers and forests were under siege from dam builders and loggers.

. . .

It was a time of major ferment on many sides: the war in Vietnam was becoming increasingly unpopular, the civil rights movement was gaining steam. The conservation movement had not been particularly political up to this point and had not participated in demonstrations to the extent the antiwar and civil rights communities had. That was about to change.

The Exhibit Format books combined politics and art in a new and compelling way and reached an audience that was both relatively well-to-do and willing to get involved in public policy in a variety of ways. Brower had an abiding faith in the power of words, and the multiplying effect of fine, often poetic writing combined with excellent photography attracted admirers.

At the same time, the experiment was expensive, and it troubled the more cautious in the Sierra Club hierarchy. Depending on who did the calculations, the publications program either caused the club's membership to soar and its influence to increase by orders of magnitude, or it came close to bankrupting the organization. Both might be true.

Brower's critics in the club continued to praise the publications program; they simply wanted it to slow down and lower its ambitions a little. Brower did not agree: if some is good, more is better, and besides, there was a world to save.

NINE

Growing Pains and Saving the Grand Canyon

If my voice sounds shrill at the moment, or strident, it is only because it is one of those used on behalf of conservationists to overcome the epidemic of laryngitis in the several federal agencies you are not hearing from on the most important conservation battle of this century.

In the early sixties the Sierra Club and David Brower were frequently in the news. A counterpoint to the glowing reviews of the Exhibit Format books were the articles and news items about clashes with agencies on the conservation front and friction in the boardroom.

At the time, the club was working hard for a new national park in the redwoods and another in the North Cascades in Washington State. Internally, there was friction over David Brower's style. Hardly anyone questioned his vision, his energy, his determination, or his devotion to the cause, but some members of the board of directors were unhappy with his penchant for confronting federal bureaucrats who were not doing their jobs as he thought they should. Others worried about his management of budgets and his habit of seeking approval from the board only after a project— often a book—was well down the road. It is better to ask for forgiveness than permission, as the old saw goes, and this might have been his subconscious motto.

The publication of Rachel Carson's *Silent Spring* in the *New Yorker* in 1962 swept the matter of pesticides and other poisons into the public consciousness. Brower reports reading the whole thing between planes in the Salt Lake airport and having his view of agriculture changed on the spot. He would urge the Sierra Club to become active in a campaign to protect nature and people from the effects of these chemicals and would run head on into

Jerry Mander and David Brower, 1980. Photograph courtesy Brower family.

some scientists on the board and in the membership who thought Carson was a fraud, or, if not a fraud, then woefully naïve. One of these was Thomas Jukes, a founder of the Atlantic chapter and an employee of American Cyanamid, who became famous for eating teaspoonsful of DDT at press conferences to prove how safe it was.

One possible buffer against the growing worries of the more conservative elements on the Sierra Club board was to diversify its membership. To that end, Brower persuaded several people with national reputations to run for seats on the board. These included Supreme Court Associate Justice William O. Douglas, an outspoken conservationist from the Pacific Northwest who had worked closely with Brower and the Sierra Club on matters of common interest; *New York Times* editorial page editor and columnist John Oakes; Houghton Mifflin editor Paul Brooks, Rachel Carson's editor for *Silent Spring;* Martin Litton, travel editor of *Sunset* magazine and uncompromising champion of the redwoods and a dam-free Grand Canyon and Echo Park; Luna Leopold, chief scientist for the U.S. Geological Survey and son of the great naturalist Aldo Leopold; Eliot Porter, the photographer; and the novelist, biographer, and professor Wallace Stegner.

Mike McCloskey, the organization's second executive director, at the time saw the expansion of the board as in part an attempt by Brower to consolidate his base and weaken his opponents. In the early sixties, McCloskey was representing the Sierra Club in the Northwest, and in 1965 he would move to San Francisco. "Brower tried to shore up his position with the board by recruiting well-known national figures to stand as candidates for election to the board," McCloskey writes. Brower figured that their reputations would help them get elected even though they had not been active in the organization. McCloskey reports, "Some of these new board members did support Brower for a while, but others did not.... But thanks to this recruiting stratagem, Brower did barely manage to maintain a supportive majority on the board through most of the 1960s."[1]

What McCloskey says is certainly true, but it is also true that Brower was genuinely trying to stretch the horizons of the Sierra Club, to bring in new blood and fresh perspectives. He felt the new directors could open new doors for the organization and attract new members and supporters—and bring in new ideas. Having the *New York Times* on your side, for example, could only help. In any case, management of the club's affairs was the rightful province of the staff, which was better equipped to handle such mundane matters than the board. And, after all, the members elected the new directors; they must have agreed with Brower's purpose in bringing new people on board.

McCloskey, however, is certainly correct in his assertion that not all the new directors stuck with Brower. Justice Douglas resigned after just over a year. His formal reason was that the Sierra Club might well wind up as a litigant before the Supreme Court, and if and when that happened, he'd have to recuse himself from the proceedings, though that had always been the case. It seems unlikely that the justice hadn't considered that possibility before he agreed to be a candidate for election to the board, though the Sierra Club wouldn't get into litigation for some years yet.[2] One suspects that the more urgent reason was, as he wrote to Brower in early 1962, "The Board meeting depressed me. You and Ed [Wayburn] apart, I felt as if I were on the mourner's bench."[3]

Of the other relative outsiders, Litton, Leopold, Porter, and Oakes stuck with Brower, though Oakes resigned partway into his term, having missed two consecutive meetings and fearing he would miss more; he may have become weary of the bickering that was on the rise. Wallace Stegner stepped down from the board in 1966, but reemerged in 1968 when internal matters blew sky high, and he became one of Brower's more influential critics. Paul Brooks remained friendly with Brower, but in the end he sided with Brower's foes.

These directors were looking at an executive director with an overloaded plate: publications; the ongoing saga of the wilderness bill; difficult campaigns to create new parks in the North Cascades, at Point Reyes, and in the redwoods; and efforts to stop construction of a nuclear power plant at Bodega Head on the California coast, the proposal by Walt Disney to build a large ski resort in a wild valley in the southern Sierra Nevada, and, the biggest one of them all, the proposal by Stewart Udall and the Johnson administration to build two hydroelectric dams inside the Grand Canyon. Brower was at the center of these efforts, which were significant in different ways—to David Brower, the Sierra Club, and the conservation movement. One of the first involved a proposed nuclear power plant.

BODEGA: A HOLE IN THE HEAD

As the fifties moved into the sixties, the Pacific Gas and Electric Company (PG&E)—the privately owned public utility that serves most of Northern

California—had plans to build seven to ten new electric power plants to meet projected demand. Most of the plants would be nuclear, and most would be sited near the coast so that seawater could be used for cooling the reactors. The garland of atomic plants would decorate the coast from near Santa Barbara to the Oregon border.[4]

The first plant was planned for Bodega Head, fifty miles north of San Francisco. Edgar Wayburn, president of the Sierra Club, got wind of the proposal as early as 1958 and went to investigate. The area had been considered for acquisition as a state park, but interest had been withdrawn and the state Public Utilities Commission, with the power of eminent domain, would have the power to seize the land if it so chose. So confident of its plan was the company that it spent several million dollars digging a hole at Bodega Head to prepare for construction. Wayburn urged local Sierra Club members to oppose the project on scenic grounds, but PG&E had courted local political leaders, and club members' opposition, such as it was, was tepid.

Dave Brower had recently hired David Pesonen, the forestry graduate from Berkeley who had recruited the Wilderness Letter from Wallace Stegner, to work as "conservation editor," a suitably vague title that would allow Pesonen to find his sea legs. It was a pattern that Brower followed throughout his career—he would spot talent in an eager young person, hire him (or her, though the hims vastly outnumbered the hers) for a pittance, and turn him or her loose. Many of them lasted only a few months or years, but some stuck around and made careers out of what Brower helped start.

As Pesonen recounts the tale, Brower handed him a sheaf of clippings by Karl Kortum of the San Francisco Maritime Museum and Harold Gilliam of the *San Francisco Chronicle* lamenting the impending loss of this spectacular stretch of coastline. Pesonen read through the material and immediately strolled a few blocks from club headquarters to PG&E's office and asked a clerk if he could have a look into the company's files on the project. He could. The files hinted at the pressure the company was exerting on local officials and the University of California, which had expressed interest in the site for a marine laboratory.

The articles by Kortum and Gilliam had led the Public Utilities Commission to reopen the hearings on the project, on which preliminary excavations had already occurred. By this time, Pesonen had helped organize a small, scruffy band of opponents who testified against the plant for a variety of reasons, mostly having to do with its location. At the point in Pesonen's testimony when he mentioned improper pressure being brought to bear by

PG&E—he went as far as to call it "corruption"—a fellow whom Pesonen had planted in the audience asked a question: "How do you know all this?" Pesonen went on the describe the contents of the files he had examined at PG&E headquarters, which caused major turmoil among the PG&E officials in attendance, who had assumed that the files were confidential. PG&E was startled by Pesonen's testimony but was still determined to proceed with the project. Shortly thereafter, a seismologist quietly suggested to Pesonen that he read a report on earthquake faults near Bodega Head, namely the San Andreas Fault, which runs right through the center of the proposed plant site. This looked like potent political ammunition.

Soon, club board members learned of Pesonen's activities and hauled him to a meeting in Brower's office. Pesonen recalled, "It was a small group of officers of the club—the president, the vice president, secretary. Three or four members of the club's board and Dave and me. And they asked me to tell them what's going on with Bodega. I described briefly what had happened at the Public Utilities Commission hearings. And I said, 'I think we can stop this thing. But we have to develop and explore further the earthquake hazard.'"[5] This did not sit well with all the directors, especially Dick Leonard. "At that point Leonard just exploded," recalled Pesonen. "He shook his finger at me and he said, 'Don't you dare mention earthquakes. Don't you dare mention public safety. The Sierra Club can talk about scenic beauty, and maybe the loss of scenic beauty, but not about public safety. That's not our job.'"[6] Brower kept quiet, which he later lamented. The club, and he personally, had argued that nuclear power plants could make it unnecessary to build dams in Dinosaur National Monument, the Grand Canyon, and elsewhere. Public concern over atomic safety was rising, sparked by fallout from bomb testing and the growing understanding of what had been unleashed at Hiroshima and Nagasaki. But the technology was still poorly understood by people outside the nuclear establishment, which was occasionally dubbed a "priesthood."

Pesonen considered his position for a week. The club would continue its opposition to the project based on its location but could not mention earthquakes. So Pesonen resigned his job, determined to carry on the fight he knew he could win. The club's campaign was handed to another young man, a newly minted lawyer named Phillip Berry. Berry said that matters had grown rather tense between Pesonen and Brower, despite their amicable history. "In that Bodega fight," he said, "Dave Pesonen was commissioned to fight the project. Dave and Dave were at each other. Pesonen accused Brower of caving, going along with the executive committee, and not fighting on the safety issue. This is what caused Pesonen to become a lawyer later."[7]

Brower respected Pesonen but was hamstrung by his early position on nuclear power and his allegiance to the board. Brower chose to stay quiet, a rather unusual behavior for him, though he tacitly cheered Pesonen on from the sidelines.

Pesonen took several months off, hitchhiking around the West. When he returned, Joel Hedgpeth—the eminent marine biologist and activist—gave him a scrapbook with four years' worth of clippings about the Bodega struggle. "When you read it all compressed, the whole story came glaringly clear," recalled Pesonen. "This was a big, big deal. It had been a big deal from the beginning. And it had been obscured from the public."[8]

Pesonen decided to write the full story, which became a four-part series, titled "A Visit to the Atomic Park," in a small weekly paper called the *Sebastopol Times*. Brower quietly arranged to have four thousand pamphlets containing the article printed for distribution all around the Bay Area. The board refused to allow the club to sponsor the publication but was willing to help with distribution. Not long after, another seismologist investigated the site and said it was riddled with earthquake faults, probably the worst possible location for a nuclear reactor. Shortly the Atomic Energy Commission weighed in with another study questioning the wisdom of Bodega Head as a nuclear site, and PG&E quietly withdrew its proposal and turned its sights elsewhere. From this experience Brower learned what a single determined person—Dave Pesonen—could do against long odds. He referred to Pesonen frequently in speeches to young audiences, encouraging them to become active, not to be afraid to go up against formidable opponents.

The Sierra Club saw that perhaps it should take public safety into account as well as scenic beauty when a development was proposed in a wild or nearly wild place. Brower, meanwhile, became determined not to cave in to orders from a board that he felt was wrong, which would get him into plenty of hot water as the months and years went by. He had followed orders in the army, but this wasn't the army.

A NATIONAL PARK IN THE REDWOODS

As the battle over Bodega Bay was reaching its peak, another contentious campaign was percolating a few hundred miles north near the California coast, just south of the Oregon border. At stake were old-growth redwoods. Unfortunately, the campaign to protect the trees pitted the Sierra Club against another venerable conservation organization, the Save the Redwoods League.

Most national parks are created from land owned by the federal government and managed by the Forest Service, the Bureau of Land Management, or the Fish and Wildlife Service. That wouldn't work for creating a national park in the redwoods in northern California. To encourage development in the Pacific Northwest, the federal government had granted huge blocks of land to the railroads in a checkerboard pattern, giving half to the companies and keeping half in public ownership. The railroads then sold their holdings to lumber companies and used the proceeds to finance rail lines to open up the country. In other words, if a Redwood National Park was to be created, much of it would have to be bought, and it wouldn't come cheap.

The Save the Redwoods League had already preserved numerous stands of old-growth redwoods and donated them to the state, which turned them into state parks. The league had bought the stands from the timber companies with contributions from Rockefellers and other philanthropists. This was a noble public service, but it wasn't perfect: the league's donations tended to be beautiful stands of forests with the biggest trees, which generally were found along streams in the bottoms of valleys. The hillsides above the parks were left in private hands and, eventually, were logged. That left the parks vulnerable to landslides in heavy-rain winters, which happened more than once and toppled some of the tallest trees in the world.

For this reason, the Sierra Club wanted the federal government to acquire a whole wild watershed as a new park to protect the upslope areas from logging as well as the old-growth giants along the stream. The league preferred to acquire Mill Creek, which had a fine stand of old-growth, stream-bottom redwoods, as the showpiece of the new national park. This provoked some rather unpleasant confrontations between the league and the club. The league was, after all, the original organization to work to preserve redwoods; the Sierra Club was a relative latecomer to the crusade. But the Sierra Club was convinced that its approach was the better one.

The Sierra Club's plan, hatched and promoted with leadership by Martin Litton and Edgar Wayburn, suggested that the Redwood Creek watershed was the least damaged of the watersheds in redwood country and that acquiring it should be the primary goal—though it was a bit of a catch-22. They feared that if they were too loud and too public about the suggestion, the timber companies would simply begin preemptive logging and skin the slopes above the creek. Partly owing to the squabble between the club and the league, that is what happened. The land above the Tall Trees Grove on Redwood Creek was largely clear-cut before the park could be created.

Dave Brower's main contributions to the redwoods battle were, not surprisingly, an Exhibit Format book and a newspaper ad. Inspired by the success of the *Denver Post* ad that helped quash the Dinosaur dams, he wrote an ad headlined, "An open letter to President Johnson on the Last Chance Really to Save the Redwoods." It ran in the *New York Times*, the *Washington Post*, the *San Francisco Chronicle*, the *Los Angeles Times*, and the *Sacramento Bee* in late 1965, arguing that Redwood Creek was the best place to create a new national park.

The book was *The Last Redwoods*, by François Leydet. Color and black-and-white landscape photographs by Philip Hyde were interspersed with historic pictures of the redwood country, teams of loggers, and contemporary photos of stripped hillsides and wounded streams. The book served its purpose, stirring up considerable support for the Sierra Club's vision for a Redwood National Park, but it didn't sell as well as some of the other books in the series. Brower always thought that including the ugly shots suppressed sales: "People didn't want that much carnage on their coffee tables."[9]

The argument between the club and the Save the Redwoods League was public and bitter. The Johnson administration was clearly in favor of a park somewhere and would eventually spend more to create it than had ever been spent on land acquisition for a national park. The club's view eventually prevailed, though inevitable political compromises left the new park vulnerable to erosion from logging on adjacent lands, even lands within the new park, including the hillsides above Redwood Creek. President Johnson signed the bill creating the park in 1966. Litigation forced its expansion several years later. Today, Redwood National Park is a showpiece of environmental restoration.

For Brower, the redwoods battle confirmed his belief in the power of the printed word, both in books and in newspaper advertisements. The campaign moved the Sierra Club away from the more old-fashioned and conservative Save the Redwoods League, though the split troubled some Sierra Club directors. Dick Leonard, for example, had served for decades on both the Sierra Club's board and the league's board and was deeply troubled by the public falling-out. Eventually the rift between the two organizations was mostly repaired, but some bruises remain.[10]

STORM KING: CONSERVATION GOES TO COURT

Three thousand miles to the east, at the opposite end of the country, another battle was brewing that drew in the Sierra Club and David Brower and would begin opening courthouse doors to conservation organizations.

In the early sixties, Consolidated Edison proposed building a pumped-storage power plant at Storm King Mountain on the Hudson River about thirty miles upstream from Manhattan. This would involve hollowing out part of the mountain to serve as a reservoir and building a power plant at river level. When demand for electricity was low, water would be pumped up from the river to the reservoir, then let down to run through the power plant to generate electricity when demand was high. The plan horrified many people in the Hudson River valley and elsewhere, who banded together as the Scenic Hudson Preservation Conference. The Sierra Club was a member of the group, as were the Appalachian Mountain Club and the Association for the Preservation of the Adirondack Forest Preserve.

The Sierra Club's board had established an Atlantic chapter in 1950, the first chapter outside California, as the club's membership and influence steadily grew and members wanted to get into various issues and controversies. The Atlantic chapter, as established, covered most of the eastern seaboard from New England to the Southeast. It was slowly broken up as statewide chapters were created in the New England states and elsewhere. The Atlantic chapter remained strong and vigorous, and when it learned of the proposal for Storm King, it was not pleased.

A young lawyer named David Sive had been recruited into the chapter, and he, along with several others, decided to challenge the utility company's project before the Federal Power Commission (FPC), which would have to issue a permit for the plant before it could be built. There was a huge hurdle to overcome, however. Until that point, courts and agencies had refused to allow conservation organizations to participate in the resolution of such disputes on the grounds that they had no financial interest in the outcome. This is what stopped the lawsuit that sought to force the government to live up to its promise to protect Rainbow Bridge National Monument from the waters of Lake Powell behind Glen Canyon Dam.

Sive and his colleagues proposed to argue that an aesthetic interest should suffice: If a project were going to ruin scenic beauty, or wreck a beautiful hiking area, or damage wildlife habitat, the people who enjoyed the area should have the right to present their arguments to the body charged with making the decision in the matter and later challenge the decision in court if it was not to their liking. If successful, this would be a major development in the evolution of the movement, allowing the organizations to use the law and the courts as potent weapons in their campaigns.

Sive by this time had met David Brower and asked him whether the club could pay a nominal fee to hire his small firm to take on the case before the court of appeals, having been dismissed by the FPC. Brower said yes, though he had no budget for hiring lawyers. Brower says in his oral history that the figure was $1,500; Sive said in an interview that it was $10,000. Some members of the club's board soundly criticized Brower for the expenditure, whichever it was. Sive says his firm put at least $150,000 worth of effort into the case. He later recalled, "Two or three years later, the one uncomfortable part of the Brower controversy for myself was a charge, I think by Tom Jukes [the pro-DDT Rachel Carson critic], that I had made a lot of money from Storm King. . . . I didn't like that."[11]

Sive and his colleagues won the case after battling before the commission and in the courts for two years and thus established the foundation of modern environmental litigation. Brower won bragging rights for having kept Sive on the case. Several of the attorneys involved with the Scenic Hudson case, including David Sive, went on to participate in the founding of the Natural Resources Defense Council (NRDC), now one of the country's leading environmental organizations. Sive would remain close to Brower.

The discretionary fund used to keep David Sive in the Storm King fight was one of Brower's main tools. He would use it to support things he didn't have time to ask the board for permission to pursue or things he feared the board might refuse to allow him to pursue. Tensions were growing steadily between the old guard on the board, who were increasingly uneasy over Brower's expanding efforts, and Brower and his allies on the board, who would push the Sierra Club's horizons ever outward. Brower immediately saw the potential in the courts. Indeed, he had discussed the potential of bringing conservation disputes to court a decade earlier, but it wasn't until Storm King and David Sive came along that that ball started rolling, never to stop.

The success of the Storm King litigation caught the eye of many public-spirited attorneys and helped inspire the later creation of not only NRDC but also the Environmental Defense Fund, the Sierra Club Legal Defense Fund (later renamed Earthjustice), and the Conservation Law Foundation of New England, among others.

Back out west, another King, Mineral King in the southern Sierra, again attracted the Sierra Club's attention and, coincidentally, would provide the next key building block in the evolution of environmental law.

Despite—or maybe owing to—his convictions, Dave Brower was only too willing to admit to lapses in judgment on the part of himself and the Sierra Club through the years, advocating nuclear power and coal plants to fight dams being the most prominent. One such instance came along in a remote valley called Mineral King.

In the late 1940s, acting for the Sierra Club, Brower and Richard Felter had hired a small plane to explore the southern Sierra in search of a site for a potential new ski development to serve people in Southern California. Skiing had grown rapidly in popularity after the war, partly with the return of the mountain troops Brower had helped train, and the only ski resorts available to Los Angelenos were Big Bear, too small to accommodate big crowds, and Mammoth Mountain, an eight-hour drive on the east side of the Sierra, nearly as far away as Yosemite.

Felter and Brower, after a careful survey, judged that the most promising site was Mineral King, served only by a narrow, twisting, dead-end gravel road, built seventy years before to serve several mines in the valley that had quickly gone bust. They submitted their report to the Forest Service, which managed the land. The Sierra Club board resolved that it supported some sort of development at Mineral King, despite the fact that it was surrounded on three sides by Sequoia National Park. In fact, save for old mining scars and debris, Mineral King surely would have been part of the park.

Nothing much happened for the next fifteen years until the Forest Service announced that it would entertain proposals for the development of an all-year resort at Mineral King, with an emphasis on skiing. Three proposals were submitted. The one favored by the Forest Service came from Walt Disney and was of breathtaking dimensions, on a scale to rival Sun Valley in Idaho, then the largest such resort in the country.

When the proposal reached the Sierra Club, some of the officials were stunned at the scope of the project but felt bound by their prior approval of the plan from the 1940s. Brower was ready to go along until Martin Litton got wind of it and went on the warpath. He argued forcefully—and no one could argue more forcefully than Martin Litton—that the Sierra Club, the *Sierra* Club, was duty bound to oppose Disney's planned desecration of the

Sierra. He turned Brower around, as he would do many times as they worked together on myriad projects. He also turned around a majority of the club's directors, though by no means all of them. The old guard insisted, as it had before and would again, that if the Sierra Club changed its position, its word would never be trusted again. Litton responded by saying just because you were wrong, you didn't have to stay wrong.

Immediately after Brower's departure from the Sierra Club staff in 1969, the organization filed suit against the project, building on what had been started at Storm King. The Mineral King case went to the Supreme Court and firmly entrenched the right of citizens' groups to take environmental disputes to the federal courts.[12] Mineral King was spared the Disney development, later incorporated into Sequoia National Park, and still later designated a wilderness. Brower was only one of many people who spared Mineral King from becoming an outsized ski resort, but he was a key player.

THE NORTH CASCADES: WRESTING A PARK FROM THE FOREST SERVICE

Another of the big conservation struggles that stretched from the 1950s to the mid-1960s was the effort to create a national park in the North Cascades in Washington State. Because the Sierra Club's resources were skimpy, Brower encouraged and participated in the creation of the North Cascades Conservation Council. His main contributions were made in the ways he knew best: book and film.

The book, in Exhibit Format, was *Wild Cascades: Forgotten Parkland*, by Harvey Manning with photographs by several photographers. It, like many of the other titles, was given to every senator and member of congress with strong urging to support the national park's creation. The film was *Wilderness Alps of Stehekin*, Stehekin being a tiny settlement at the north end of Lake Chelan, gateway to Image Lake, Glacier Peak, and other beloved features of the North Cascades. The stars of the movie were Brower's children. The scriptwriter and narrator was Brower himself.[13] The film was shown to legislators, bureaucrats, and citizens repeatedly.

In this case, as in Kings Canyon, Mineral King, and many other places, the sought-after land was within a national forest. The trick, Brower and others hoped, would be to persuade—more likely force via legislation—the Forest Service to turn management over to the National Park Service for preservation as mostly wilderness. It worked. The North Cascades National Park came into being in 1968.

Unlike some of Brower's other projects, the club board wholeheartedly supported his endeavors here. The campaign had resulted in the creation of the North Cascades Conservation Council, or N3C, which remained to watch over the management of the new park and to work to save other wild areas in and near the North Cascades. Brower had made many strong friends and allies during the campaign with whom he would work both within and outside the Sierra Club for the rest of his life.

POINT REYES: AN ISLAND IN TIME

Here again, Brower and the Sierra Club played a key supporting role in persuading Congress to block the development of the Point Reyes peninsula north of San Francisco and acquire the land for a park. Point Reyes had been owned by a San Francisco law firm, which leased land for twenty-six separate dairy farms named for the alphabet: Ranch A through Ranch Z. The rest of the area was undeveloped and a prime magnet for developers who had plans to build homes and golf courses and shops and roads. It was also a prime attraction for people from the Bay Area who enjoyed spectacular hiking and camping and birding. The local congressman, Clem Miller, was a fan of the peninsula and led the effort to create a park—in this case a national seashore managed by the Park Service. George Collins, a retired Park Service employee, had set up Conservation Associates to fight for a park; he was a key player as well. Brower's contributions were again a book—*Island in Time: The Point Reyes Peninsula*, text by Harold Gilliam, a reporter for the *San Francisco Chronicle*, and photographs by Philip Hyde—and a film he also organized, though this time Laurel Reynolds's hand held the camera rather than his. It was called *Island in Time* as well. Gilliam had, at Brower's request, written an article on Point Reyes for the *Sierra Club Bulletin;* the book was an expansion of the article. *Island in Time* was slightly smaller than Exhibit Format and copublished with Charles Scribner's Sons. Brower even managed to persuade Stewart Udall, then secretary of the interior, to write a preface. Again, copies were sent to all members of congress.

It was a real horse race. Bulldozers had already started grading lots and carving roads just above Limantour Spit, one of the favorite destinations on the peninsula, near spots favored by harbor seals, elephant seals, sea lions, white pelicans, and other creatures. One sticking point was the dairies: Do cows belong in a national park? In this one they do. The dairy farmers—who had bought their farms from the law firm years earlier—were bought out by the federal government and then allowed to lease their farms back in perpetuity. Many of the parts of Point Reyes that are not dairy farms are protected as wilderness. The book and film *Island in Time* were widely acknowledged as key elements in the successful campaign to preserve Point Reyes. The Sierra Club had clearly become the publishing arm of the conservation movement; that role would continue and expand as long as Brower was running the show.

GRAND CANYON: FREE-FLOWING RIVER OR HYDROELECTRIC SITE?

The sixties were a busy time for Brower. In addition to the campaigns for the redwoods, the North Cascades, Mineral King, and other places, he was deeply embroiled in a battle to save arguably the most spectacular natural feature on the North American continent, the Grand Canyon.

The floodgates at the Glen Canyon dam were scheduled to close on January 21, 1963. Dave Brower went to Stewart Udall's Washington, DC, office to make one last entreaty to the secretary to cancel the event, to leave the dam unfinished and the river running free. But Udall wasn't there. He was across town at a press conference announcing an administration plan to build two dams inside the Grand Canyon. And not just that. The plan, called the Pacific Southwest Water Plan, included a proposal to transfer water from the Columbia River Basin and Northern California to the thirsty Southwest. All hell was about to break loose.

The Sierra Club and David Brower may have sacrificed Glen Canyon to save Dinosaur, but they weren't about to roll over in the face of this invasion of a national park and a natural wonder known throughout the world. Brower took it as his personal duty to stop this outrage, and his board, this time, was in total agreement. He would organize, recruit, testify at hearings, publish books, and participate in the making of two films. He would stop the plan no matter what.

The Grand Canyon dams themselves, in fact, would supply no water to anyone—by the government's own reckoning, the dams would waste enough water through evaporation each year to supply the residents of Tucson. The administration, in the person of Floyd Dominy, the commissioner of reclamation, referred to the dams as "cash registers," implying they were a fund-raising scheme to finance the Central Arizona Project, which would bring water to Phoenix and Tucson.

Brower and his allies attended and testified at the hearings—three in the House (1965, 1966, and 1967) and one in the Senate (1967)—and worked the media. The *New York Times* editorialized repeatedly against the dams, as did other papers. Public sentiment nationally appeared to be running against the dams, but legislators from the Southwest held key positions on the congressional committees that would determine the fate of the project. They had little regard for what someone from the East might think. An additional wrinkle was that California's political leaders tended to oppose the dams, which led to charges that the Sierra Club was in league with California water interests, who wanted more Colorado River water for themselves, a charge the club vigorously denied.

The Sierra Club had published a successful book to challenge the dams—*Time and the River Flowing: Grand Canyon*—by François Leydet, but even a book selling a more-than-respectable 45,000 copies could hardly be expected to stop such a giant project by itself. An earlier book, *The Place No One Knew: Glen Canyon on the Colorado*, was both a remembrance of canyons lost and a call to arms to save Grand Canyon. Again, books alone couldn't turn the tide.

Life magazine had put some wind in the dam fighters' sails with a big spread featuring Brower ("Knight Errant to Nature's Rescue") with photographs of him and his family in what was left of Glen Canyon and calling him "His country's No. 1 working conservationist."[14] Brower thanked the writer, Hal Wingo, writing, "The spread in *Life* was so flattering as to be highly embarrassing, but I can't say I don't like it or am ungrateful for what you did for the cause in the beautiful piece you put together. It was a pleasure working with you on it."[15] In answer to a fan letter from Allan Kitchal of Connecticut, Brower wrote, "Thank you very much for your note. . . . I shall be walking around the streets of New York next week incognito because I don't want to be mistaken for the Number 1 Conservationist I am not."[16]

Recruiting the Next Generation

Meanwhile, a young MIT graduate in mathematics and political science and Columbia doctoral dropout named Jeff Ingram had fallen in love with the Grand Canyon on a trip out West a year or two earlier with his wife, Helen, and their small baby. They moved to New Mexico, where Helen finished her own political science doctorate and landed a teaching job at the university in Albuquerque. Jeff got a low-level job at Los Alamos. Gas-station road maps were already showing the Bridge Canyon dam site in the Grand Canyon, and that inflamed Ingram. But he didn't know that anyone was resisting the dams until he happened upon a copy of *The Place No One Knew*. For him, as for thousands of other people, this was his first exposure to the Sierra Club.

In late 1964, Ingram heard about a Sierra Club conference to be held in Santa Fe, with the club's executive director as the key speaker. Ingram showed up and met Brower and his wife, Anne, who were accompanied by Eliot Porter, the author and photographer of *The Place No One Knew*, who lived just outside Santa Fe. Ingram went to lunch with Porter and the Browers and that evening was mesmerized by what he termed "Brower's charismatic oratory."[17] He set out to learn as much as he could about the rationale for the dams and the campaign to oppose them.

A year later Ingram attended a second Santa Fe conference, and again Brower was there, this time without his entourage. As they chatted about conservation work, Brower told him the club was thinking of hiring someone to represent it in the Southwest. "What would this person's responsibilities be?" Ingram asked. Brower pulled out an unlined pad of paper and a ballpoint pen with green ink. He wrote what might have been his shorthand manual for an organizer: "Sharpshoot in the area. Observe. Analyze. Influence.... Get into areas being reclassified, recommend additions (invariably!). Carry the philosophy shared by The Wilderness Society, National Parks Association, Audubon, Nature Conservancy.... Help inform and build up cooperation from local organizations. Get to know local administrative and legislative people—*and editors*. Travel fairly widely through the region, talk, show films ... *develop the SW conservation force.*" Then, almost as an afterthought, "How about getting involved yourself? Any interest? I've had this in mind ever since I saw you here last year. DB."[18] Ingram, needless to say, was interested. Ecstatic was more like it. What he didn't know was that Brower had no authority to make such an offer (as so often he didn't), but Brower (as so often he could) was able to convince his executive committee that this was a smart move. Ingram began work the following January and was immediately blown away.

Ingram recalled, "We went to Washington. One evening Dave and I were talking in his hotel room. I left to go back to my hotel room almost staggering because I was so carried away by his charisma. This grasp he had of all this stuff that I was only starting to learn about. I didn't stagger; I had wings." He then added an insight about Brower's character that is profound but often overlooked: "It's not unusual in environmental, conservation, and other do-good kinds of things, for people to act out of anger. 'I hate that they're chopping down redwood trees.' 'Why do they treat little kids so badly in public schools?' I don't think Dave was a hater. I won't say he didn't get angry. I think he was a lover. He loved wilderness, he loved wildness. He loved his wife. He loved his kids." And one other thing particularly impressed him: "Dave was a great public speaker. An orator in the best sense of touching all those strings and being funny and not appearing in any sense rehearsed, almost spontaneous, but never lost. He was a phrase turner, always delightful."[19]

This technique—hiring young talent more or less on impulse—would be repeated many times in years to come. Indeed, just months later Brower recruited Gary Soucie to join the Sierra Club staff as its representative in New York. Soucie, who had also discovered the Sierra Club in a bookstore window, was volunteering at the club's New York office and helping with publicity—he had been a public relations specialist for Swissair. Brower wooed him for some months and finally Soucie agreed. Little did he know that Brower was under explicit orders *not* to hire anyone in New York, orders he cheerfully disobeyed. Soucie, who now says he would not have accepted the job had he known, flew to San Francisco, charmed the club's directors, and began work.

A third regional rep, Brock Evans, was hired more conventionally in Seattle, to replace Mike McCloskey, who had moved to San Francisco to become assistant to Will Siri, who was then club president. Evans's story is a little different, but sheds light on Brower's theory of planning and of delegation. He had met Brower and was in awe.

> I went down to San Francisco to get my marching orders. The North Cascades Park was on the Sierra Club's list of priorities. So surely, I thought, there must be a master plan. I had been in the Marine Corps, so I had a little military background. I got down to Mills Tower [club offices], the holy of holies.
> "Private Evans reporting for duty, Sir!"
> "What are you talking about, Evans?"
> "Sir, please show me the battle plans and the maps. Where are they?"
> "What are you talking about?" There was no battle plan, there was no nothing. I was on my own.[20]

Typical.

In addition to Jeff Ingram, two other MIT grads volunteered to help the Save Grand Canyon crusade. They were the nuclear engineer Laurence I. Moss, who would go on to win election to the Sierra Club board and later become president of the club, and the economist Alan Carlin, then working for the Rand Corporation.[21] Each carved off a piece of the argument: Ingram demonstrating, for example, that the main aims of the Central Arizona Project could be achieved without building *any* dams in the Grand Canyon, but instead using revenues from existing facilities to pay to have the water for Phoenix and Tucson pumped from Lake Mead downstream. Carlin attacked the economic analysis justifying the cost of the project. Moss calculated that the dams' lost power could be fully replaced by nuclear reactors. But momentum, in early 1966, was still heavily on the side of the dams, in large measure owing to the power of the chairman of the House Interior Committee, Wayne Aspinall of Colorado. It was early 1966. Something dramatic needed to happen.

The Grand Canyon Campaign

It is never easy to get newspapers to pay attention to your press releases and testimony and books. It was extra difficult in those days. The civil rights movement was in full swing and anti–Vietnam War protests were in full flower, with huge demonstrations happening all across the country. The Summer of Love was about to bring young people to San Francisco with flowers in their hair. The Free Speech Movement in Brower's hometown of Berkeley was barely over. A tough time for a crusading publicist for nature. Brower, thinking back on the newspaper ad that had helped save Dinosaur, and one he had written on behalf of a redwood national park, wondered if a big, bold, splashy ad or ad campaign might work. If it wouldn't, the canyon might be a goner.

As Susan Senecah points out in her fascinating study of David Brower's discourse, Brower, at least subconsciously, decided to bring the public into the argument. "It is at this point that David Brower decided to invite the American people to leave their spectator positions and become agents of change," she writes. "Until that time, the pros and cons of the dams were debated in the media, and each side took shots at each other. The public was being informed as viewers from the sidelines, not as invited participants." Brower blamed the loss of Glen Canyon partly on the fact that it was so little known by the public. "Brower had sworn, however, that the Grand Canyon would not become another Glen Canyon, dammed because people did not know or feel empowered to do something about it."[22]

Brower had noticed ads written and designed by the San Francisco agency Freeman and Gossage. He admired the style of the ads: their spirit, their erudition, their design, and their typography. A famous series for the makers of Irish whiskey run in the *New Yorker* struck a chord, particularly because it used Brower's favorite typefaces—Centaur and Arrighi—ones he used in the Exhibit Format books. Brower, in fact, was very opinionated on the topic of typefaces, beginning with his days at UC Press and then as editor of the *Sierra Club Bulletin*. He liked elegant, classical fonts like Bodoni, Old Style, and especially Centaur and Arrighi. He had no use for sans serif fonts.

Brower drafted copy for an ad, put it in his pocket, and strolled the half-dozen blocks from his Financial District office to the Freeman and Gossage office in an old firehouse in the Barbary Coast neighborhood, which had been largely taken over by fancy interior design studios.

Brower had read an *Advertising Age* article by Howard Gossage that was critical of the advertising profession and revealed that he and the adman shared an aversion to Smokey the Bear, which seemed a promising start.[23] He showed the ad copy to Gossage, who summoned the newest member of the agency, a young New York transplant named Jerry Mander, to have a look.[24] The men were interested in the project but hated Brower's draft, which was gentle where they felt forcefulness was required. "We immediately had a big fight, the first of dozens," Mander remembered.[25] They finally compromised with a contest of sorts. The *New York Times* agreed to split the run—that is, it would print half the papers with Brower's ad and half with copy written by Mander and edited by Gossage. Brower said later, and frequently, that this was a first for the *Times*. Mander says it was nothing unusual.

The ads appeared in the *Times* on June 9, 1966. The Brower version, headlined "Who Can Save Grand Canyon? You Can . . . and Secretary Udall can too, if he will," had a single coupon to return to the Sierra Club with a contribution to support the campaign or to ask for more information. The Gossage-Mander version, "Now Only You Can Save Grand Canyon From Being Flooded . . . For Profit," had six coupons addressed to various key players in the struggle: President Johnson, Interior Secretary Stewart Udall, Representative Wayne Aspinall, the reader's senators and representative, plus a Sierra Club coupon soliciting memberships and donations and selling the Grand Canyon book *Time and the River Flowing*. Coupons returned from the pros' ad outnumbered the amateur's by two to one, a clear victory for Gossage and Mander, setting a pattern for dozens more ads that would spring from this collaboration over the next three decades.

The response was fast and substantial. Secretary Udall's office logged upward of ten thousand letters protesting the dams, many with coupons attached, an utterly unprecedented occurrence. Dan Dreyfus of the Bureau of Reclamation put it this way: "I never saw anything like it. Letters were arriving in dump trucks. Ninety-five percent of them said we'd better keep our mitts off the Grand Canyon and a lot of them quoted the Sierra Club ads."[26]

Others professed surprise for different reasons. Utah senator Frank Moss, a dam proponent, said, "I frankly don't know what the Sierra Club and other conservationists talk about when they say they want to 'Save' Grand Canyon. Save it from what? A little more water in a dry, arid country. A little easier access to an exciting canyon? A little more beauty for people to enjoy?" The senator said he could neither understand nor sympathize with "frenzied, irrational opposition" to the project, "particularly when we are doing our development in a thoughtful, careful way which will preserve and even enhance our natural beauty and make the outdoors more accessible to more people."[27]

Where the redwoods ad had elicited no backlash from the government, which favored a national park in the redwoods, the Grand Canyon ad sparked a visit to the club's San Francisco office by an agent of the Internal Revenue Service, who delivered a letter informing the club that the agency was troubled by the ad and its attempt to influence a governmental decision, possibly in violation of IRS rules. Contributions to the Sierra Club might no longer be tax-deductible pending a review of the situation by the agency.[28]

Exactly what piqued the IRS's interest is hard to pin down. Everyone, it seems, has a slightly different story. Suspicion fell immediately at the feet of the Udall brothers—interior secretary Stewart and Arizona congressman Morris (Stewdall and Modall, as they were known informally)—who denied it. Some suggested that IRS commissioner Sheldon Cohen had seen the ad and acted on his own. Brower said that Mo Udall eventually admitted sending the IRS after the club and called it his biggest mistake. That may well be so, though Mo did not say as much to one of his biographers, who put it this way: "Although Udall never confirmed it, Brower was convinced that Mo was behind the IRS action. Brower insisted that Udall had confided to him in Udall's office that he had indeed sicced the IRS on the Sierra Club but refused to admit it publicly because of the public reaction that would have followed.[29] Udall later denied he played any role in the IRS action. Even Floyd E. Dominy, the head of the Bureau of Reclamation, said Udall called in the IRS."[30]

Mike McCloskey, then conservation director of the Sierra Club, on the other hand, writes in his memoir that when Mo Udall saw the ad in the

Washington Post, he telephoned Joseph Barr, undersecretary of the treasury, to ask what could be done about this outrage. Barr, according to McCloskey, then called the commissioner of the Internal Revenue Service: "In less than twenty-four hours the decision was made, and that day a notice revoking the Club's tax deductibility was hand-carried by IRS agents to our offices. Rarely—even in times of war—had the federal government acted with so much dispatch."[31] Stew Udall puts yet another spin on the story: "The ads caused a furor on another level when the White House ordered the Internal Revenue Service to revoke the Sierra Club's tax exemption as a nonprofit organization."[32]

There's an odd twist to the story in Mo Udall's memoir: "The ad caused a stir, but it might have been short-lived had the government not made a monumental blunder. A day later the Internal Revenue Service notified the Sierra Club that it might lose its tax-exempt status if it continued lobbying against the dams."[33] If he was responsible, would he have called it a "monumental blunder"? That seems a little unlikely. Jeff Ingram, however, who came to know Morris Udall well, thinks it's not unlikely at all: "In fact, if Udall had done it, it would have been in character for him afterwards to have made a rueful joke at his own expense."[34] A bit further on in the same account Mo says, "Together, the two ads and the IRS's blatant attempt to muzzle the Sierra Club sparked a firestorm of protest. It was phenomenal. The republic was nearly two hundred years old and we had finally found something everybody could agree about."[35]

The IRS action was big news across the land. Here the mighty Internal Revenue Service was picking on the little Sierra Club, which was only trying to protect the Grand Canyon. As Brower remarked later, people may or may not have had strong feelings about the canyon, but they certainly did have strong feelings about the IRS. New members joined in a torrent. Books sold like crazy. Small contributions flooded into the Mills Tower headquarters, boosting club membership from 39,000 in June 1966 to 67,000 by October 1968. And if the IRS expected to discourage the Sierra Club from this sort of advocacy advertising, it had miscalculated, and badly. Over the next few months three more ads appeared in newspapers and magazines across the country urging the administration and Congress to abandon the plans to put two dams into the canyon and suggesting that if Grand Canyon were at risk, no public park was safe.

The second ad in the series, published July 25, 1966, expanded the ambit of the club's concern:

Dinosaur and Big Bend. Glacier and
Grand Teton, Kings Canyon,
Redwoods, Mammoth, Even Yellowstone
and Yosemite. And
The Wild Rivers, and Wilderness.
How Can You Guarantee These, Mr. Udall,
If Grand Canyon Is Dammed For Profit?

More letters and coupons (which were printed across the top of the ad this time) poured into Washington, DC, and more donations and memberships into San Francisco.

The third ad, the most famous of all, widened horizons even more:[36]

SHOULD WE ALSO FLOOD THE
SISTINE CHAPEL SO TOURISTS CAN
GET NEARER THE CEILING?

The government had argued that reservoirs in the canyon would make it easier for visitors in boats to appreciate the beauty of the canyon walls. The ad was a compact, one-page history of life on earth. "Earth began four billion years ago and Man two million. The Age of Technology, on the other hand, is hardly a hundred years old. . . . It seems to us hasty, therefore, during this blip of time, for Man to think of directing his fascinating new tools toward altering irrevocably the forces which made him. Nonetheless, in these few brief years among four billion, wilderness has all but disappeared."

The ad went on to enumerate five pending proposals, all of which Brower and the Sierra Club thought were lousy ideas: dams in the Grand Canyon, logging the last redwoods, a power plant at Storm King mountain on the Hudson River, "a proposal to flood a region in Alaska as large as Lake Erie," and a plan to fill an area the size of Manhattan in San Francisco Bay for a new air cargo terminal. Yet more letters deluged Washington.

Morris Udall, Wayne Aspinall, and their allies, though stunned by the public outpouring of sentiment against the dams, continued to push for their approval. As the weeks wore on, a debate was ginned up between Mo Udall and Dave Brower. The congressman recalls that "it became increasingly apparent that the bureau's rationale for the dams was flawed on the merits, even if one completely disregarded the larger question of whether dams belonged in the Grand Canyon." He describes having a debate with Brower "in front of a gaggle of national press" on the rim of the Grand Canyon: "This was a tough assignment—comparable to debating the merits of chastity in

Hugh Hefner's hot tub in front of an audience of centerfold models, and me being on the side of abstinence."[37]

Clever as this account is, it is not how the debate happened. Instead it took place in Albuquerque (not at the Grand Canyon) before a pro-Reclamation audience in November 1966. It featured Brower and Udall, with a Brower-Aspinall confrontation beforehand. Brower, not Udall, was the one being boiled in the hot tub.[38]

At one of the many congressional hearings on the dams, Brower did get into a wrangle with Mo Udall that would finely etch Brower's aversion to compromise, a theme of his philosophy. Here's a sample:

MR. UDALL: What would the Sierra Club accept? If we have a low, low, low Bridge Canyon Dam, maybe 100 feet high, is that too much. Is there any point at which you compromise here?

MR. BROWER: Mr. Udall, you are not giving us anything that God didn't put there in the first place, and I think that is the thing we are not entitled to compromise. . . .

MR. UDALL: You say that you will continue the fight and try to defeat the bill unless it contains a provision setting aside that damsite once and for all in the Grand Canyon National Park.

MR. BROWER: We have no choice. There have to be groups who will hold for these things that are not replaceable. If we stop doing that we might as well stop being an organization, and conservation organizations might as well throw in the towel.

MR. UDALL: I know the strength and sincerity of your feelings, and respect them.[39]

Not long after this exchange, Representative Udall conceded defeat, and the bill authorizing the dams died without ever coming to a vote in the House of Representatives. Refusal to compromise had carried the day

Stewart Udall definitively turned against the dams in late 1966. "The burden of proof, I believe, rests on the dam builders. If they cannot make out a compelling case, the park should be enlarged and given permanent protection"—as it eventually was.[40] Udall ordered the Bureau of Reclamation to conduct studies showing there were other ways to finance and pump water for the Central Arizona Project (CAP). And in 1967, he selected a Reclamation alternative to buy a share of a thermal power plant's output to pump CAP water.

Some people, including the historian Donald Worster, say that the killing of the dams proposed for the Grand Canyon led to the building of the Navajo

Generating Station, a coal-fired power plant, near Page, Arizona, and that the conservationists who fought for the canyon were partly to blame. Here's Worster: "Once more, the environmentalists buckled down to battle to save a last piece of the natural river, and once more—for the second time in a century—they were victorious. Once more, however, they lost something as well, for the energy to make the CAP go would be derived instead from coal strip-mined on Hopi sacred lands at Black Mesa in northern Arizona and burned in the Navajo Generating Station near Page, polluting the crystalline desert air with ash and poison gas."[41]

Jeff Ingram forcefully disputes this account, arguing that the coal plant was already being planned (by private utilities), and power to pump water would have come from it even if the dams had been built.[42] The revenues from the dams were most importantly to finance water import schemes from Northern California and the Columbia River for Southern California. The Central Arizona Project did not need the dams, and with the Northwestern senators (and the administration) against them because of the threat to their water, plus the Sierra Club's success in publicizing what would be lost, the Grand Canyon dams were goners.

But it didn't stop the pro-dam forces from trying one last ploy. In 1967, they would expand Grand Canyon National Park, eliminate Grand Canyon National Monument, and settle for just one dam. This sparked the final Sierra Club ad in the series run in the *New York Times* and other papers on March 13, 1967:

> (Better Hold Up On The Flowers and Cheery Wires, Just A Bit Longer)
> "Grand Canyon National Monument Is Hereby Abolished."
> —from a bill submitted to Congress 15 days ago by Rep. Wayne Aspinall.

More letters, more coupons, and the proposal was shelved. A year later, in 1968, the Central Arizona Project legislation was signed into law, and it included a ban on dams in the Grand Canyon.

· · ·

These six battles and others put the Sierra Club and the conservation forces on the map, especially the fight over the Grand Canyon dams and the concurrent tussle with the Internal Revenue Service. They began to lead the club into new arenas and certainly introduced it to a national audience. The Bodega fight, as ambiguous as the club's role had been, put nuclear power on the organization's agenda and began to force it to rethink its hope that the atom would make big dams unnecessary. Mineral King and Storm King opened courthouse doors to conservation activists, never to close again. Point Reyes, the redwoods, and the North Cascades honed Brower's and the Sierra Club's campaigning techniques, particularly publishing and working the media. All in all, they led to a doubling of the club's membership—still small, but everything was smaller in those days—and an amplification of its influence.

Despite Brower's labors and successes, however, the division on the Sierra Club board over Brower's leadership style and fiscal activities reached fever pitch in the spring and summer of 1968.

TEN

Uncivil War

Process is that which gets between where you are and where you want to be.

Despite Brower's successes protecting wild places and raising the Sierra Club's reputation as one of the world's most influential conservation organizations, a determined fraction of the club's board was bent on removing him from the position of executive director. Although the board had refused to discuss firing Brower at the infamous Clair Tappaan Lodge meeting in September 1968, the three leaders of the anti-Brower movement and their allies elsewhere in the Sierra Club were anything but dissuaded from their crusade.

Ansel Adams, the great photographer, had been close friends with Brower for well over thirty years, and in fact had been instrumental in Brower's being hired as the Sierra Club's first executive director in 1952, an idea he had first proposed a decade before. But the two had drifted apart for complicated reasons. Among them, Adams argued that Brower was a danger to the survival of the club through financial recklessness, mostly having to do with the publications program. Brower, for his part, thought that Adams was jealous of the attention being paid to Eliot Porter as the club published more books in color and fewer in black and white. Brower's papers contain many letters between the two men, with very complimentary letters from the photographer slowly giving way to more and more critical ones, to the point where Adams called Brower a "dictator."[1]

After one particularly vituperative missive from Adams was circulated throughout the club hierarchy, Brower wrote back demanding an apology for severe damage to his reputation and club's: "Dear Ansel, I wish this

David Brower, Ansel Adams, and Edgar Wayburn, early 1960s. Photograph courtesy Colby Library, Sierra Club.

disastrous dialogue could end. . . . You, Dick Leonard, and Dick Sill have greatly damaged the club and indirectly the conservation movement." He enumerated lost grants and many other alleged results of the attacks launched against him. He concluded,

> I consider your letter and your charges actionable, libel, and slander, consisting of untrue statements made with the intent to injure me in my profession and to destroy my reputation in the publications field, and as such to have caused tremendous damage, both financial and emotional, not only to me but also to my family. I believe that the least you can do to try to undo this wrong is: a) Withdraw your letter. b) Apologize for the irrevocable damage you have done. c) Cease and desist from further participation in this destructive scheme.[2]

No apology was forthcoming.

Dick Leonard, the lawyer, likewise had been very close with Brower in the thirties; many times the men had depended on each other and a rope swung between them as they scaled vertical granite walls in Yosemite and the Sierra high country. Leonard, who had originally sponsored Brower's application to join the Sierra Club, had also been an enthusiastic supporter of Brower's being hired as executive director but now shared Adams's fear that Brower was out of control and a threat to the survival of the club. He too thought that Brower was willing to risk the future of the club on behalf of his lofty ambitions. Neither man, nor any other of Brower's critics, charged that Brower was out to enrich himself ("He has never taken one dime for himself. One look at his house shows that—how shabby it is, aluminum pans catching the rain," Leonard would tell John McPhee).[3] He might also have pointed out that Brower was his own barber: he cut his own hair.

Dick Sill, the physics professor, it was said by some Brower partisans, was jealous of Brower's fame and felt that he should get more recognition for his work in Nevada. He resented the fact that to much of the public and the press, Brower *was* the Sierra Club. He was by far the least temperate of the Brower critics. He was a recent arrival on the Sierra Club board but was hardly reticent about expressing strongly held beliefs. Phil Berry, a former climbing protégé and close friend of Brower, then on the board and later to serve two terms as president, said, "Sill was always the guy with the sharpest knife. He was a little nuts. Sill was unbalanced. Implacable. He moved Leonard and Ansel to positions of implacability."[4] On the other hand, perhaps to balance things out, Berry said of Brower, "He had some good ideas and some bad ideas. If there was one thing that was Dave's fault, it was not being able to tell the difference between those two. Some really great ideas and some really bad ideas, and because they were his ideas, the ability to filter them out wasn't very good."[5]

At the September 1968 meeting, once the attempts by Sill and Adams to sack Brower were tabled or voted down, the debate turned once again to Diablo Canyon.

DIABLO CANYON: SUITABLE FOR A NUCLEAR PLANT?

In 1963, the Pacific Gas & Electric Company (PG&E) had announced plans to treble its electric generating capacity over the coming decade. Two thirds of the new capacity would be nuclear, and most of those facilities would need to be on the coast, close to vital cooling water.[6] The company identified several possible sites for new plants. One, for which it had received preliminary approval, was at Bodega Head north of San Francisco, discussed in chapter 9. A second was at the Nipomo Dunes near Pismo Beach south of San Luis Obispo.

The Sierra Club had long wanted to see the dunes acquired for a state park and appealed to PG&E to find another site. PG&E, reluctant to get into another fight like the one it had lost at Bodega, asked the Sierra Club to participate in the site selection process. Dick Leonard, whose law practice specialized in the law of corporate finance, was friendly with people at PG&E, and he and club president Will Siri, a physicist, began informal discussions with representatives of the company. Eventually they took a proposed policy motion to the Sierra Club board. It read, in part, "The Sierra Club considers Diablo Canyon, San Luis Obispo County, a satisfactory alternate site to Nipomo Dunes for construction of a Pacific Gas & Electric Company generating facility" and then put in a few inconsequential provisos hoping to minimize damage to marine resources from hot water discharges and to ensure that views would not be badly affected by power lines. In the discussion preceding this resolution, Kathy Jackson, a Sierra Club activist from the area, famously called Diablo Canyon "a treeless slot."[7] In fact, the canyon harbored many large live oaks, and the reactors would not be in the canyon but out on the shelf next to the Pacific Ocean and its cool water.

None of the directors voting on the resolution had been to Diablo Canyon, nor had David Brower. Brower urged board members to defer voting on the resolution until they could visit the site (shades of Glen Canyon), but PG&E was getting impatient and Leonard and company argued that a vote then would be timely. The resolution was adopted. It was May 1966. The one director who *had* seen Diablo was Martin Litton, but he was abroad at the time of the vote. When he returned and learned what had been done, he was outraged both at his fellow board members and at PG&E, which he felt had perpetrated a fraud.

He fired off an angry letter to Shermer Sibley, the president of the utility, which read, in part, "As a director of the Sierra Club, I was deeply shocked upon my recent return from Asia to learn that the remainder of the directors, by a split vote, had indicated what amounts to actual Sierra Club approval of the installation of a nuclear power plant at Diablo Canyon, in the middle of the very last fragment of California Coast south of Humboldt County that is not already irrevocably defaced by highways and other works of man." He went on to allege that the board's understanding of the area was based on "misleading information" and reported that he had investigated the site by air and on foot and found it wild and worthy of preservation. Then he said, "The membership of the Sierra Club can be expected to prevail over the fraudulently obtained vote of the Board of Directors in this matter, and I myself am doing all in my power to bring about a reversal of the unfortunate position assumed by the Board at its last meeting." He then argued that there was in fact no need for yet another power plant in the area, citing the "gigantic installation" at nearby Moss Landing, a natural-gas-fired plant.[8]

Copies were duly sent to the Sierra Club hierarchy, and all hell broke loose. "Fraudulently obtained" was the phrase that most incensed the pro-power-plant forces. George Marshall, then president of the club, wrote on June 25, "Dear Martin: Your stating that the vote of the Board of Directors of the Sierra Club on May 7, 1966 on the Nipomo Dunes-Diablo Canyon Resolution was obtained 'fraudulently' is outrageous. . . . To have written this to an officer of another organization and thus making this slanderous statement public is unfair."[9] Marshall then demanded an apology from Litton and asked him to retract the letter he had sent to Sibley. Litton ignored Marshall's letter and vowed to press on with his campaign to overturn the board's approval of the Diablo site.

Dave Brower kept his head down during this stage of the argument. Trouble was brewing around him, and while he was firmly in favor of the Litton position, he didn't publicly enter the fray until February 1967. On February 7, Sill, then chairman of the Sierra Club Council and a candidate for election to the board of directors,[10] sent an open letter to Litton and to Fred Eissler, a director who lived in Santa Barbara and was a staunch ally of Litton in most matters, including Diablo. Sill wrote, "You are undermining confidence both within and without the club in the Board of Directors and in the reliability of the club's positions and you may as a side effect destroy the career of David Brower as an effective voice in conservation.[11] I am sure beyond any reasonable doubt that these are not your goals.... Your actions suggest belief in unrealities. Power development near San Luis Obispo cannot be halted."[12]

The reference to Brower finally forced his hand. He wrote an open letter to "Dear Dr. Sill," dated February 13, 1967: "If I am lost it will be in part owing to any of several of my failings, but it will be primarily because people who should have had the courage to stand for policies the club believes in were fooled by one of the commonest ploys in the business: an organization that becomes effective is bound to make its opponents uncomfortable; the opponents seek ways, often by flattery, to split the organization and to hamstring whatever people are making the organization uncomfortably effective." Here Brower suggests that PG&E may be inserting itself into internal Sierra Club matters. Directors Siri and Leonard were both friendly with the utility and had helped select the Diablo site. Brower was suspicious of these relationships and became convinced that PG&E was a prime player in the campaign to oust him from his job. He went on, "It is not our obligation to make P. G. & E., or the AEC, or Arcata Redwoods, or the Bureau of Reclamation, or Consolidated Edison comfortable. It would be the easy way to operate the Sierra Club, and the sure way to fail. We have a different obligation. One of these is to ascertain facts about scenic damage, and also about alternatives. I would like to see you help the club do just this. You are doing the opposite."[13]

Amid all the upheaval, the directors decided to take the matter to the members of the club in response to a petition circulated by the Litton-Eissler faction within the club as hinted at in Litton's letter to Sibley—the group that wanted to keep Diablo Canyon reactor-free. The petition asked that the ballot contain two items for voters to choose between. The first, "I desire the Sierra Club to urge that the Diablo Canyon region remain unaltered...." And the second, "I favor the construction of power generating plants at the Diablo Canyon region...."[14] Will Siri, the board president, concluded that the two statements were not parallel and that "to put them on the ballot in this form could not result in a meaningful vote."[15] He changed the sentence to read, "The Sierra Club . . . considers Diablo Canyon, San Luis Obispo County, a satisfactory alternative to the Nipomo Dunes for construction of a PG&E generating facility. . . . "—yes or no. Much later, Siri admitted to having influenced the outcome by changing the wording of the proposition: "The petition was submitted in one form that clearly biased the vote—you could only vote one way. To my everlasting discredit, I managed to get it biased the other way."[16] Phil Berry took the long view: "It was a typical Sierra Club flap. A typical Sierra Club flap requires both sides to be right. Usually it was split between being right substantively or being right procedurally. Both sides had a claim to that. Sierra Club people are rational but they're also emotional. They wouldn't be Sierra Club people unless they were both."[17] To complicate matters, another question was presented to the membership, a proposal to allow Brower a voting, ex officio seat on the board, though he'd be forbidden to serve on the executive committee. Such a change would require a two-thirds vote in favor.

The directors ordered Hugh Nash, editor of the *Sierra Club Bulletin*, to present both sides of the Diablo argument to Sierra Club members in the February issue, with the election to be conducted by mail in March and April. Litton and company duly submitted their copy and photographs ahead of the deadline set by Nash. Siri, who had agreed to prepare the argument in favor of the status quo, dithered, asked for several extensions, and finally submitted copy to Nash more than three weeks after the agreed-upon deadline.[18] Siri, in his oral history, claims he turned in the pro-power-plant argument "late by a day or two."[19]

Nash, Brower, and Litton were beside themselves. Time was slipping away. The *Bulletin* with the Diablo arguments in it was in danger of arriving in members' mailboxes *after* the election ballots did. In desperation they decided on a stunt that would later be seen as a monumental blunder: Nash had seven hundred copies of the eight-page *Bulletin* printed with two blank pages where the pro-status-quo argument was to appear. Copies were distributed to chapter officers in the hope of exposing the alleged delaying tactic of one side, but it seemed to backfire. What came to be known as the "half *Bulletin*" was roundly condemned as a cheap trick. Not so cheap, in retrospect—rather expensive. The initiative reaffirming Sierra Club approval of the Diablo Canyon site passed by a comfortable margin. The attempt to let Brower join the board was approved by about three to two, less than the two thirds needed for passage.

As always, there were five seats on the board of directors to be filled in the election. The winners were Dick Leonard, Dick Sill, Martin Litton, Paul

Brooks, and Pat Goldsworthy. Sill was growing ever more strident in his criticism of Brower; Litton and Goldsworthy were reliable allies; Leonard was becoming ever more critical of Brower; Brooks was more or less neutral. For the next year, an uneasy cease-fire prevailed on the board, with pro-reactor forces holding a scant majority.

The election of spring 1968 would see a dramatic change. Directors elected then were Luna Leopold, son of Aldo Leopold, a scientist with the U.S. Geological Survey; incumbent Eliot Porter, the photographer of several successful Exhibit Format books; Laurence I. Moss, MIT-trained nuclear physicist prominent in the Grand Canyon campaign; Phillip Berry, attorney, longtime leader of club High Trips, and a key member of the club's legal committee; and incumbent Will Siri, physicist and former board president. Leopold, Porter, Moss, and Berry were admirers and, mostly, supporters of Brower, though Berry would soon turn against his longtime mentor. Siri was solidly in the anti-Brower camp, though he had many complimentary things to say about Brower, especially in the realm of publications. The election marked a clear change in the balance of power on the board.

Once again Diablo took center stage. Brower, Litton, Eissler, and others drafted a new letter to Sibley of PG&E alerting him to the fact that the board would be asked to reconsider its policy on Diablo when it held a regularly scheduled meeting in September 1968. Wayburn, who had been elected president at the May meeting, asked Brower not to send the letter, and Brower agreed; Litton sent it instead. This stirred up the hornets who had been quiescent for most of a year. They were out in force for the Clair Tappaan meeting, where we started this story.

When Diablo was discussed at the Clair Tappaan meeting in September 1968, members in attendance took turns denouncing or praising the new board majority and its questioning of the Diablo decision. The discussion ended with the board's adopting a resolution drafted by director Phillip Berry: "The Sierra Club Board of Directors regretfully acknowledges its belief that it made a mistake of principle and policy in attempting to bargain away an area of unique scenic beauty in its prior resolutions in regard to Diablo Canyon and environs."[20] The board stopped short of resolving to oppose the project, thereby satisfying no one. In fact, Berry took it upon himself soon after the meeting to write the chairman of PG&E to say that in his opinion the club's position was unchanged. He suggested to the board that the matter be referred to Sierra Club members in a second referendum the following spring. This suggestion was accepted, grudgingly.[21]

Immediately following the September 1968 meeting, Sill wrote to president Wayburn demanding that he call a special meeting of the board for October to "Discharge the Executive Director. Set up a separate trust for the permanent fund, selling [book] inventory or the color separations, if necessary, in order to obtain the money. Call for a special election to be held this fall at which no incumbent or former director is eligible for election. All members of the current Board must resign in a body at the special meeting, effective on the day the election results are adopted."[22]

Wayburn acquiesced and called a special meeting for October 19, 1968, in San Francisco. A large banquet room at the Sir Francis Drake Hotel was packed with Sierra Club members and staff and reporters from most of the city's news outlets, plus the *New York Times* West Coast reporter, Gladwin Hill, who filed many stories on the Sierra Club and Brower before, during, and after the fracas. Sill, Adams, and Leonard had put together a series of three charges against Brower: "1. He has unlawfully attempted to divert Sierra Club funds." This had to do with an attempt by Brower to write for himself a small royalty—10 percent of the author's 8 percent royalty—to be used at his discretion for Sierra Club purposes. Phillip Berry and other attorneys had thought this improper—as did Eliot Porter—and Brower had dropped the plan.

"2. He will not accept a position subordinate to the legally and duly constituted authority of the Sierra Club." This had to do with the Galápagos books and the opening of a club office in London. Recently, the club had been given a large anonymous donation in blocked sterling—British money that had to be spent in the United Kingdom—to support publication of the two-volume Exhibit Format set on the Galápagos, the first in what Brower envisaged as "The Earth's Wild Places" series of international books. The club's publications committee had discussed the project over many meetings before giving final approval on June 7, 1968. When the grant appeared, Brower promptly opened a London office with two brothers, Alan and Robert Horlin, to staff it, mainly to arrange for and oversee production of the Galápagos books as a first assignment, though Brower clearly had ambitions to spread the club all around the globe. The Horlins had come to San Francisco and had met with the executive committee January 21, 1968. Eliot Porter had made an interest-free $10,000 loan to the Sierra Club to allow the project to get started and allow him to travel to the Galápagos to make the pictures and Brower's son Kenneth to accompany him and eventually to write part of the text and gather material for the rest.

"3. He is financially irresponsible." This was based on disputed audits of the publications program that showed losses of $230,000 over the previous five years and dire projections for the year 1968. Brower argued that the estimates were skewed, allocated no value to color separations, got no credit for attracting new members, and likewise assigned no value to conservation achievements, including a dam-free Grand Canyon, a new Redwood National Park, and a new North Cascades National Park.

The board summarily rejected the first charge and gave Brower a month to answer the other two. The opening of a London office had caused grumbling among some board members, including, most loudly, Dick Leonard, who said it was illegal: the Sierra Club was a domestic organization, he argued, and any foreign activities were a violation of its bylaws. Brower and others pointed out that the club was a member of the International Union for the Conservation of Nature and other international organizations, that its Northwest chapter included members residing in British Columbia and Alberta, Canada, and that its outings program had included foreign trips since 1963.

David Sive, a board member and an attorney himself, disputed Leonard's legal analysis. This spat later led Anne Brower, Dave's wife, to pen a series of limericks to pass the time at board meetings, including this:

> An astute New York lawyer named Sive
> At meetings can often contrive
> From within the profession
> To wring a confession
> That Leonard's *lex lingua* is jive.[23]

One of the persistent criticisms of Brower was that he was devoting too much of his energy—and the club's resources—to the publications program. As noted, the numbers were matters of hot dispute, with Brower arguing that the books achieved far more than the money people spent to buy them. August Frugé, the University of California Press director, chairman of the Sierra Club's Publications Committee, and soon-to-be candidate for the club board, was quite harsh in his criticism of Brower and the book program at the board meeting held December 11 and 12, 1968. This provoked a letter to the board from James Moorman, a lawyer who would go on to become the first executive director of the Sierra Club Legal Defense Fund and a member of the Carter administration. Many others would tell the same story.

Moorman wrote that he learned about the Sierra Club when he noticed two Exhibit Format books in a New York bookstore window: "These wonderful, transcendent books touched me as have few other things. I am not ashamed to say they restored hope." He said that until that moment he had felt alone, "regarded myself as something of a crank, with a lonely, frantic anxiety over the devouring destruction of earth and life which, I believed, I alone perceived and cared about. Then these books! Others also saw and cared! If man created such books, then perhaps man could be persuaded to stop the destruction." He then appealed to the directors to stand by Brower, his books, and the powerful impact they had had on himself and others: "I beg of you, the Board of Directors of the Sierra Club, not to listen to Mr. Frugé, and not to let him stand in the way of the publications program which has given me and others like me hope."[24]

At this same December board meeting, Brower answered the charges from Sill, Leonard, and Adams. The board dismissed them and then went into executive session and awarded Brower a raise, from $21,000 to $25,000 per annum, presumably over the objections of Brower's detractors on the board. The charges of insubordination, financial irresponsibility, and financial impropriety, however, though dismissed by the board, would continue to circulate far and wide. Feeling besieged, Brower began to think about stepping down from his job and running for election to the board, hoping for a change in the bylaws that would allow him to serve as paid president.

The pot boiled over on the morning of January 14, 1969, when the *New York Times* published a page-and-a-half advertisement signed by Brower on behalf of the Sierra Club under the headline

> New Sierra Club Publications advance
> this urgent idea: An international program,
> before it is too late, to preserve the Earth as a
> "conservation district" within the Universe; a sort of
> EARTH NATIONAL PARK

The text went on to talk about the international book series and the urgent need for people and their governments to face up to the mounting international environmental problems facing them. Jerry Mander, Brower thought, had written the ad "beautifully."[25] Kudos poured in from all over, including a congratulatory phone call from the poet Grace Paley, along with orders for the Galápagos books, at fifty-five dollars for the boxed set. Edgar Wayburn, club president, didn't know about the ad, however, until he received a phone call from George Dusheck, a reporter for the *San Francisco Examiner*. Wayburn, who had tried to remain neutral in the mounting battle between pro- and anti-Brower forces on the board, hit the ceiling. After hurried consultation with the club's volunteer legal committee, he fired off a telegram suspending Brower's ability to spend Sierra Club money:

> In accordance with the legal advice I have received, I am by means of this memorandum immediately suspending any and all authority in you to make or fulfill financial commitments of any kind on behalf of the Sierra Club or with club funds until the end of the Board of Directors meeting February 8–9, 1969. The immediate cause of this suspension is the recent deliberate disregard of Board directives not explained by your memoranda of January 20, 21 and 23. My action is also based in part on the entire prior record of your failure to follow Board policy.[26]

Wayburn hadn't been much Impressed with the ad, either: "A hodgepodge account of international environmental threats. . . . The language was flighty and unfocused—fodder for the kind of criticism routinely flung at conservationists."[27]

Brower challenged Wayburn's power to suspend his fiscal authority, and there was legal skirmishing on that topic for a few weeks, but the suspension was upheld at the board's February 1969 meeting. Phil Berry, who had issued the legal opinion justifying Wayburn's act, wrote to Brower, "You have forced us all to the brink and pushed the moderates into belligerency."[28]

Brower insisted that it had been within his authority to run the ad as a promotional announcement for the international series. He said that he had been encouraged to go ahead by Larry Moss, a new director. He also said that he had asked the sales and promotions manager, Jack Schanhaar, to inform Wayburn of the imminence of the ad, which he and Mander had been working on for weeks. Schanhaar didn't make the call. One can only speculate why Brower didn't phone Wayburn himself, though it seems quite likely that Wayburn would have ordered him to pull the ad and he didn't want to do so. It was clearly an act of major defiance; Brower was picking a fight. Mander, for his part, had no idea that the ad hadn't been properly authorized.[29]

The day the ad ran in the *Times*, Brower was on a plane to Washington, DC, to attend confirmation hearings for Walter Hickel, nominated for the position of secretary of the interior. Richard Nixon had just been elected president, and his choice for interior secretary troubled conservationists across the country. Hickel, the governor of Alaska, was what was sometimes called a "boomer," meaning that he was in favor of development and more development. The Sierra Club, whose core principle was the preservation of wilderness, was horrified at the prospect of a boomer in charge of the national parks, wildlife refuges, and other public lands. Brower, conservation director Michael McCloskey, and president Wayburn had resolved to oppose Hickel's nomination. The club dipped into reserves and hired a private detective to sniff out skeletons in Hickel's closet, without success. It wrote letters to editors and went on radio and television to denounce the nomination. As a measure of how public this contest became, the confirmation hearings were broadcast on public television.

Brower spent three days at the confirmation hearings making extremely detailed notes, as was his lifelong habit: eighteen pages of minute-by-minute shorthand notes on January 15 before racing to New York for an appearance on the *Tonight Show*, next day back to Washington for more hearings and fourteen pages of notes on January 16, nineteen more on January 17.

Hickel was eventually confirmed, but both he and his boss seemed to have been chastened by the experience. According to Gary Soucie, then the New York representative of the Sierra Club, "Opposing Hickel's nomination was one of the Sierra Club's great coups. Because we knew we had no chance [of blocking the appointment] we had to do it. Mike [McCloskey] announced that we'd spent our entire contingency fund opposing Hickel. Out of the blue Sheila Piper of Piper Aircraft sent ten thousand dollars because the club had been brave enough to oppose Hickel. So Hickel set out to prove he wasn't as bad as we said he was. And he was actually very good."[30]

Meanwhile, Wayburn, incensed by Brower's defiance over the Earth National Park ad, was drafting a bill of particulars against Brower to present to the February 1969 board meeting. His report to the board read, in part, "I have always felt that our Executive Director is a man of genius, as well as a prodigious worker. He has produced some of the most beautiful books in the world. He has made a major contribution to the Nation's conservation effort. At the same time, he is a man who finds it very difficult to work within the confines of authority in any form—whether it be the authority of the Board, of the club Bylaws, the club President—or the unarguable authority of fiscal facts."

Wayburn added that he had tried to work with Brower for many years, thinking that his virtues outweighed his limitations. But he had come to the end of his tether: "Recently, certain club leaders have made charges against the Executive Director that could not be kept in the confines of a meeting room. They—and in turn the Executive Director—have taken our club difficulties to the public through the news media. Perhaps as a penalty of our success, the press, radio and TV have considered our problems news. What happens within the Sierra Club now is public property, and this fact must be recognized."[31] He then went on to enumerate what he saw as Brower's insubordination—Earth National Park, the international series of books, and general defiance of board directions. The charges weren't new, and the directors already knew where they stood on the issue of Brower. The next step was to consult the members.

"The Brawl"

Brower concluded that his only hope was to take his case to the members of the Sierra Club. He asked for and was granted a leave of absence from his position as executive director to last until the mail-in ballots were due at club headquarters—April 14, 1969—and had his allies circulate a petition to nominate him as a candidate for election to the club's board. Brower was the lead candidate on a slate of five. Others on the slate were former board member Polly Dyer of Seattle, long a conservation leader in the Northwest; incumbent Fred Eissler, a Santa Barbara schoolteacher and leading opponent of the Diablo Canyon nuclear plant; and incumbent David Sive, a New York lawyer. Filling the fifth slot was a problem. A number of Brower confidants, including Sive, argued that they should invite Wayburn to join the slate. He was the president of the club, after all, known as a moderate, and a popular leader. Others argued that Wayburn had already turned against Brower and what he stood for. The latter view prevailed, and it seems highly unlikely that Wayburn would have accepted such an invitation anyway. The fifth slot was finally filled by George Alderson, a cofounder of the Southeast chapter of the club, headquartered in Washington, DC, who had been recently discharged from the U.S. Air Force. The slate called itself ABC: the Committee for an Active, Bold, Constructive Sierra Club.

Brower's adversaries put together a slate of their own, calling it CMC: Concerned Members for Conservation. It consisted of incumbent Ansel Adams; August Frugé, director of the University of California Press, where he had been Brower's boss, and chairman of the club's publications committee, where he often clashed with Brower; Raymond Sherwin, a superior court judge in Vallejo, California, and a rock climber; and Maynard Munger, a real estate broker in Lafayette, California, and chairman of the San Francisco Bay chapter of the club. The four also urged members to vote for Wayburn, though he was not formally a member of the CMC.

The fight—Michael Cohen in his Sierra Club history calls it "the Brawl"[32]—was conducted largely within the pages of chapter newsletters across the country, and there the Brower forces were at a fatal disadvantage. Anti-Brower forces were firmly in command of most of these chapters, notably the chapters headquartered in and near San Francisco and Los Angeles, where most members lived. The chapters all had newsletters that were paid for out of members' dues. These carried a steady drumbeat of anti-Brower news and commentary. The pro-Brower forces had no such platform to use to present their case to the membership. The pro-Brower slate was able to send a single mailing piece to the whole membership list but had no way to match its adversaries' access through the newsletters, though its members would write numerous and extensive letters to editors in an attempt to refute charges and portray Brower in a favorable light.

It was almost a Greek tragedy, with old friends with histories going back as much as thirty-five years turning on each other. One small exchange of correspondence is poignant. It started with a couple of members' letters to the editor commenting on reports of the September 1968 board meeting carried in the *Yodeler*, the San Francisco Bay chapter's monthly newsletter. One, by Cicely Christy, lamented the inclusion of "vague and imprecise accusations against Dave Brower," with no chance afforded to Brower to answer them.[33] Another, from the newsletter's editor, James McCracken, said, "I was startled, and many listeners shocked, by several attempted assaults by innuendo on the reputation of the executive director. If he has done things that are wrong or are against club policy or against directions given him by the board, then let open charges be made and documented. Then he can make his defense and a decision can be properly reached. But please, gentlemen, no more sniping."[34]

These observations prompted a letter from Anne Brower to Dick Leonard, who had been one of those leveling accusations and assaults. Remember he had been a close friend and climbing partner of Dave Brower, and his wife, Doris Leonard, had been a go-between in the courtship-by-letter that resulted in the Browers' marriage. Anne wrote, "Dear Dick, A copy of *The Yodeler* is enclosed in which I have marked two paragraphs for your attention. I concur with the sentiments Cicely Christy and James McCracken express here. When I hear from old friends reports of similar allegations I feel equally, if not more, strongly that specific charges should be made and an opportunity offered to respond to them."[35]

Dick replied, "Dear Anne, As a lawyer, I fully agree that the record should be complete. However, the 'record' was brutally suppressed by Larry Moss's motion to shut off any discussion of the charges." He said that the matter was therefore out of the hands of the directors. "I am sorry indeed, Anne, that you were so distraught at the Directors Meeting that you were unable to accept my offer to talk to you. [signed] Still a friend, Dick."[36]

To this, Anne replied,

> Dear Dick,
> Thank you for your letter of October 1, 1968. I am sorry that it was not more responsive to my letter to you of September 30. I am amazed that you would feel it proper to take the matter of firing Dave to the open meeting of the Board on September 15.... From the course you elected to pursue I am forced to infer you were not so much interested in having your charges answered as in securing for the charges themselves the widest possible audience. This is an old and familiar technique, but I think not a very honorable one.... You are mistaken that I was "distraught" at the Directors meeting. I was not so much distraught as disgusted.[37]

The board had tried to discourage electioneering, but without success. Both sides prepared for a bitter and quite public fight. The CMC—the anti-Brower faction led by Adams, Leonard, and Sill—sent a brochure to the entire membership with a full-page photograph of Tenaya Lake by Ansel Adams under the line "—to save the Sierra Club." It claimed that all living past presidents of the club supported their slate and then listed about two hundred "dedicated members" in support as well. There were several surprises on that list: Alan Carlin, the MIT economist who had helped defeat the Grand Canyon dams; Raffi Bedayn, a former climbing partner of Brower (the Browers' daughter, Barbara, was named for Bedayn's wife); Horace M. Albright, former director of the National Park Service; and H. Stewart Kimball, another old friend (the Browers' youngest son, John, took his middle name from Kimball). Inside the six-page flyer were thumbnail descriptions of the CMC candidates plus Edgar Wayburn and then a long "Anatomy of a Crisis—documented facts," under the headings "Financial Problems," "Book Publication Losses," "Conservation Budget Slashed," "Focus on David Brower," "Profligate Spending," and "Brower's Libel Threats." Each was elaborated in considerable detail, an effective and damning indictment, if seriously unbalanced.

The ABC committee answered with its own flyer, which was produced by Freeman, Mander, and Gossage, the agency that had done the Earth National Park and Grand Canyon ads and others. It ran eight pages on glossy stock under a mock ballot:

- [ ] Shall the Sierra Club revert to its days as a society of "companions on the trail"
- [ ] Or, shall it be an eloquent, *successful* voice for causes that might otherwise have no voice at all
  You decide.

The copy went on to outline a series of campaign slogans:

1) Our most basic position: "In the struggle to save the Earth's wild places and environment, it is now the 11th hour. Anything short of total commitment in this battle wherever it is joined, is reprehensible."
2) On compromise: "The land is not ours to compromise."
3) On *winning* the conservation struggles: "When faced with Goliath, try to find something better than a slingshot."

And so on, in that vein.

The final two pages, in smaller type, were a detailed refutation of allegations of financial improprieties and other specific charges leveled at Brower by Ansel Adams, Dick Leonard, Dick Sill, Edgar Wayburn, and others. It was a closely argued and well-documented argument, put together principally by Anne Brower.

Meanwhile, Hugh Nash, then the editor of the *Sierra Club Bulletin*, tried to publish material in the magazine to explain the controversy and Brower's rationale for taking a leave of absence. President Wayburn, who by this time had taken command of the *Bulletin*, exercising editorial authority over its contents, ordered Nash to publish an article that Nash thought unfair to Brower and overly helpful to Wayburn's own campaign. Wayburn further ordered *Bulletin* staff to prepare a rebuttal based on minutes, letters, and memoranda for Brower, who was out of town. Nash refused, arguing that Brower should have the right to prepare his own rebuttal. Wayburn suspended Nash from his job.[38]

Brower even went as far as hiring a lawyer, Henry M. Siegel of San Francisco, to send stern letters to the editors of the chapter newsletters and other anti-Brower club leaders saying that what they were publishing was coming dangerously close to libel, but it was too late—and the tactic was denounced as intimidation by some of the newsletter editors.[39]

Brower was accused of financial recklessness, insubordination, and arrogance, among other sins. In a very damaging letter to the *Palo Alto Times*, reprinted and circulated far and wide, the novelist and historian Wallace Stegner, once a collaborator and staunch ally of Brower and editor of *This Is Dinosaur*, wrote:

> Brower has ceased to be what he was. He has been bitten by some worm of power. . . .
>
> Those whom his recklessness and insubordination have driven into opposition are not senile fuddy-duddies—he almost calls them birdwatchers—but some of the most distinguished, experienced, and dedicated conservationists on the planet. They oppose him, as I do, because they fear that in his grab for absolute power he will wreck the Sierra Club.
>
> I do not think the current problems will be solved by packing the board of directors with people who will give Brower carte blanche to extend the publication and conservation programs to the borders of the known universe and beyond the borders of both the by-laws and the budget. I think Brower a kind of genius, but I do not think the publication program or the club's effectiveness will collapse if he is forced to act within his legal authority.[40]

The charge of a "grab for absolute power" was but one symptom of a major subtext to this struggle: Should the Sierra Club be run by volunteers or by professionals? As it was, the board of directors was composed of volunteers who hired a professional staff led by Brower and oversaw club operations and activities. Board members saw their duty as oversight; Brower often considered it meddling. His critics accused him of wanting a rubber-stamp board. He often responded with the image of a volunteer fire department where a professional one is called for: "We're still trying to operate like a volunteer fire dept long after we knew the conflagration was too big for that. . . . Our present trouble happens because a few volunteers want the equipment to stay in the firehouse until the bell rings the way it used to. Meanwhile, some houses have burned down."[41]

Anne Brower joined the fray with a letter to a member who had attacked her husband in a Southern California club newsletter: "The dichotomy you set up between a professional staff with a rubber stamp board of directors to run the Club or a democratic, member oriented Club is utterly false and absurd. Moreover it is insulting to the members of the Board." She then asked, rhetorically, "Can you really believe that people like Edgar Wayburn and Will Siri . . . Pat Goldsworthy . . . John Oakes . . . Paul Brooks . . . Martin Litton . . . could ever be a rubber stamp board! You must know if you think about it at all that the idea is absurd." She pointed out that the directors of the club are elected and that "the majority of the Sierra Club Board (none of whom could be described as yes men of Dave's) has been bold enough to back a creative and very hard-working staff. The position of the Club in the country today attests that their faith is justified."[42]

Ansel Adams stirred the pot by writing to the California attorney general demanding an investigation into Brower's behavior, calling Brower "aggressive, imaginative, power hungry, and self-oriented."[43] The attorney general evidently declined. Adams also tried to enlist Arthur Godfrey, on whose national radio program Brower was a frequent guest. Godfrey sent Brower a note in early 1969 saying, "Meanwhile, I received a letter from the chap who did the print in the upper left-hand corner of your letterhead recently. He asked me not to publicize your efforts. Is he some kind of a nut?"[44]

Brower's family rallied around the embattled patriarch. Anne wrote to Dave's brother Joe and Joe's wife, Gayle: "It was nice to talk with you last night and tonight. One nice thing about this horrid affair has been the evidence of family solidarity that has appeared. . . . Our husband and brother, for all his array of fautes, is so much worthier than these creatures who snap at his hamstrings. Is it not so?"[45] And in another letter, two weeks later, "We are over the pain of seeing old friends behave this way and last Saturday I was able to sit next to Dick Leonard without poisoning his salad. One advantage will be much curtailed Christmas card lists."[46] She went on to observe that she and Dave and their allies were bruised but optimistic. "Ghastly though this business is we seem to feel pretty cheerful. They are such lying sons of bitches that there isn't much pain in their disapproval. We think the tide is turning, perhaps just from a surfeit of crap. But if we lose, it will be with the comfortable knowledge that we are intact, while their ethics have been spilled all over the floor."

The election campaign raged for more than three months. Newspapers across the country, including the *New York Times*, the *Wall Street Journal*, the *Washington Post*, the *Los Angeles Times*, the *San Francisco Chronicle*, and the *San Francisco Examiner* carried stories, as did the *Nation, Sports Illustrated*, and other magazines. The Sierra Club's elections committee mailed ballots to the seventy thousand members of the club, to be marked and returned.

In the end the contest wasn't close, even though Brower was the most prominent conservationist alive, the most famous and effective since John Muir. Sixty percent of Sierra Club members had voted, an extremely high percentage for a mail-in ballot like this one. With five directors to be elected, Brower came in sixth, six thousand votes behind Maynard Munger, the realtor from Lafayette. The CMC slate plus Edgar Wayburn swept all the seats.

"A Fallen Giant"

The new board met for its organizing meeting on May 3, 1969. On the front page of that morning's *San Francisco Chronicle* was an old photograph of the Wawona tree in Yosemite National Park. The tree, which had had a tunnel cut through it years before so tourists could drive cars through, had succumbed to age and its wound and fallen and shattered the previous winter. The photo showed an automobile in the tunnel with a tiny figure standing next to it. The caption above the picture read, "A Fallen Giant." The photographer was Ansel Adams. The figure—though he was too small to be made out—was David Brower.

Brower had written to the new board members at the end of April suggesting a reorganized club that he might still lead, but his heart wasn't in it and the new directors weren't interested. Brower made a graceful and eloquent resignation speech, wherein he announced that he would create a new organization:

> Because of my long commitment to the club, I am reluctant to leave it but will serve it as well as I can as a member of thirty-five years' standing. Many have urged the setting up of a splinter organization to step up the broadly based expanding program the club has developed in my sixteen years as executive director, but I don't like splinters, dividing what should be unified. This I will not do. But we feel it imperative to go in a direction implicit in the Earth National Park ad which troubled many directors. It also aroused wide public support. We feel it imperative to go in a direction Aldo Leopold, Paul Ehrlich, William O. Douglas, Stewart Udall, Joseph Wood Krutch, and George Wald have been talking about. So we are today announcing that there will be formed, after careful study, a new organization to augment this and existing groups, even as the Pacific Northwest Chapter [of the Sierra Club] has augmented the Mountaineers, and as the North Cascades Conservation Council has augmented the Sierra Club. . . .[47]

He went on, needling gently,

> The conservation movement needs organizations in which ideas have a reasonable life expectancy, in which indecision is not rife, in which an ethical sense toward the land, toward the many races dependent on it, and toward fellow members, has a reasonable life expectancy too. There is an enormous amount to be done, for the old addiction to growth will grind up our wilderness, our forests, mountains, and streams in a decade. We cannot be dilettante and lily-white in our work. Nice Nelly will never make it. . . .

And he ended,

> I thank those of you who gave it for all the good effort you put in while I was
> your chief of staff. I hope to make many more speeches praising good Sierra
> Club achievement. I intend this to be my last speech as a Sierra Club employee,
> and it has ended.

The applause was loud and sustained, and there were many tears.

Martin Litton immediately moved that Brower's resignation be rejected.
The motion failed, ten to five. Then Will Siri moved to accept the resignation;
"I offer this motion in the deepest sense of sadness and reluctance.... It is
done with the recognition that two giants have come to a parting of the ways.
The two giants are the body of the Sierra Club and the other embodied in the
person of Dave Brower." [48]

Then Larry Moss and Litton offered what the minutes call a "Eulogy":

> David Brower has served the club with dedication and brilliance first as a
> director and then since 1952 as Executive Director. More than any other per-
> son he has involved the public in our fight to preserve a livable world. He has
> pioneered in the effective use of films, Exhibit Format Books, paperbacks,
> posters, full page newspaper ads and other of the mass media. He has sought
> to expand the concerns of the club to include all of the environment. David
> Brower has been a leader. He has tried to bring along those who have lagged
> behind, not always with success. And now his role in club affairs must dimin-
> ish. We are saddened by this prospect. We wish him well in his new efforts to
> save and restore the quality of our environment (in ways which the Sierra
> Club is not yet willing and able to pursue). We salute David Brower and wish
> him to know that his unique contribution to the Sierra Club is
> appreciated. [49]

The motion was approved on a vote of ten to five after the parenthetical clause
was deleted.

Mike McCloskey, named acting executive director immediately upon
Brower's resignation and then getting the job permanently soon after,
summed it up this way: "In many ways, Brower was growing faster in his
grasp of the field than was his board." He mentioned Brower's travels, where
he met a diverse variety of people and was exposed to new kinds of thinking
and acting. "He wanted the Sierra Club to be in the forefront of meeting
these challenges. He felt a sense of urgency to act and resented having to
bring along a board that was not ready. He took chances and plunged ahead,
ignoring restraints that the board tried to impose upon him." [50] He added,

"I thought it was remarkable that the club was able to transform itself from an outing organization with a conservation program to a conservation organization with an outing program. And then into an environmental one. From California to national. A tremendous transformation."

McCloskey mused on how things might have turned out differently: "In the normal way the transformation of the club would have involved big discussions over policy and scope and mode. Instead, the issue became Brower's management stewardship and everyone let off steam and the kinds of pressure that would have attended got transferred onto him. Brower helped build the organization, and it became less suited to him. More people wanted to get in on the action. Brower wanted to run it himself and not be bound by too many rules and regulations and procedures."[51]

Phil Berry, protégé-turned-persecutor, said, "He was a great man with faults. He did a lot of good. Probably the greatest cheerleader conservation ever had because he was able to draw in people from outside the club. He had a great ability to draw in people who'd never heard of wilderness, never been there, get them interested in going." Berry concluded, "Without his ego he wouldn't have been what he was on the positive side. It was driven by this deep-seated desire to be heroic. Without that he wouldn't have accomplished what he did. It's what drove the books. It's what drove the tough positions. It's what drove his pioneering ideas on purity and all that. It was also his ego that would get him into colossal trouble. And often with close friends."[52]

Martin Litton, Brower's staunchest ally on the club's board, thought otherwise:

> Dave Brower was working for the earth. Sometimes he had too much to think about and he couldn't always stay on track, on every little issue. But in large sense he created the Sierra Club as a fighting organization and a lot of people didn't want it to be that. "We just want a comfortable club, we want to be happy, and we want to pretend that everything's all right in the world." Well everything wasn't all right. Dave had been in a war. We knew a lot of things that were wrong in the world. Our role was to keep the world productive and beautiful.[53]

. . .

Brower in a sense had outgrown the Sierra Club, and vice-versa, but he never really severed his ties. He rarely talked about the ordeal of 1968–69 and was loath to complain or criticize his critics. He continued to attend Sierra Club board meetings now and again and to give speeches to Sierra Club gatherings. Indeed, he would seek and win election to the club's board of directors in the 1980s and again in the 1990s. The organization was in his blood. His leaving the Sierra Club staff certainly marked the end of an important era in American conservation—and the beginning of another era, every bit as important as the one it supplanted.

It also marked the beginning of a shift from strong, charismatic leaders like Brower and Zahniser to more behind-the-scenes technicians and schmoozers like Mike McCloskey in the Sierra Club and John Adams, longtime executive director of the Natural Resources Defense Council. Brower would continue his prominence in Friends of the Earth, but the larger, more mainstream—some would say practical and moderate—groups would choose to become more organized and less spontaneous, somewhat to the dismay of Brower and his adherents.

ELEVEN

From Archdruid to
Friend of the Earth

We have lately been playing a game of strip poker with the American earth. A relatively few people have been winning the early hands—people interested in quick profits from the sale of conveniences—and all but guaranteeing that our children will lose as the game goes on. The future will lose not just conveniences but necessities as well.

In the audience that Saturday morning in May 1968 when David Brower became the first former executive director of the Sierra Club was a staff writer for the *New Yorker*, just setting out to write a three-part profile of Brower. His name was John McPhee.

Before the project, McPhee had known nothing of Brower and little of environmental topics, but he saw the burgeoning environmental movement as a growing force that might be interesting to explore. "It was becoming muscular,"[1] he said. "Brower seemed to be the best [candidate]—the least reasonable, the feistiest, the most outspoken." And to another reporter, "He was an early preacher of the environmental movement, and he was the right choice."[2]

After years of writing profiles of individuals, McPhee had decided to try a slightly different approach: he would profile one person interacting independently with three others "to see if one plus one might add up to more than two."[3] The eventual three-part article—and subsequent book—titled "Encounters with the Archdruid" marked a turning point in Brower's career and the expansion of his influence in the environmental movement beyond the confines of the Sierra Club.

Sam Candler, a resident of Cumberland Island who later became head of the Georgia Natural Areas Council, David Brower, John McPhee, and a turkey vulture, Cumberland Island, Georgia, 1969. Photograph courtesy John McPhee.

On March 26, McPhee placed a call to Brower and explained what he had in mind. Brower's first response was to say that he'd have to check with his son Kenneth, who had asked about writing a profile of his own of his father. Ken's memo, dated June 18, 1968, said in part,

> For some time I have been thinking about doing a profile of you, for the New Yorker if possible. The treatment I am thinking of would fit best in that magazine, it seems to me. It would fit in, or begin, in the "Talk of the Town" tradition—little do you New Yorkers know that the silver-haired man who just passed you in the street, or is sitting across from you at La Fonda, carries a map of the Sierra around in his head. The profile would be the best way for me to bring together and make good use out of my observations in your shop for the past four years and as your son for longer, and if it got published might even entrench your position and scare the board.[4]

When the inquiry came in from McPhee, Dave asked Ken for guidance, and Ken said he'd withdraw.

Once McPhee confirmed Brower, he set about choosing the three people that Brower would interact with in the making of the piece. Naturally, he chose Brower's adversaries ("His Natural Enemies" the subtitle read in some versions of the publication). At one point the candidate list reached seventeen. The final roster consisted of Commissioner of Reclamation Floyd Dominy, a Nebraska native who had overseen the construction of many large dams in the West but had been thwarted in his quest to put two reservoirs inside the Grand Canyon; Charles Fraser, a land developer then planning a series of golf courses, condominiums, and hotels on Cumberland Island off the Georgia coast; and Charles Park, a career geologist with the United States Geological Survey who had retired to become a professor of geology at Stanford. Park was a last-minute substitute. The original choice had been Harry Burgess, a vice president of Kennecott Copper. Burgess's "backpack was packed," McPhee says, when a call came in from the Kennecott president ordering Burgess not to go. Park was available and knowledgeable and so got the nod.

So began a year of travels, highlighted by trips to the North Cascades, where Brower argued with Charles Park about whether copper under a protected area—Miner's Ridge, in this case—should be left unmined. Park said copper is so vital to society that the White House should be moved if copper were discovered beneath it. Another trip was to Cumberland Island, where Charles Fraser planned his large new development in bird habitat that Brower wanted left alone—in fact, he wanted the whole island left alone.

The third encounter was a float trip down part of the Grand Canyon with Floyd Dominy, whose plan to build two dams inside the canyon Brower had just defeated. Dominy had accused Brower and the Sierra Club of playing dirty pool, of exaggerating, even lying, about what the dams and reservoirs would do to the canyon. Brower stood firm, denied exaggerating or lying, and insisted that man had no right to ruin an irreplaceable treasure like the Grand Canyon. He cited Teddy Roosevelt, who, upon seeing the canyon for the first time said, "Leave it as it is. The ages have been at work on it and man can only mar it,"[5] a favorite line that Brower would repeat frequently.

"Encounters with the Archdruid" appeared in three consecutive issues of the *New Yorker* in March and April 1971, when Brower was chest-deep in launching Friends of the Earth and rousing public concern and action on various issues. The Archdruid moniker was coined by McPhee based on Charles Fraser's remark that "I call anyone a druid who prefers trees to people. A conservationist is too often a preservationist and a preservationist is a druid."[6]

At least two Sierra Club people were definitely not pleased with the profiles. Ansel Adams fired off a postcard to Dick Leonard on March 22, 1971, which read, in part,

> D.B. and a gent named Parks got a *Profile* in the last New Yorker (1st of 3 articles!!!)[7] He neglected Nancy Newhall—takes credit for the design of This is the American Earth, etc. It is the truth that *she* did the design of the exhibit and the Book Layout. He has been copying it!!! DB was also on the Arthur Godfrey show the other morning. I think he is shifting into high gear, and I feel the Club should not overlook it. I sense the Dictator emerging again. I suggest we all watch out.[8]

Adams was clearly not ready to bury the hatchet just yet, though Brower had been off the Sierra Club staff for almost two years and was focused on his new endeavors.

Another old club hand, Philip Bernays, who had served as the club's president from 1931 to 1933, sent an angry letter to William Shawn, the *New Yorker*'s editor, with this: "Too bad John McPhee didn't learn the true facts from the Sierra Club before being charmed by Brower.... Brower is not another JOHN MUIR altho ambitious to be. Neither was he ever the life blood of the Sierra Club."[9] He suggested that the *New Yorker* should give the Sierra Club equal space to reply, which the magazine declined to do.

Reviewers in the mainstream press were kinder, especially to McPhee, "one of the nation's finest reporters—uncanny in locating the significant fact, the colorful fact, and clear and graceful in setting them down on paper. He is at his unfaltering best in *Encounters with the Archdruid*."[10] The reviewer then observes, "If there is a hero in the book, Brower is it, though he rarely wins an argument hands down and more often than not seems to lose, if there must be winner and loser. He loses single engagements in his grand cause—on points alone. He is never knocked out. And his opponents here are just about the best one might imagine—knowledgeable, forceful, honest, witty, and wholly engaging, more than a jot druid themselves."[11]

Still, showing a trace of thin skin, Brower took serious issue with two of the passages in "Archdruid." One had to do with a line McPhee ascribed to him to the effect that the copper mine Kennecott wanted to dig into the North Cascades would be visible to the naked eye from the moon. In the book it goes like this: "Brower said he could see the hole in the ground that would be there in the future. He said that it would be a man-made crater so large it would be visible from the moon."[12] McPhee continues, "While Brower was executive director of the Sierra Club, the organization became famous for bold full-page newspaper ads designed to arouse the populace and written in a style that might be called Early Paul Revere. One of those ads called attention to the Kennecott Copper Corporation's ambitions in the Glacier Peak Wilderness under the headline 'AN OPEN PIT, BIG ENOUGH TO BE SEEN FROM THE MOON.'" To make matters worse, McPhee concludes, "The fact that this was not true did not slow up Brower or the Sierra Club. In the war strategy of the conservation movement, exaggeration is a standard weapon and is used consciously on broad fronts."

It was a pretty damning charge and did not go unnoticed. The *Wall Street Journal* seized the opportunity and published an editorial quoting from McPhee's piece and sermonizing: "Many public issues today, particularly those that deal with ecology or environment, already are complex without the added complication of deliberate distortion. The counter-argument," the editorial writer went on, "is that relatively weak groups [adding insult to insult], such as conservation societies or public-interest law firms, have to resort to dramatic over-statement to be heard when the mass media are dominated by the ads of the giant corporations they often are attacking." The *Journal*, never a friend to environmental concerns, proclaimed, "But we have the feeling that everyone, weak and powerful alike, could make his point more forcefully by sticking to the facts. If a real problem exists, the facts usually support the claim that it exists. If the facts are scarce, maybe the problem isn't all that great."[13]

The other passage that sparked Brower's ire was in the Grand Canyon section and touched a similar theme. McPhee wrote that people in the Bureau of Reclamation, which Dominy headed, "felt that Brower capitalized on literary hyperbole and the mystic name of the canyon. He implied, they said, that the dams were going to fill the Grand Canyon like an enormous bathtub."[14] And elsewhere in the story, McPhee quotes Dominy quoting Brower: "All's fair in love and war."

Brower sent McPhee a long letter commenting on the series, along with an annotated set torn out of the magazine: "The notations are of all kinds, as you will see. Some relate to errors in fact that I didn't clarify well enough for the checking editors. One is fairly serious—the implication that stands unchallenged that neither the Sierra Club nor I were particularly worried about facts and that we used exaggeration as a weapon. Exaggeration as a weapon you demonstrated with an ad I did not write, did not review, did not sign, and which the Sierra Club did not run."[15]

He also heatedly denied claiming that the Grand Canyon would be flooded out, and denied ever saying—or believing—that all's fair in love and war: "I am in love and have been in war and 'anything' is definitely not fair in either."[16] He insisted, "McPhee did wrong by me in leaving that impression, that allegation by Dominy—even though I had said that it was not true to the publisher's facts editor and to McPhee—letting that stand because he wanted just the right form for his story there. . . . So I think that there was damage done and that McPhee should have cleared it up, but he didn't think so and that's the way the book reads."[17]

Brower told McPhee he also wondered about the title: "Ken and Anne, and I guess others, have commented that the title 'Archdruid' does not seem to be explained. What was so arch? I find only two possible archnesses."[18]

McPhee replied, "The word is Archdruid, not arch druid. I don't know how arch you are, pretty arch, sometimes, I guess—but that's not what I'm saying. This is not arch the cunning or arch the Gothic. This is arch the prefix—'first, principal, chief.' Archbishop. Archduke. Archfiend. Archenemy. Archdefender. Archdavid. Archdruid."[19] And he said that he'd changed the reference to the big-enough-to-be-seen-from-the-moon ad from "one of those ads" to "one such ad" for the book version of the series. He closed the letter, "I am already nostalgic for the project. Where do I go next? Do not answer that."

It is at least arguable that *Encounters with the Archdruid* has kept David Brower's name alive more effectively than anything Brower himself wrote or published. It certainly helped Friends of the Earth get off to a flying start. The book is still in print, forty-plus years after it appeared in the *New Yorker*. Despite the alleged errors or distortions Brower complained about to McPhee, Brower said whenever asked that *Archdruid* was the best thing ever written about him—and dozens of books have touched on aspects of his life and career.

BROWER'S NEW VENTURES: JMI, FOE, AND LCV

At the same time that the *New Yorker* pieces were stirring up controversy among the old guard of the Sierra Club, Brower was out front, marching as a leader of the new order of environmentalists: political, gaining in influence, concerned with public health as well as with wilderness and wildlife, and increasingly international. It had begun a couple years earlier, with the creation of the John Muir Institute for Environmental Studies.

The John Muir Institute

A year before his resignation as executive director of the Sierra Club, Brower had joined up with Edgar Wayburn and Max Linn, a public-relations specialist with Sandia Laboratories in Albuquerque, to launch the John Muir Institute (JMI) as a tax-deductible, nonlobbying organization. Linn was president, Brower vice president, Wayburn treasurer. The secretary was David Sive, and the chairman was Robert O. Anderson of the oil company Atlantic Richfield.

The idea was that conservationists, now slowly morphing into environmentalists, needed better information in order to win their arguments. JMI would, according to plan, eventually become a provider of sound, solid studies and other material to bolster efforts to force environmental sanity into the public debate. Such an organization might also serve as a lifeboat if Brower were ever forced to jump off the good ship Sierra Club. In fact, Brower would often characterize his last act as a Sierra Club employee as walking the plank.

Immediately after his forced resignation, Brower got together with Linn to chart a course for the immediate future. Linn prevailed upon Anderson to make a grant of $80,000 to the new institute to hire Brower to organize a conference he called "Forum for a Future," in Aspen, Colorado, in the autumn of 1969. It brought together politicians, scientists, and conservation activists to discuss a broad range of issues. Brower was expected to devote 60 percent of his time to the John Muir Institute for pay and the remainder to organizing his new non-tax-deductible organization as a volunteer.

The grant from Anderson was not widely publicized at the time but began to raise eyebrows later: What was David Brower doing accepting money from an oilman? There's no evidence that Anderson ever tried to pressure Brower to moderate any of his stances, and Brower allayed any suspicion when he filed suit to block construction of the trans-Alaska oil pipeline a year and a half later.

Friends of the Earth Is Born

The new, no-holds-barred organization was formally created with the signing of incorporation papers in the Manhattan law office of David Sive on July 11, 1969. The site was not an accident: Brower wanted to make sure that it was clear he was not trying to compete with the Sierra Club but planned to augment what it was doing. Thus, the new organization would be a New York corporation and its first headquarters would be there, though it might be more accurate to say that there would be two headquarters: The executive director, Gary A. Soucie, would run the New York headquarters office and oversee lobbying activities in Washington from a distance. David Brower would run the San Francisco headquarters, where publishing and campaigning activities would take place.

The directors of the new organization consisted of Brower, president; Max Linn and Stewart Ogilvy, a former writer for *Fortune* now working for the Population Institute, vice presidents; Perry Knowlton, head of the literary agency Curtis Brown, secretary; attorney Al Forsyth, treasurer; and Donald Aitken, David Sive, John Milton, Frank Fraser Darling, and Ray Dasmann.[20]

The name of the new outfit was Friends of the Earth. The name was simple, easy to remember, and easily translated into other languages. This last point was important to Brower because one of his principal objectives was to spread his gospel internationally via publications and the establishment of groups throughout the world, something that had troubled some Sierra Club directors, who felt that the club should limit its activities to the United States.

There were some objections to the new name, particularly to the inevitable shortening of the name to FOE. Some thought that sounded too negative. Marget Larsen, the graphic designer at the Gossage agency, who designed the letterhead, was among these people, and the original letterhead she designed for the organization rendered the name as Friends of The Earth to discourage readers from using FOE as a short handle. It didn't work.

From the outset, Brower encouraged informality among his staff and volunteers. He stopped wearing a suit and tie every day, opting instead for a woolen Norwegian jacket. He managed staff with a light hand, always encouraging initiative and creativity and delegating authority freely.

A technique he developed at the Sierra Club was working lunches at an establishment called In the Alley near the Sierra Club's Mills Tower offices. He usually invited a half dozen or so of his top lieutenants—nearly always men—and would buy everyone's lunch out of his discretionary fund. Conversation would revolve around work, and much was accomplished, more than would have been achieved by a series of one-on-one meetings in the office.

With the establishment of Friends of the Earth, lunches moved to Enrico's on Broadway. Mr. Banducci, the restaurateur and former proprietor of the hungry i (a nightclub where Lenny Bruce, Phyllis Diller, Bill Cosby, the Kingston Trio, the Limelighters, and many other acts got their start), would frequently serenade lunchers on his violin. At In the Alley, lunch had generally begun with a martini or two; at Enrico's, wine and beer were the normal libations. Again, serious business was discussed, with Brower picking up the tab with money earned from speaking engagements.

The relative informality around FOE was reflected in the frequent parties the group threw. Gary Snyder, Michael McClure, and other poets (once including Allen Ginsberg) might turn up, along with the *San Francisco Chronicle* columnist Herb Caen, the *Newsweek* bureau chief Jerry Lubenow, the *Whole Earth Catalog* founder Stewart Brand, and others. Once, when Pete Seeger was in town for a concert, he and Malvina Reynolds dropped into the FOE office for homemade soups and salads provided by the staff. After the simple supper, Pete and Malvina pulled out banjo and guitar and sang into the wee hours, sitting on the floor. Interest in the environment— "ecology," as it was often called then—was spreading rapidly and attracting people from many walks of life, especially the arts. Brower was seen as a trailblazer.

FOE occupied the streetside office on the ground floor of the old firehouse that housed Freeman, Mander and Gossage. Behind that office was Warren Hinckle and his short-lived *Scanlan's Monthly*. Behind that was a small courtyard with a fishpond. One day someone from *Scanlan's* rushed into the FOE office distressed because a baby bird—a sparrow, most likely—had fallen into the pond. Dave Brower strode back to the courtyard, plucked the near-drowning bird from the water, and held it, warmed it, and talked softly to it until it recovered. Important phone calls received during those fifteen minutes would simply have to wait.

Brower set up an office, and Hugh Nash and I, recently fired by the Sierra Club for being too closely tied to Brower, started work, answering letters and otherwise planning for the launch of the new organization. We were soon joined by Connie Parrish and several other volunteers, plus Joan McIntyre and Patricia Sarr, hired on at minuscule salaries to do whatever needed doing. David Chatfield, an early FOE volunteer also active in the American Friends Service Committee, later recalled an episode when he ran an errand for Brower and got a parking ticket. Brower paid it: "He was just incredibly generous."[21]

We called a press conference for September 16, 1969, to announce the existence of Friends of the Earth and its partnership with the John Muir Institute for Environmental Studies. Brower and Linn spoke and answered questions before a packed room of journalists from newspapers, radio, and television. Brower outlined his vision of a worldwide network of independent but affiliated FOE groups, a robust international publications program, and a vigorous lobbying operation centered in Washington, DC.

But what most captured the interest of the press was the announcement of a new effort to inject environmental concerns into elections. Brower had been thinking along these lines for at least ten years but couldn't get the Sierra Club interested. He even had come up with a name—League of Conservation Voters—based on the League of Women Voters, though the LWV does not generally endorse candidates or work toward their election, as Brower hoped the LCV would do.

League of Conservation Voters

Within a week of Brower's resignation from the Sierra Club staff, providence had stepped in. Marion Edey, a young woman on the staff of Representative

Lester Wolff of New York, sent Brower a letter at his home in Berkeley. "Dear Mr. Brower, I suggest that conservationists start a frankly political organization that is in some ways analogous to a political party, although it does not run its own candidates for office." She noted that conservation organizations "operate like narrowly based pressure groups" when their real source of strength is much broader. "They tend to concentrate on persuading office holders to vote the right way rather than to change the very makeup of legislative bodies. And because they are not active in campaigns, they have no political clout when they do try to influence a Congressman who is not receptive to their ideas in the first place."[22]

Edey described how the organization might work, raising money for its chosen candidates from donors all across the country, not just in selected districts. And she stressed that the operation must be nonpartisan: "This organization would only be successful if it declared itself non-partisan . . . and endorsed a spectrum of candidates, both Republicans and Democrats." She then added, "If I became involved in trying to start such an organization I should be able to round up from $30,000–$50,000 to help finance it."[23]

Brower immediately telephoned George Alderson, one of his slate mates in the recent Sierra Club board election, who lived in Washington, DC. Alderson met Edey for lunch in the House Office Building and was extremely impressed with her intelligence and determination. Later in May or early June Brower met with Edey in Washington. She outlined her idea and Brower suggested the name League of Conservation Voters. They discussed the idea and what it would take to make it happen, how it might operate, what it might look like. Both were convinced that it was a splendid idea. "So are you going to do it?" Edey asked. "No. You are," Brower replied.[24]

And so, when FOE was announced to the world two months later, Brower also announced the creation of the League of Conservation Voters, a political arm that would endorse candidates, raise money for them, rate incumbents on their environmental performance, and work to defeat the worst of them and replace them with more earth-friendly candidates.

In a *New York Times* story headlined "Naturalists Get a Political Arm," Lawrence F. Davies reported Brower's announcement of the creation of the League of Conservation Voters, which "would take part in political campaigns, all the way from local fights to the Presidency."[25] Soon after this,

Brower and the FOE board learned that it wasn't legal for LCV to be a division of Friends of the Earth, as they had planned. That would violate the Corrupt Practices Act, which at the time barred nonprofit, tax-exempt corporations from participating in political campaigns. Therefore, LCV had to be an independent campaign committee, though its steering committee included leaders from many environmental organizations.

But the league continued to have a special relationship with Friends of the Earth. Marion Edey later recalled, "I am forever grateful to David Brower for helping me so much, and for making the League of Conservation Voters possible. Not only his encouragement and leadership, but providing a base of operations in the FOE offices, and all his contacts. He knew the best and boldest environmental activists around the country who weren't afraid to be active in elections. I was more than willing to do the work, but without him I wouldn't have known where to start."[26]

It didn't take long for LCV to have an impact. In 1970, it played a key role in helping a young Paul Sarbanes defeat George Fallon, chairman of the House Public Works Committee, founder of the Highway Trust Fund, and a staunch opponent of public transit. In 1972, LCV raised half the money Alan Merson used to defeat Representative Wayne Aspinall in the Democratic primary in Colorado. Aspinall was a staunch opponent of wilderness who had delayed passage of the Wilderness Act by years, had championed the Grand Canyon dams, and was generally in favor of everything conservationists opposed.

LCV's electoral activity began well before the Watergate scandal led Congress to rewrite campaign laws, which duly led to the creation of political action committees. Many environmental groups then established their own PACs, but LCV continues to this day.

As Edey's letter to Brower said, it would be important to find people from both major parties to endorse. Back in the early seventies, there were plenty of moderate Republicans whose environmental records were stellar: Representative Paul N. "Pete" McCloskey, of California, coauthor of the Endangered Species Act and other green laws; Representative John Saylor, of Pennsylvania, hero of the Wilderness Act effort; Senator Bob Stafford, of Vermont, a clean air champion; and many others. As the parties have drifted apart, environmentally speaking, over the past several decades, it has become more difficult for LCV officials to find Republicans to endorse, with the result that LCV is frequently dismissed as an arm of the Democratic Party.

An early decision in the organization of Friends of the Earth was not to establish chapters, because the Sierra Club has chapters and Brower was trying mightily to avoid being seen as competing with the club. Instead the FOE leaders decided that they would establish "branches," which would, it was hoped, be organized around issues rather than simply the institution. FOE started fairly quickly, reaching the thousand-member mark within about six months, but it was still tiny compared to older groups and lacked the foundation support that the Natural Resources Defense Council and the Sierra Club Legal Defense Fund, for example, enjoyed. Gary Soucie thinks branches were a mistake, and chapters could have helped get FOE established and growing. Brower would quip, however, that "a chapter doesn't often know what a book is doing, but a branch has inside genetic information about the tree it is part of."[27]

Whether called chapters or branches, they were made up of members who needed to be communicated with. About a year after launching Friends of the Earth in San Francisco, Dave Brower decided that the organization needed a proper publication. FOE had published and distributed three issues of a newsletter called *Muir and Friends* to its members, but more was needed. Membership had risen to more than five thousand, still tiny compared to more established groups. But FOE's activities were expanding in all directions, and people needed to know about them.

Various names were suggested, but Brower was the decider-in-chief. He selected *Not Man Apart*, a fragment from a Robinson Jeffers poem called "The Answer," which Brower had used as the title of a Sierra Club Exhibit Format book with Jeffers's poetry and photographs of the Big Sur coast. The relevant lines of "The Answer" are these:

> the greatest beauty is
> Organic wholeness, the wholeness of life and things, the divine beauty
> of the universe. Love that, not man
> Apart from that, . . .

It was a typical Brower creation, no funds to back it but no shortage of energy and enthusiasm. Three members of the San Francisco staff, Patricia Sarr, Hugh Nash, and I, were assigned to write, gather, and edit copy for the publication, a quarter-fold newsprint tabloid to save money. Chris Condon, from *Northwest Passage*, a free weekly in Seattle, whom Brower had met after a speech, did the design and layout for the first two issues, after which he was replaced by Brower's son Robert.

The goal was decidedly ambitious: to be the *New York Times* of the environment, a tall order with a tiny staff and tinier budget. Still, we had almost complete freedom and wrote stories about a wide variety of topics, including many that had nothing to do with what Friends of the Earth was working on. The publication was decidedly activist, with dozens of suggestions of actions readers could take, mostly involving letters to editors and politicians, urging one course of action or another.

There was no prior censorship, no review of story lists or copy before we went to press. Some environmental-group CEOs wanted a look at copy before publication, but not Brower. He would occasionally gripe about a story after it appeared or, more often, insist that something be included at the last minute, but he never asked what was going in, never asked to see stories before publication. The paper attracted a small but fiercely loyal readership.

The name *Not Man Apart* caused predictable problems. It was confusing. It was also, some argued, sexist, which would provoke calls for a change of title as the years went by. But was it pornographic? The first edition did have a naked male wolf cub on its cover, lolling on its back. This may have inspired William Murray to call San Francisco's underground press "the country's liveliest and . . . unashamedly pornographic" in his *New York Times Magazine* story about San Francisco, "The Porn Capital of America." He listed as examples "*The Berkeley Barb, Tribe, The Organ, Aquarian Age, Freedom News, Body Politic, Psychic, Not Man Apart*" and noted the youthfulness of their staffs. "To get the message across and publish only what they like," he observed, "the underground staffers are prepared to make material sacrifices and, if necessary, live like incontinent monks."[28]

This in turn prompted a somewhat gleeful memo from executive director Gary Soucie to Friends of the Earth's directors and the staff of *NMA:* "I hate to say 'I told you so,' but . . . you will recall my voicing concern that, by virtue of its folded-tabloid size, *Not Man Apart* would be shelved on the newsstands alongside the underground and porno papers. . . . With two issues behind us, I don't think *NMA* looks significantly different from a number of San Francisco publications, present and past. Nor, apparently, does writer William Murray. One good thing, though: so long as the San Francisco staff is going to live like monks, it's good they're being incontinent."[29]

Friends of the Earth was one of several new environmental organizations to spring to life in the late sixties and early seventies as the public became ever more aware of environmental deterioration and Earth Day grabbed headlines. Congress passed the National Environmental Policy Act, thereby creating the President's Council on Environmental Quality, and President Nixon created the Environmental Protection Agency by executive order. In addition to FOE, the new organizations included Greenpeace, the Environmental Defense Fund, the Natural Resources Defense Council (NRDC), and the Sierra Club Legal Defense Fund. The latter was created by people active in the Sierra Club, but it was an independent organization, which caused endless confusion until the name was changed to Earthjustice in 1997. The people who had defeated the power plant proposed at Storm King on the Hudson created NRDC. They were mainly lawyers, and the organization would begin by focusing on litigation.

Greenpeace grew out of concern over nuclear weapons testing among activists in Vancouver, who soon expanded its activities to confronting Japanese whaling ships on the high seas, trying to save whales by putting themselves between the whales and the harpoons. Some of those active in forming Greenpeace were in fact expat Sierra Club members then living in British Columbia, who may have turned to the new, more radical organization out of worry that the club, by dumping Brower, might be becoming more conservative.

Greenpeace engaged in civil disobedience, wearing its arrest records with pride. Brower would participate in demonstrations beginning about this time but stopped short of deliberate lawbreaking himself, though he didn't criticize those who chose that tactic. As resistance to the construction of nuclear power plants began to attract people interested in this sort of direct action, the Friends of the Earth board had a debate about whether the organization should endorse such activity. David Sive and other attorneys on the board argued that if the organization was going to file lawsuits to force government agencies and others to obey the law, it should obey the law itself, and this argument carried the day.

· · ·

FOE was off and running and would undertake a wide variety of campaigns on very thin shoestrings. These would involve transportation, energy, and wildlife, among other topics, sometimes in concert with other organizations, sometimes alone. The organization never officially condoned direct action in violation of the law, but many of its members and a few of its staff and directors would participate in picket lines and sit-ins from time to time, and the organization developed a substantial body of lawsuits, some of which had considerable impact.

TWELVE

Friends of the Earth
Takes on the World

Any environmental organization will always be short of funds if
it's doing anything right.

In the early days—indeed throughout the early years—Friends of the Earth's
campaigns grew from the interests of individuals rather than from long
debates or focus groups. Dave Brower led many of them but tended to delegate authority freely and oversee the work of others with a light hand.

Some of the campaigns involved issues that were of interest to the broad
public already, while others sought to bring important matters into the public consciousness.

THE FIGHT AGAINST FUR

One of the earliest FOE campaigns launched the organization into politics
and high society, distinguishing it as a creative provocateur as well as an
influential conservation force. The campaign was the brainchild of Joan
McIntyre, who joined the small FOE staff shortly after the organization
came into being. She was one of many people Brower would hire on impulse
over the years. She had watched the Sierra Club struggle from the sidelines
but had come to admire Brower's style and his unswerving determination.
Soon after the press conference announcing the birth of Friends of the Earth
in September 1969, McIntyre strolled into the firehouse and happened
to catch Brower there. "I've got a slogan for Friends of the Earth," she

David Brower and Max Linn, president of the John Muir Institute for Environmental Studies,
announce the creation of Friends of the Earth, the John Muir Institute for Environmental Studies,
and the League of Conservation Voters in San Francisco, September 15, 1969. Photograph by
Tom Turner.

proclaimed: "A Man on Earth by 1980." This was an obvious play on Kennedy's pledge to put a man on the moon by 1970. Brower loved it and asked McIntyre to join the staff.

Her first love was wildlife, and she decided to shake up the fur industry, then ostentatiously advertising cheetah jackets and leopard-skin pillbox hats. She studied the society pages of the *San Francisco Chronicle* over several weeks and noted the names of women who appeared most often. She then started making phone calls. "Hello, Mrs. Hamm, this is Joan McIntyre from Friends of the Earth. How would you like to lead a fashion revolution?"

Her idea was to persuade opinion leaders to sign a pledge that they would never again buy or wear "the skin, fur, or feathers of wild or endangered species." She figured this could eventually reduce demand and ratchet down pressure on wild species. Her first target was San Francisco society, and once she had signed up a dozen or so movers and shakers, she called a news conference. The speakers were herself, Dave Brower, Candace Hamm (married to one of the beer Hamms), and Mrs. John Fell Stevenson, Adlai Stevenson's daughter-in-law. The resulting story was carried in papers across the globe. This was something new, and the fur industry could not fail to take notice.

Journalist and author Tom Wolfe didn't fail to notice, either. In his 1970 book, *Radical Chic*, he described the campaign, with considerable embellishment:

> Some of the most prestigious young matrons in San Francisco and New York were into an organization called Friends of the Earth. Friends of the Earth was devoted to the proposition that women should not buy coats or other apparel made from the hides of such dying species as leopards, cheetahs, jaguars, ocelots.... On the face of it, there was nothing very radical about this small gesture in the direction of conservation, or ecology, as it is now known. Yet Friends of the Earth was Radical Chic, all right.
>
> The Friends of the Earth actually took to the streets, picketing stores and ragging women who walked down the street with their new Somali leopard coats on. A woman's only acceptable defense was to say she had shot the animal and eaten it.[1]

Following the success of the press conference, McIntyre spread her net wider, far beyond San Francisco and the cosseted world of high society. A few months later, with funds donated by her well-heeled friends, she bought a page in *Women's Wear Daily* to hammer home the burgeoning fashion revolution. The message was the same as the original one in San Francisco, but this time the signatories were far better known, among them Lauren

Bacall, William F. Buckley, Truman Capote, Dick Cavett, Jules Feiffer, Dustin Hoffman, Hal Holbrook, Danny Kaye, Ali McGraw, George Plimpton, and Joe Namath. The fur industry definitely noticed, and the fake fur market got a big shot in the arm.

This was by no means the first time people had objected to the killing of wild creatures for fashion—the Audubon Society was created in the latter half of the nineteenth century to save egrets and other species of birds from the depredations of the makers of ladies' hats—but the melding of celebrities with conservationists was new and made a major impact.

FOE was off to a great start in the United States, but Brower had promised to make the organization international. He had been moving in that direction in the Sierra Club, one of the things that got him in trouble in that organization. FOE was all his and had self-professed international ambitions, but it would need a help and a fair measure of luck.

FRIENDS IN ALL THE RIGHT PLACES

Brower first came across Edwin Matthews in 1963 when he was a young attorney, fresh out of Yale and working for the Coudert Brothers law firm. He had volunteered to work on a case against a developer's proposal to build a bar and restaurant in Central Park that would involve filling in a lake at the corner of Fifty-Ninth Street and Fifth Avenue in Manhattan. Tiffany's and the Pierre Hotel had hired the Coudert Brothers to fight the project, and Matthews went at it with relish.

Matthews reasoned that his case would be bolstered with some less-self-interested parties than Tiffany's and the Pierre. He'd become aware of the Sierra Club through the Exhibit Format books and thought the club would be the perfect counterbalance in the case. He telephoned the club's New York office, outlined the situation, and suggested a meeting. Dave Brower was in town and suggested lunch at the Biltmore, where he was a fixture. David Sive was there, as was Stewart Ogilvy.

David Sive prepared a friend-of-the-court brief for the Sierra Club arguing that the city should not be allowed to turn over a large area of the park for a private five-hundred-seat restaurant. The judge was not impressed and ruled in favor of the restaurant. The lawyers appealed and lost. They appealed to New York's highest court and lost again. The litigation, however, delayed the project for years. In the end, the restaurant was never built, owing to a change in New York politics. In 1966 John Lindsay was elected mayor. He named Thomas Hoving parks commissioner. Hoving's father, Walter, was president of Tiffany's. Hoving the younger scotched the project.[2]

Matthews and Brower had several meetings in the course of the litigation and became friends. In 1965, Coudert transferred Matthews to its office in Paris. After a trip to Libya and a visit to Leptis Magna, a Roman city buried by the Sahara, an early environmental catastrophe, Matthews wrote to Brower saying that environmental problems were everywhere, that they didn't respect national boundaries, and that the Sierra Club should get active internationally. He received no answer, Brower then being embroiled in what Matthews characterized as his "death struggle," with the club. It was 1968.

Several months later, Matthews's phone rang. "Hi, this is Dave Brower. I'm answering your letter." He was calling from Lausanne, where he had gone on publishing business. "I'm coming to Paris. I'll be there in the morning. Can I see you?" Matthews said sure, and Brower turned up at his apartment for breakfast. They talked all morning about issues and organizations, especially Brower's ideas about Friends of the Earth, then a few months old. They then went for lunch with the head of the International Union for the Conservation of Nature.

Upon his return to California, Brower wrote a letter asking Matthews if he would be willing to join the board of directors of FOE. Matthews said yes. He went to New York for the first FOE annual meeting and met various staff members and other directors. Back in Paris, Matthews went looking for people he might interest in forming a French version of FOE, to be called Les Amis de la Terre. That group was incorporated exactly one year after the creation of FOE in the United States.

It got off to a slow start, but then serendipity stepped in. A French journalist named Alain Hervé dropped in on the FOE office in New York, and Gary Soucie urged him to get in touch with Matthews when he returned to Paris. He did, and Matthews began paying him a modest stipend out of his back pocket to get Les Amis de la Terre going.

One of the early campaigns was to stop the building of an expressway along the left bank of the Seine in the middle of Paris. This caught the interest of Brice Lalonde, who was president of the student body at the Sorbonne during the May 1968 demonstrations that very nearly brought down the French government. Lalonde, a political animal to his very core, gave impetus to the young organization, which started growing rapidly. He organized rallies and demonstrations and brought the tiny organization to the attention of the public. He aligned himself with Les Amis de la Terre because he agreed with FOE's antinuclear stance and various other positions. He would go on to team up with Greenpeaceniks trying to halt French nuclear bomb testing in the South Pacific, run unsuccessfully for president of France, serve as his country's environment minister twice, and remain active in environmental matters thereafter, most recently as special advisor on sustainable development to the United Nations.

Ed Matthews's eye then turned to England. He organized a meeting at the Travelers Club in London, which was attended by about twenty people including Dave Brower, and out of that grew Friends of the Earth Limited. Sweden followed soon, then the Netherlands and others. As of this writing, Friends of the Earth has affiliated but independent groups in more than seventy countries, operating under the umbrella of Friends of the Earth International, set up by Matthews.

One common beginning activity among the early FOE groups abroad, often assisted by Matthews, was publishing, as pioneered by Dave Brower. Not lavish picture books—of which FOE in the United States would eventually publish ten—but with small, inexpensive paperbacks such as the *SST and Sonic Boom Handbook, Defoliation, Nuclear Dilemma, The Voter's Guide to Environmental Politics*, and *The Environmental Handbook*. Brower had developed *The Environmental Handbook* as a guide for Wisconsin senator Gaylord Nelson's national "teach-in," which became Earth Day, in 1970. It was an instant hit and would eventually sell a million copies in the United States. Matthews succeeded in persuading publishers in several European countries to adapt these titles for their own audiences. These first books would provide modest but vital initial seed revenue for FOE's endeavors worldwide and would earn the new organization public exposure, which attracted more members.

BANNING THE BOOM

In the late 1960s a race developed between Boeing in the United States and Air France and British Airways in Europe to see who could build the first supersonic passenger aircraft. This might not have been a political issue in the United States save for the fact that Boeing needed a large subsidy from the federal government to proceed. A small but determined group of people thought that a fleet of supersonic passenger planes was a terrible idea for a variety of reasons. An anti-SST campaign fit right into the growing FOE docket and would give the organization an opportunity to build important alliances with other public-interest groups.

David Brower's interest in the debate over supersonic travel began a year before his ouster from the Sierra Club, when he hired a young man named Charles Shurcliff to work for the summer in the club's San Francisco office. Shurcliff's father, William Shurcliff, was a physicist and the founder of the Citizens League against the Sonic Boom, an organization trying to block federal subsidies for Boeing's supersonic passenger plane. The younger Shurcliff spent the summer building a dossier against the Boeing SST, but the Sierra Club had other matters on its agenda, not least of which was ridding itself of its executive director. FOE might pick up that torch.

Once FOE got going, Brower's thoughts again turned to the SST, and he quickly persuaded Shurcliff the elder to write and Ian Ballantine to publish the *SST and Sonic Boom Handbook*. Meanwhile, Gary Soucie, who had left his Sierra Club job to become Friends of the Earth's first executive director, based in Manhattan, thought that an anti-SST campaign was just what the doctor ordered for the new organization. Senator William Proxmire, of Wisconsin, who had made a career of ferreting out extravagant and wasteful federal spending, had jousted with his colleagues over the gigantic subsidy being suggested for the Boeing project but hadn't had much success. A number of environmental organizations were opposing the project but had many other fish to fry, so the field was relatively clear. And the plane as proposed was a clear environmental villain. It would blanket the country with sonic booms; it would be preposterously inefficient in its fuel consumption; and it threatened to weaken the already compromised protective atmospheric ozone shield, thereby having a serious effect on people's skin, not to mention the skin of frogs, other amphibians, and other sensitive derma types.

Brent Blackwelder, then a volunteer and graduate student at the University of Maryland, who would go on to become FOE president many years later, said in an interview that the anti-SST campaign was in fact the first real effort to protect the climate, laying the groundwork for the crusade that has taken over the environmental movement and much of the scientific community forty years later.[3]

George Alderson, recently discharged from the Air Force and setting up an FOE presence in Washington, DC, liked the idea as well. He began meeting with his counterparts in other organizations and building what would become the Coalition against the SST. Arthur Godfrey, the ukulele-strumming radio personality on whose program Brower was a frequent guest, was honorary chairman.

An early initiative, which vaulted Friends of the Earth into the leadership position in the anti-SST battle, was another of Jerry Mander's full-page *New York Times* newspaper ads. This one blared:

> BREAKS WINDOWS, CRACKS WALLS,
> STAMPEDES CATTLE, AND WILL
> HASTEN THE END OF THE
> AMERICAN WILDERNESS.

Mailbags full of coupons and checks with membership applications poured in to the Friends of the Earth office in the firehouse in San Francisco, and the membership of FOE began to swell. The emphasis on the sonic boom became a bit of an issue inside the anti-SST coalition. Dr. Shurcliff had his Citizens League against the Sonic Boom, but pro-Boeing forces suggested that the plane could simply travel more slowly across the American landmass and upon landing. The waste of fuel and the damage to the atmosphere were at least as serious but were downplayed to some extent by the Citizens League. And although FOE was an important player in the successful effort to kill the plane in the United States, the FOE groups in Great Britain and France were powerless to stop the Concorde from being built and being flown in and out of Dulles and John F. Kennedy airports; the planes were forbidden to cross the North American landmass.

The diseconomics of the enterprise finally killed the Concorde after a quarter century, just as some had predicted. Summing up later, Brower said, "The damage to the ozone, plus the extension of inequity—everyone else's inconvenience for a few people who want, as the ads for the Concorde said, 'The gift of time.' 'The gift of time' to them—a tiny difference—at everybody else's expense. The SST is immoral, that's all."[4] "What's the use of getting to Paris ahead of your judgment?" he would tongue-in-cheekily ask.

In the end, one notable benefit of FOE's involvement in the anti-SST campaign was the building of alliances among diverse groups. These floating coalitions would become a hallmark of activist efforts in Washington, DC. The Coalition against the SST was made up of sixteen national and fifteen state and local groups,[5] which included the Sierra Club, the Wilderness Society, and other environmental groups, plus the Federation of American Scientists and the National Taxpayers Union as well as the International Longshoremen's and Warehousemen's Union and the Oil, Chemical and

Atomic Workers International Union. It had long been mooted that environmental groups might make common cause with organized labor. Here was a start.

PROBLEMS WITH PIPELINES

With the Boeing SST vanquished, the demand for jet fuel was held in check slightly, but the demand for oil to power the nation's fleet of cars and trucks was growing quickly, and oil companies were searching far and wide for new deposits to tap. If they could find new domestic deposits, thereby lessening dependence on the Middle East and other foreign sources, so much the better.

In 1968, Robert O. Anderson's Atlantic Richfield Company was the first to strike oil at Prudhoe Bay on the Arctic coast of Alaska.[6] The strike looked promising, but the conditions were daunting. Prudhoe was nearly eight hundred earthquake-fault-riddled miles from the nearest ice-free harbor, which was all the way across Alaska at Prince William Sound in the Gulf of Alaska southeast of Anchorage. How to move the oil? ARCO and British Petroleum engineers suggested a pipe and set up the Alyeska Pipeline Service Company to design it. It would be a major project. The pipe would be four feet in diameter and would have to cross innumerable rivers and streams, including the mighty Yukon River, plus the Brooks Range. And there were migrating caribou and other animals that might not be well adapted to pipelines, in addition to the possibility of sabotage, both of the pipeline and of the tankers that would bring the oil to refineries. In the early stages, the plan was to bury the pipe over most of its route, which threatened to melt the permafrost, with unpredictable consequences.

Dave Brower argued that the risks were simply too great. He calculated that if all American automobiles had standard transmissions rather than automatic, the need for Prudhoe crude would disappear. He argued that a superior plan would be to transport the oil in railcars through Canada to U.S. markets. This would avoid most of the pipeline's problems and would obviate the need for sending the oil via tanker from Valdez on Prince William Sound to refineries on the west coast of the United States. This suggestion was not taken seriously, though its merit was made clear when the *Exxon Valdez* went aground on Bligh Reef in 1989, spilling eleven million gallons of crude into the sound, causing damage to wildlife and the fishing industry still being felt twenty-five years later.

As crude-by-rail operations are expanding in the early twenty-first century, accidents are becoming common, and opposition to transporting both oil and coal is building rapidly. One guesses that Brower would have rethought his support for the rail alternative and argued that the oil and coal should simply be left in the ground. In any event, when the pipeline proposal became formal and the process of applying for various federal permits for the project began to move forward, Brower telephoned Jim Moorman, at that point still with the Center for Law and Social Policy in Washington, DC, prior to his move to the Sierra Club Legal Defense Fund, and asked if he'd heard about the trans-Alaska pipeline.

Moorman had read a *New York Times* story about what a horrible mess the pipeline would make. He agreed to see if he could find any way to challenge the project in court. Prospects were bleak. The only law Moorman could find was one governing rights-of-way across federal lands. As he read the law, it appeared to say that for a project such as this, a right-of-way could be only the width of the project—the pipe in this case—plus twenty-five feet on either side. He doubted this pipeline and its accompanying haul road could be kept to such a narrow corridor, but was equally confident that the Interior Department could find a way around that law. He called Brower back with this discouraging news.

That was in the fall of 1969. On January 1, 1970, President Nixon signed the National Environmental Policy Act (NEPA), which had loped through Congress with little notice and no controversy. It was the brainchild of Senator Henry "Scoop" Jackson, Democrat of Washington State. Most people, if they were aware of the legislation at all, thought it was just window dressing to make Congress look good as public concern for the environment grew in anticipation of the first Earth Day, scheduled for April 22.

NEPA seemed straightforward. It required projects with "a major impact on the human environment" that involved federal money or federal permits to undergo an examination of their likely environmental impact and a consideration of alternatives. The law also required that the public be given an opportunity to weigh in on the project by means of hearings or written comments.

Moorman read the new law and consulted with colleagues including Joe Sax, a leading environmental law professor then serving on the board of the Center for Law and Social Policy. They thought they might be able to force the government to at least delay the project pending the writing of an environmental impact statement. He phoned Brower and said that he'd be willing to file a lawsuit and that his services would come free but expenses would be considerable for travel to Alaska and the deposing of experts and other costs.

"I wonder if there are any other groups that might join the case," Brower answered. "We don't have any money." He then mentioned Stewart Brandborg, head of the Wilderness Society, which had had a long interest in Alaska. Moorman suggested they might also approach the Environmental Defense Fund, which Moorman shortly would represent in anti-DDT litigation. Moorman phoned Brandborg, who agreed to shoulder the costs of the litigation if the society could be listed first on the suit. EDF and FOE would play second fiddles.

The first environmental impact statement (EIS) for the pipeline appeared on March 5, 1970. All of eight pages long, it found that the pipeline would have no appreciable environmental impact.[8] It was clearly inadequate and possibly illegal. So *The Wilderness Society et al. v. Hickel* was filed on March 26, the first major lawsuit to be filed under the National Environmental Policy Act. It accused the Interior Department of violating NEPA by not producing an adequate estimate of the environmental impact of the pipeline and its associated haul road. The case was assigned to Judge George T. Hart in Washington, DC. As Jim Moorman later described it, this was an incredible windfall for his clients—Judge Hart had been stationed above the Arctic Circle at a DEW (Defense Early Warning) station in his Air Force days and understood the arguments about permafrost and caribou and the rest.[9] Judge Hart enjoined the pipeline project on April 13, even though pipe had been ordered, fabricated, delivered, and stacked at various points along the proposed route.

The Interior Department, with input from the oil companies, thereupon got serious about writing an environmental impact statement, though this second attempt was met with scorn and derision by fans of the Alaska wilderness. Brower wrote in an op-ed piece in the *New York Times*, "Beside me is the draft statement the National Environmental Policy Act requires about the environmental impact of the proposed Trans-Alaska pipeline. The kindest comment I can make is that the draft leaves unprecedented room for improvement."[10]

As the federal government and the companies worked to write an environmental impact statement that would satisfy Judge Hart and the law, debate moved to Congress and into the media. Further drafts were produced, eventually covering thousands of pages. Still, the environmentalists were not mollified—to them, the studies proved that indeed the pipeline would be an environmental disaster. Finally, a bill was introduced into Congress ordering the Interior Department to finalize the latest draft EIS, to waive the project's duty to comply with NEPA, and let construction proceed. The bill passed the House, then deadlocked in the Senate, on a forty-nine to forty-nine vote. Vice President Spiro Agnew, who would resign his position in disgrace six months later, cast the deciding vote in favor of the pipeline on April 27, 1973.[11]

The pipeline was duly built. The litigation and public opposition to the pipeline didn't stop it, but certainly resulted in a safer pipeline—specifically, one that was built above ground along its entire route, with provisions to allow caribou to pass beneath it and for avoiding the slumping-permafrost problem.

The pipeline battle, along with the successful struggle to deny federal subsidies for development of a supersonic passenger aircraft and other front-page efforts, launched Friends of the Earth into the public consciousness along with many other organizations, most of them far larger. That in turn continued to build public interest in things environmental.

REVISITING GLEN CANYON AND RAINBOW BRIDGE

In late fall 1970, while Brower was still embroiled in the fight against the trans-Alaska pipeline and the SST, he turned his attention back to Glen Canyon, the loss of which still haunted him after a decade. He jumped at a chance to atone for Glen Canyon's destruction in some small way, and he would use the power of the courts, at which he'd become adept.

It started when Brower's eldest son, Kenneth, and two FOE staff members were backpacking in Coyote Creek, a tributary of the Escalante River in southern Utah and a vestige of the Glen Canyon watershed. On the trip, they ran into Ken Sleight, an outfitter and guide. Sleight bemoaned a plan by the Utah Department of Highways to build a road on the tableland above Coyote Creek and a bridge across the Escalante—"and there's no Dave Brower around to stop them." Ken Brower and his friends assured Sleight that indeed Dave Brower was still around and busy stopping things like that project. The four vowed to explore working together.

The Escalante road and bridge faded quietly away with no pushing necessary, but Dave Brower and Jim Moorman, by this time head of the Sierra Club Legal Defense Fund, cooked up another plan: a lawsuit to protect Rainbow Bridge. Recall that the act of Congress that authorized the building of Glen

Canyon Dam and other edifices expressly said that Rainbow Bridge National Monument must be protected from the reservoir: "As part of the Glen Canyon Unit, the Secretary of the Interior shall take adequate protective measures to preclude impairment of Rainbow Bridge National Monument.... It is the intention of Congress that no dam or reservoir constructed under the authorization of this Act shall be within any national park or monument."[12]

The bridge, the largest known natural bridge in the world, soars over a tributary of the Colorado River several miles from where the river once ran free. The law couldn't have been clearer, but the government simply ignored it. Lake Powell was very nearly lapping the walls of the inner canyon below the bridge. Not only was this patently illegal, but it also caused some worry that water might slowly seep into the sandstone and weaken the bridge abutments: if and when the reservoir filled to capacity, the water would stand about fifty feet deep below the bridge.

Moorman thought a lawsuit might work. Brower was more than enthusiastic. FOE was a plaintiff, along with the Wasatch Mountain Club of Salt Lake City and the river guide Ken Sleight. The suit was filed in Washington, DC, on November 4, 1970. FOE's membership stood at around one thousand nationally.

The government immediately moved to have the case transferred to Salt Lake City. Motion granted. Moorman scrambled to find an attorney he could bring into the case in Utah and found Owen Olpin, then a law professor at the University of Utah. The judge they drew was Willis Ritter, a colorful federal jurist in Salt Lake. Olpin enlisted his students to help prepare the case and recruited James Lee, a seasoned litigator and son of a legendary former Utah governor, J. Bracken Lee, to sit with him at counsel table.

As the trial opened, Olpin said to Judge Ritter that this was a simple case; all the court needed to do was interpret a single sentence in the statute. Ritter interrupted, "Don't you tell me that this is a simple case, Mr. Olpin. There's a huge federal investment in waterworks at stake on one side and a magnificent sandstone arch on the other."[13] Olpin didn't argue. That afternoon the Justice Department attorney, who had been listening intently during the morning session, rose for his own opening statement. "Your honor, this is a very complicated case." Ritter again interrupted. "Weren't you listening to Mr. Olpin this morning? He explained that this is a simple case. All I have to do is interpret the meaning of a single sentence."

On the second or third day of the trial, Dave Brower turned up at the courthouse and asked Olpin if he could testify. Olpin said sure. Brower took the witness stand and Olpin asked him to explain his position and his interpretation of the law and the facts. Ritter, Olpin remembers, had already telegraphed that he was sympathetic toward the plaintiffs' arguments, so when the judge started asking Brower questions, Olpin withdrew from the conversation: "Here was the legendary judge in awe of the legendary environmentalist. It was a love-fest. Brower was in rare form, very respectful, a wonder to watch. One of those incredible moments in the courtroom."

Ritter ruled for the plaintiffs on all counts, finding that the government had blatantly broken its promise to protect Rainbow Bridge and that it would have to stop impounding water behind the dam until measures could be taken to protect the national monument and the bridge. A full year's worth of runoff would be allowed to continue its way downstream rather than being trapped behind Glen Canyon Dam.

The government immediately filed an appeal with the Tenth Circuit Court of Appeals in Denver, which, on its own motion, decided to hear the appeal en banc—that is, with all seven judges hearing the case rather than the usual three. Congress had rebuffed several attempts to repeal the provisions of the law that required protection of Rainbow Bridge and had repeatedly refused to appropriate money for protective measures—a coffer dam, for example, to keep reservoir water out of the monument—so the court had to come up with some other rationale for overturning Ritter's injunction. What the judges came up with was the notion that Congress had repealed the protective language "by implication," a creative if rather fanciful bit of judicial legerdemain.

So Judge Ritter's ruling and injunction were overturned on appeal, and the Supreme Court declined to review the case. Water invaded the national monument in the late seventies. The bridge seems to be stable, and persistent drought has lowered the lake level dramatically; some experts predict that it will never again reach capacity, known as "full pool" in the trade. Time will tell. "It was an utterly outrageous decision," Olpin still maintains. "I could have won that case in any other circuit in the country."[14]

THE GLOBAL POWER OF PRINT

About the same time Rainbow Bridge was being shunned by the Denver court, the United Nations was getting ready to host the first international Conference on the Human Environment in Stockholm in June 1972. In order to participate in an informal way, Friends of the Earth teamed up with the *Ecologist* magazine in England to undertake yet another innovation that would become a fixture of environmental rabble-rousing.

When David Brower had been at the annual Frankfurt book fair, as was his habit, in the fall of 1971, looking for publishers to form alliances with, he and his team had cooked up the idea of publishing a daily news-sheet for the conference. Its purpose would be to make sure that the proper slant was put on the deliberations and that important topics were not omitted or glossed over.

By coincidence, Teddy Goldsmith, Robert Allen, Mike Allaby, and Peter Bunyard of the *Ecologist* had hatched the same idea, independently, at about the same time. Somehow, probably via the FOE office in London, the two groups learned of each other's plans and decided to join forces. The positions of the groups seemed compatible. FOE would supply about half the personnel, mostly from FOE-UK in London plus Walt Patterson, editor of the small journal *Your Environment*, and the *Ecologist* would supply the rest, including a brilliant editorial cartoonist named Richard Willson, whose work had appeared in the *Guardian*, the *Washington Post*, and other papers. Funding would come mainly from Goldsmith. Jordens Vänner, the Swedish Friends of the Earth group, would provide people to help typeset copy for the paper (on electric typewriters) and headlines (from Letraset ruboff sheets) and see that copies of the paper were delivered, in time for morning coffee, to the hotels where the delegates would be staying. The paper would be called the *Stockholm Conference ECO*. (The Brits tended to pronounce it EE-koh, the Americans, EH-koh.)

The matters that concerned the *ECO* reporters coincided with the interests of many of the thousands of people who came to Stockholm to have their say: Hopi elders angry about coal strip-mining on their sacred lands; residents of Minamata, Japan, who were grossly disfigured by mercury-laden discharges from a nearby factory; antiwar activists protesting the use of 2,4-D and 2,4,5-T as defoliants in Vietnam and trying to end the war altogether; people opposed to the continued slaughter of whales; people against nuclear power; and many, many others. Some of these matters were on the conference agenda; most were not.

On the first Thursday of the two-week conference, the UN's newest member, the People's Republic of China, threw a curveball in the proceedings, demanding that a secret session be convened of all participants to debate an alternate declaration China had already proposed. The United Nations had circulated and negotiated a bland, feel-good, utterly toothless declaration about how it is the responsibility of every nation to protect the global environment, hoping to have it ratified by all parties by the end of the conference. What was China up to?

The next day's *ECO* had the answer, an exclusive scoop, reporting a story that the *New York Times, Asahi Shimbun, Dagens Nyheter*, the *Times* of London, and every other paper in the world had missed. *ECO* had had a reporter inside the secret session, who reported on the Chinese. China had pronounced, "Man is the most precious of all things on earth. Man propels social progress, creates social wealth, and advances science and technology. There are no grounds for any pessimistic views on population growth and the preservation of the environment." It then went after the United States, its First World allies, and the dominant economic system, saying, "We hold that the major social root cause of environmental pollution is capitalism, which has developed into a state of imperialism, monopoly, colonialism, and neocolonialism—seeking high profits, not concerned with the life or death of people, and discharging poisons at will. It is the policies of the super powers that have resulted in the most serious harm to the environment." And then it brought up the specter of the Vietnam War: "The United States has committed serious abuses in Viet-Nam, killing and wounding many of its inhabitants. These facts are known to the world and should be included in the Declaration. The Declaration should also be comprehensive on the nuclear threat."[15] The *ECO*, in reporting the Chinese declaration, caused a major sensation. *ECO* immediately became a must-read for delegates, observers, even the conference secretariat. It would become a staple at various international conferences from then on.

BROWER BREAKS RANKS

Joan McIntyre, of fur-coat fame, was at Stockholm rabble-rousing on behalf of the great whales. Joanna Gordon-Clarke was there for the same purpose on behalf of FOE Ltd from London. Though whaling was not on the official agenda of the environmental conference, the two managed to get a resolution introduced and passed that put the conferees on record in favor of a ten-year moratorium on commercial whaling, a major coup. The annual meeting of the International Whaling Commission (IWC) was to take place in London soon after the Stockholm clambake ended, so McIntyre and Gordon-Clarke and others trooped off to London to make sure that the IWC was made aware of the resolution approved at Stockholm.

This launched FOE into the anti-whaling crusade in a big way, joining it with Greenpeace, the World Wildlife Fund, the International Fund for Animal Welfare, and several other international bodies in trying to bring pressure on the IWC to end commercial whaling while there were still a few whales left to save. It would be a long campaign. It would also cause rifts within the environmental community, frequently finding Dave Brower taking positions at odds with friends and allied organizations who were usually in agreement with him and Friends of the Earth. The whale savers made little headway in London in 1972, but they kept up the pressure, got the public concerned, and recruited allies.

The 1977 meeting of the International Whaling Commission was held in Canberra, Australia, and *ECO* was there to record the proceedings and put in its two cents' worth. In spite of growing and vocal opposition, the IWC was still issuing dangerously high quotas for killing great whales. But in Canberra that year a new and awkward twist was added. The commissioners voted to ban all whaling for bowhead whales, a subspecies of right whale that lives in the Arctic Ocean and the Bering Sea and had been nearly wiped out by commercial whalers in the preceding decades.

Alaskan Inuits—Eskimos—had taken a few bowheads each year for millennia, and they considered the IWC's action both scientifically unjustified and racist. The United States, the leader of the anti-commercial-whaling bloc, was put in a difficult position. How could it maintain its position against whaling by Japan, Norway, Iceland, Chile, and the rest and approve whaling by some of its own citizens on a stock of whales that was seriously depleted, though the depletion had come at the hands of commercial whalers?

Most of the environmental community fell in line with the ban on taking bowheads, including, initially, Brower. His mind was changed by Pam Rich, from Fairbanks, a member of the FOE staff in Washington, and her colleague Anne Wickham.[16] They argued that the Inuit had lived in harmony with their environment for millennia and that whales are vital to both Inuit culture and diet. If bowheads are to be saved, it will be Inuit who do the saving. And the Inuit insisted that there were far more bowheads in the sea than the scientists had been able to count.

Brower went to visit Inuit whalers in Alaska and joined the U.S. delegation to the IWC as an advisor. He also, with some difficulty, persuaded

Friends of the Earth in the United States to side with the Inuit (FOE in London remained opposed to any whaling for bowheads). Brower argued that it would have to be the Inuit who figured out how to reduce their take of bowheads anyway, and that there was a far greater threat to the whales' survival, one that is becoming acute as this is being written in the summer of 2013. Brower saw it coming decades ago: "The great threat was not the Eskimos, but Exxon and the other oil companies that are now [1978] rushing to do offshore drilling in northern waters, in the Beaufort Sea and other places. A massive blowout or two up there could do more damage to the bowhead whale than a lot of Eskimos could ever do."[17] The dispute faded for the time being when the Inuits' assertion that there were at least ten times as many bowheads as the scientists had been able to count was confirmed.

The other matter on which Brower and FOE broke ranks with the orthodox position had to do with a boycott of Japanese goods over whaling. Most of the rest of the environmental community had launched a boycott of all Japanese goods—automobiles, electronics, the works—to continue until Japan stopped killing whales. Friends of the Earth had initially joined the boycott along with most of the established environmental groups, including the Sierra Club. But Steve Rauh, editor of the Sierra Club San Francisco Bay chapter's newsletter, the *Yodeler*, was troubled. He noticed, for one thing, that virtually all the photographs he published were taken with Japanese cameras and wondered at the overall fairness of an across-the-board boycott. He got in touch with Dave Brower, laid out his concerns, and Brower offered to underwrite a thorough study of the situation.[18] The two hundred-page treatise reported, among many other things, that the boycott was futile: Japanese exports to the United States had risen from $18 billion to $25.8 billion during the period the boycott had been in effect.

Based partly on this study, Brower determined to have FOE boycott the boycott and helped persuade the Sierra Club and the National Audubon Society to withdraw support as well. His reasoning was that this was a secondary boycott and would have been illegal within the United States: What did a Japanese autoworker or camera-maker have to do with killing whales?[19] Finally, the boycott would make it difficult to support the fledgling environmental movement in Japan and especially difficult for Japanese environmentalists to try to persuade their government to abandon whaling.

Brower's stance angered many in the movement: his staunchest supporter in his Sierra Club days, Martin Litton, refused to talk with him for several years for abandoning the boycott and persuading the Sierra Club to pull out.

The International Whaling Commission eventually adopted a ten-year moratorium on commercial whaling, which went into effect in 1986,[20] and Brower and Litton resumed their friendship and occasional collaboration.

NO TO NUCLEAR ENERGY

As we have seen, David Brower had encouraged the building of nuclear power plants as an alternative to hydroelectric dams for two decades, most specifically concerning the dam proposals at Dinosaur National Monument and in the Grand Canyon. His was not total or unequivocal support for the nuclear option, and he began to be troubled by reports of safety problems at reactors, the danger of nuclear fuel's being diverted to warlike purposes, the damage that radiation could do to humans and other creatures, and the extremely long-lived nature of some nuclear waste products, especially plutonium. "I had high hopes for nuclear energy," Brower said, "but these were finally dashed in 1969 as I began to realize the perils that lay in every stage of the nuclear fuel cycle, from unearthing to re-earthing it."[21]

He credited two people in particular with cementing his soon-to-be adamant opposition to nuclear power: Amory Lovins, a dropout from Harvard who became the youngest-ever don at Oxford and then dropped out of that institution to work for Friends of the Earth in London, and Henry Kendall, an MIT physicist, winner of a Nobel Prize in 1990, and cofounder of the Union of Concerned Scientists. In addition to Kendall's essential work on nuclear power plants, he also ran a small family foundation that contributed generously to Friends of the Earth and other organizations.

Lovins's field of study at both universities was physics, and he soon came to believe that his greatest contribution would be in analyzing and reorganizing energy policy, which he has done with exceptional distinction. The way Lovins became wrapped into the Brower sphere is one more story of how Brower would act on impulse when he spotted talent. It didn't begin with energy but with a lode of copper under a modest mountain range in Wales, comparable in makeup if not in size to the copper deposit in the North Cascades that Brower and Charles Park fought over in *Encounters with the Archdruid*.

This mountain range is in Snowdonia National Park, where Lovins and a friend named Philip Evans were fond of hiking and photographing. Film was expensive and Lovins, a grad student, and Evans ("probably the top landscape photographer in Britain"),[22] a technician who repaired photocopy machines on campus, needed to generate some income from their photography to fund more. They had heard that *National Geographic* paid well. Lovins—who worked summers as a hut boy for the Appalachian Mountain Club in New England—decided to send a selection of photos depicting Snowdonia and other scenes to the *Geographic*'s headquarters in Washington, DC. The answer came back, "This is beautiful work, but it's really too atmospheric for us. It's not representational enough. We want pictures that are more in the style we publish, not so much like fine art. But you might send it to Dave Brower, he likes this sort of thing."[23]

Lovins telephoned Friends of the Earth in San Francisco to see if there might be interest there. Brower was not in the office, but Lovins was encouraged to send the photographs. Lovins shipped off his package. When Brower saw it, he was impressed but, as usual, he was too busy to respond. Months later, Lovins telephoned again and reached Brower, who invited him and Phil Evans to a meeting at the Travelers Club in London being set up by Ed Matthews; it just happened to be the organizing meeting for the United Kingdom Friends of the Earth. The Lovins-Evans book, *Eryri: The Mountains of Longing*, was published in 1971 and helped stop the copper mine.

Lovins would go on to revolutionize how people think about energy and, with his Rocky Mountain Institute in Colorado, help make practical and competitive solar and other sustainable energy technologies, always paying homage to Brower. "I've had some treasured mentors over the years," said Lovins, "but he was by far the greatest influence, especially in his leadership, his style of being and doing, and his ability to cause vast and lasting change."[24] One change in which Lovins played a starring role was a major effort to turn the nation away from nuclear power.

The conservation movement had always had a difficult relationship with energy. Many conservationists—Brower prominent among them—hated dams for what they did to rivers. They would come to hate coal for what mining and burning it does to hills, mountains, streams, the air we breathe, and the atmosphere itself. At first they thought the mighty atom would be their salvation. But problems mounted: uranium miners, many of them Navajo, contracting lung cancer; studies indicating that serious accidents were possible if not probable; concerns about what to do with spent fuel that would remain lethal for millennia; worries about bomb-grade material falling into the wrong hands; and calculations showing that the rosy projections of a nuclear economy (such as early claims that electricity from nuclear plants would be "too cheap to meter") were fanciful at best.

In the summer following the 1972 Stockholm conference, Henry Kendall, the physicist from MIT, was engaged with his economist colleague Daniel Ford of the Union of Concerned Scientists in Atomic Energy Commission hearings in Bethesda, Maryland. They had badgered the commission into holding the hearings to delve into troublesome studies that seemed to indicate that a key safety feature of nuclear power plants, the emergency core-cooling system, could easily fail and allow a reactor's core to melt down and release dangerous radiation. Kendall, who had become acquainted with Brower through a shared mountain-climbing past, asked Brower if he could help draw some public attention to the hearings. He felt they were being almost totally ignored by the press because the subject matter was so remote and technical.

Fresh off the success of *ECO* in Stockholm, Brower suggested that what some were calling a "hunter-gatherer" newspaper might be able to help. He recruited a team: Amory Lovins; Walt Patterson, a physicist-turned-energy-journalist and campaigner; the cartoonist Richard Willson from London; and Hugh Nash, John Diamante, and me from San Francisco, duly augmented by a handful of volunteers from Washington, DC, and environs. We set about publishing *ECO* and mailing copies to all addresses we could scrounge up of people who had demonstrated interest in matters nuclear.

The paper came out three times a week for three weeks and carried dense material about reactors, what might go awry, and what the consequences might be. Results were by no means as dramatic as they had been in Stockholm, but the light shed on the hearings helped build the nascent anti-reactor movement in the United States. When the Three Mile Island reactor's partial meltdown threatened Pennsylvania's capital, Harrisburg, in 1979, the writing was on the wall for the U.S. nuclear industry. No new reactor would be ordered for at least three decades. Cost was the main consideration, but safety problems and the lack of a solution to the waste problem were major factors in driving up the cost of plants whose output was supposed to be too cheap to meter.

ECO, under Brower's leadership, would invite itself to several of the joint annual meetings of the Atomic Industrial Forum and the American Nuclear Society in San Francisco. At one memorable meeting at the Hilton Hotel in San Francisco, Brower assembled a panel consisting of himself; Paul Ehrlich, a Stanford biologist and author of *The Population Bomb;* John Gofman, a nuclear physicist who had become a leading critic of nuclear power from within the academy; and Ralph Nader, founder of the organization Public

Citizen and the Public Interest Research Groups, who had become famous with *Unsafe at Any Speed*, a book that accused the automobile industry of building dangerous cars and resisting spending money on development of better safety features. Nader had recently made nuclear power one of his principal crusades.

Brower rented a large ballroom and invited the press. There was no real news beyond the fact that the four men were offering to explain to the world why using nuclear reactors to generate electricity was a lousy idea, but the press, always loving a fight, showed up in force. So did scores of physicists and engineers from the Atomic Industrial Forum and the American Nuclear Society, most to do battle with Gofman, their renegade colleague. The press conference went on for an hour, with the panelists hammering away at the record of the industry and a government meant to regulate it but often too willing to cover up its flaws. After Nader, Ehrlich, and Brower left, Gofman was kept for another hour fencing with his former colleagues, who were furious at his apostasy.

ECO, born and reared in Stockholm, would have many more lives and continue its mission of shedding light on matters the public should know more about. Brower, for his part, would continue to inveigh against what he then considered the biggest threat to the future of life on earth: the atom. His concerns, based on careful research and lengthy conversations with leading scientists, were at least two: First, the possibility that the release of massive amounts of radiation from a nuclear accident could—would—cause damage and injury that would interfere with human genes, plus genes in other living things. Second, terrorists or rogue nations could use nuclear material to make atomic bombs or missiles. This concern sent him off in a somewhat new direction: arguing that environmental protection was part and parcel of national security.

Brower's first reaction to the atomic bomb had been one of relief: after the German surrender in Europe, Brower's Tenth Mountain Division was preparing to be sent to the Pacific to try to end the war there. The bombs at Hiroshima and Nagasaki allowed them to go home instead, for which the troops were grateful. But later, as the horrendous carnage was revealed, Brower, along with millions more, wondered if anything could justify the bombing of so many innocents. Brower would spend an increasing fraction of his time trying to splice the peace movement and the environmental movement together. These efforts were recognized and in 1978 led to a nomination for the Nobel Peace Prize.

Steve Rauh, *Yodeler* editor, published a series of interviews with various prominent people around the Bay Area, among them Linus Pauling, winner of the Nobel Prize in Chemistry as well as the Nobel Peace Prize. In the course of that interview, Pauling and Rauh discovered a shared admiration for David Brower. Rauh wondered if Pauling might be willing to consider nominating Brower for the Nobel Peace Prize. Pauling said he thought Brower worthy of the honor but that he'd already nominated someone else.

Rauh's next interview was with Ron Dellums, the congressman who represented the district where the Browers resided. Dellums declared himself a lifelong admirer of Brower and said he would be happy to nominate him. He wrote to the Nobel committee: "I nominate David R. Brower, the world's leading voice to stop the war against the planet Earth, for the Nobel Peace Prize." He went on, "Dr. Brower has shown a prescient vision and signal persistence in developing the public conscience to the delicate balance of life on our earth."[25] Dellums spoke of Brower's dedication to peace and its relation to the environment and lauded Brower's career as "publicist for a revitalized environment and protector of an endangered planet." He finished, "I respectfully place his name in nomination for this august award—the Nobel Peace Prize. Sincerely, Ronald V. Dellums, Member of Congress."[26]

Brower did not win, though he was one of thirty finalists winnowed from a list of about seven hundred. That year's prize went jointly to Anwar al-Sadat and Menachem Begin for the Camp David peace accords brokered by President Jimmy Carter. Dellums submitted Brower's name for consideration twice more (once jointly with Paul Ehrlich), but without success. The Nobel committee got around to recognizing an environmental leader in 2004, when it gave the prize to Wangari Maathai of Kenya.

Another concern for Brower, which was closely tied to environmental degradation and the terrible impact of the arms race, was the very idea of economic growth: "A sophisticated method of stealing from future generations." This concern had weighed on him and built slowly for many years. It had informed his view looking both backward and forward. As he spoke more frequently at schools and conferences all over the country, this theme became more central. A feature of his stump speech—he came to call it "The Sermon"—was his version of the six days of creation, with the earth's history compressed into a week. There were hundreds of slightly different versions of this metaphor over the years. These are the basics: The earth is created Sunday at midnight. Life begins Tuesday noon. Millions of species come and go. Fossil fuels begin to be created Saturday morning.

Dinosaurs appear Saturday afternoon at about four. The Grand Canyon begins to take shape eighteen minutes before midnight. *Homo sapiens* doesn't show up until thirty seconds before midnight. A second and a half before midnight agriculture is invented. A third of a second before midnight, Buddha; a quarter of a second, Jesus Christ; a fortieth of a second, the Industrial Revolution; an eightieth of a second, we discover oil; a two-hundredth of a second, we learn how to split atoms. The human experiment is recent; it is moving incredibly quickly, and to assume that what has been going on for the past two or three hundred years can continue forever is dangerously foolish at best, suicidal at worst.

THE CONDOR CONFLICT

As we have seen, Dave Brower was willing to go against orthodoxy, to take positions contrary to those espoused by other environmental organizations— bowhead whaling and the Japanese boycott, to name just two. Another example involved the California condor, the largest North American bird, a scavenger with a wingspan approaching ten feet, which viewers on the ground sometimes mistook for small aircraft. Condors once soared above much of the American West, but habitat destruction and poisoning from lead shot in the animals that condors ate had reduced their population to a tiny fraction of their original numbers.

As the species dropped toward extinction in the 1970s, the National Audubon Society and the U.S. Fish and Wildlife Service proposed drastic action: capture all the condors and persuade them to breed and rear young in zoos a "captive breeding" program. This was in the mid-1970s. No one knew if it would work. No one knew whether captivity-bred condors would know how to be condors. Dave Brower and his right-hand wildlife guy, David Phillips, were leery of the plan. They consulted with the preeminent condor expert, Carl Koford, a resident of condor country, which by that time had shrunk to a patch of arid, wild, remote land in south-central California. Koford shared the worries of the Davids. If all the condors were captured, how would they learn how to scavenge, how to evade predators, how to ride thermals thousands of feet into the sky? And if condors were removed from their habitat, they worried, efforts to preserve that habitat would be far more difficult than if the birds were still there. Brower put it this way: "A condor is about 5 percent feathers, blood, and bone, and about 95 percent place. Place designs the condor, as it does the arctic tern and the monarch butterfly." He pointed out that a condor must learn to know the wind and learn where to find food and water, where to nest, where to hang out. "A young condor remains at the nest for a year, and accompanies its parents for another five, a little like a human child—but how condors can fly!"[27]

Again a book was in order: *The Condor Question: Captive or Forever Free?* was edited by David Phillips and Hugh Nash. It was released in 1981, followed by a documentary film, *Cry of the Condor*, which was put together primarily by Gar Smith, an FOE staff member and designer of the journal *Not Man Apart*. Brower tried to persuade the Sierra Club Legal Defense Fund to bring suit against the federal Fish and Wildlife Service for possible violation of wildlife-protection laws, but the attorney assigned to review the possible case judged that there were no solid grounds. The last twenty-one wild condors were all captured and sent to zoos and breeding programs. Now captivity-reared, tagged condors have been returned to central California and the Grand Canyon. It's too early to see if they'll be able to reproduce successfully in the wild.

"They've had mixed success," Phillips says. "They've raised a lot of birds. But the birds that they've released have had lots of problems. They swoop down on picnic tables and grab people's sandwiches. Wild condors would never do that in a million years. They sip antifreeze in puddles. Things that no self-respecting wild condor would ever do. I still think we were right."[28]

LEADERSHIP STRENGTHS AND STRUGGLES

Although most of FOE's staff members were hired by Brower and turned loose in the trenches, some did not have a history with the Sierra Club or Brower, and inevitably there were clashes.

Early in the life of the organization, Joe Browder, a staff member of the National Audubon Society in Florida working mainly to protect the Everglades, joined the DC staff of FOE. He had told Gary Soucie, FOE's executive director in New York, that Nat Reed, a well-to-do Florida conservationist who would go on to serve in the Nixon Interior Department, had offered to give FOE $10,000 to pay part of his salary and expenses for the first year. The money never came through, and Reed later told Stewart Ogilvy, a member of the FOE board of directors, that there had been no such promise. Browder soon clashed with both Brower and George Alderson, who had set up the DC office originally. Soucie said that hiring Browder "was my biggest mistake."[29]

In early 1972 Browder led a walkout by many of the Washington, DC, FOE staff and established the Environmental Policy Center. With him went his then-fiancée Marion Edey, founder and president of the League of Conservation Voters; Louise Dunlap, his future wife and partner in a political consultancy; Wilson Clark, an energy campaigner; and Brent Blackwelder, a graduate student who would become president of Friends of the Earth years in the future. Alderson was left at the FOE office and quickly hired new staff, including Tom Garrett, who would later serve as U.S. commissioner to the International Whaling Commission.

Two years after Alderson rebuilt the DC staff, he left to take a job at the Wilderness Society. "One of the problems about FOE," he explained, "was that our charter was the whole world—the whole environment—and I don't think that our organization had really set priorities except in the SST case. I had a feeling that we needed to be doing something on everything, which you can do and not be effective on any." He left FOE partly for this reason. "At the Wilderness Society I was able to concentrate on wilderness. Dave pretty much left us to our own devices in the Washington operation once we got started." Brower was the recruiter, the organizer: "He did his speaking around the country, and of course the activists who were inspired by him were our grassroots people. It was Dave's ability to attract people and then to thrust them forward."[30]

Here the drawbacks of the Brower style show up. He would spot talent, hire people, and turn them loose. Whether they would fit with what other people were working on was hit or miss. Team-building was not something Brower had much time for. People, depending on their personalities, would find ways to cooperate and support each other—especially on projects with clear responsibilities, such as publishing Not Man Apart—but there were plenty of lone wolves who operated independently.

Brower was suspicious of planning and setting priorities, feeling that plans and priorities were straitjackets that would inhibit flexibility and agility. He also tended to delegate much authority to those working for him, though he did keep a fairly tight rein on the book-publishing program, which included numerous paperbacks and campaign books, as well as two standout series: the Earth's Wild Places, which included ten exhibit format–style books (the Sierra Club claimed a trademark on "Exhibit Format" and refused to allow

FOE to use it, even though Brower had coined the name and invented the format), and another, slightly smaller series called Celebrating the Earth.

There is a division of opinion about Brower and delegation. Bestor Robinson, a climbing companion of Brower's, a lawyer, and a Sierra Club director in the 1950s, said, "He did not prove an adequate administrator or executive as the club grew and had to have a big staff. He just did not know how to delegate jobs, to oversee the work of others but not make all the decisions himself."[31]

Contrast that view with what Mike McCloskey, who succeeded Brower as Sierra Club executive director, said: "I learned from him to delegate pretty completely. He would inspire by his vision and his intensity. Not too interested in follow-up and details. He'd print a brochure or run an ad, but not enough attention was given to political reality. His management style was loose, but it caused people to work their hearts out."[32]

Another insight into Brower's management style comes from Gary Soucie, the first executive director of Friends of the Earth, who left the Sierra Club staff to run the FOE office in New York: "There were frequent and unreasonable calls from Dave that always worked out. One night he called to say that Colin Fletcher was to be on the *Today* show the next morning and he wanted to talk to him first.[33] 'Where's he staying?' 'I don't know.' 'How will I find him?' 'You'll figure it out.' I thought, author: New York; I called the Algonquin. Sure enough, he was there. Things just magically happened like that."[34]

Brower was sometimes accused of making unreasonable requests, far-fetched, almost naïve. To Soucie, however, "the thing about Dave was this: he would make what would seem to a reasonable person an unreasonable demand, but it always turned out to be doable and the right thing to do." Now and then Brower would come up with a flawed idea or suggestion, but in Soucie's experience, he was willing to have his mind changed. "I couldn't understand why people on the [Sierra Club] board couldn't figure this out. I think it was that the board represented people above him trying to stop him from doing something, whereas people like me—I worked for him—he thought he should listen to. I found him to be absolutely reasonable to work with."[35]

Another aspect of his personality, his shyness, has also been perceived in different ways. Two young women who worked for Friends of the Earth in the seventies and eighties offer interesting contrasts.

Juliette Majot, having helped defeat a planned nuclear power plant in Indiana, moved to San Francisco and landed a job as, in her words, "the worst office manager in history" at Friends of the Earth. She'd never heard of Brower.

> Someone described Dave Brower to me. I'd never seen him. I got in the elevator at Friends of the Earth. A white-haired man got in. The elevator got stuck. He was socially unskilled, shy, especially around women. We were both nervous. I knew he was someone important. I said, "Mr. Brower I just want you to know how proud I am to be working for your organization." We developed a friendship. I'd go into his office when I got to work, sit down and talk. We'd have a kiss on the cheek. I always thought he needed to be protected.

She elaborated, from a slightly different angle: "He lived in his own world, didn't know what was going on around him. People didn't relate to him as a person; he was Brower. He related to people as vehicles. He saw things in people that were a potential for something wonderful happening."[36]

This "shy around women" observation is a common one, but not universal. Mary Lou Vandeventer, who worked on the Friends of the Earth periodical *Not Man Apart*, has a somewhat different view: "I never noticed any unease on Dave's part around women." She pointed out that Brower had appointed Stephanie Mills editor of *Not Man Apart* and Natalie Roberts administrative director. "FOE was open. You could be whoever you wanted to be. There were no preconceived limitations. Dave was very friendly and very generous. Shy." Shy again. But inspiring: "He was just overflowing with message. We all got the benefit. He was warm, informal, encouraging. You felt like you could just go to him and talk. Ask questions, come away inspired." And a little on the paradox: "A genius is a difficult person to put up with. Geniuses like Dave are particular people. They have flaws. You have to accommodate the flaws and still cope. If you can do it, it's so worth it, and you can gain from it."[37]

And you occasionally had to put up with gentle criticism. Vandeventer had proposed starting a green literary magazine. Brower was tentatively interested and asked for a prospectus. As part of the proposal, Vandeventer suggested using a typeface called Souvenir and sent Brower a sample. He replied,

> The face in the sample is one I don't know, and I guess my impression is a negative one. I get sort of a wish-washy feeling about it, a little precious in the cut, too rounded where it needn't be, too jammed where it shouldn't be. The e tries too hard to be different. The i can't breathe. Too many of the letters look as if they had been rattled around in a box too long, and their serifs got bruised. Their descenders all got the 2,4,5-T treatment and never really took root. The y needs a lesson in family planning. On the whole, the impression

I get is that the designer really liked sanserif but didn't quite have the courage of his (her) convictions, which is easily understood.[38]

The magazine never appeared, with Souvenir or another typeface. The proposal was deemed to have problems other than the typeface.

While Brower was jetting around the country and the rest of the world, Friends of the Earth was slowly becoming a force on the national scene, playing a leading role in the debates over nuclear power, the trans-Alaska pipeline, the supersonic transport aircraft, and commercial whaling, among other matters. Under Brower's vision, FOE even began to take on issues generally outside the traditional sphere of environmentalists' concerns. One was the new technique of genetic engineering. Boosters of the technique, from laboratories and chemical companies, promised increased yields of crops that could withstand blights and diseases. They spoke of new medicines and other wonders to come. Brower was deeply suspicious of anything that would meddle in the grand scheme of evolution which, he was quick to point out, had been working perfectly since the beginning of life on earth. Each one of us is the direct product of an unbroken flow of wildness that began with the first organisms. Tinkering with that magic would be risky at best, possibly catastrophic.

To launch FOE into the fray, he arranged, in early 1977, to have *Not Man Apart* reprint a highly controversial article by Dr. Liebe Cavalieri,[39] which had originally been published in *Science* and been roundly criticized by some leading scientists within the gene-splicing community, where Cavalieri was somewhat analogous to the physicist John Gofman, a leading critic of nuclear power. The publication of the piece caused Lewis Thomas, the celebrated author of *The Lives of a Cell: Notes of a Biology Watcher*, to resign from the FOE advisory council, much to Brower's dismay. As if to balance the opposition to genetically engineered foods, FOE then pioneered the encouragement of organic agriculture through the brilliance and determination of Bob Scowcroft, who had earlier organized retailers selling outdoor gear to support a campaign to preserve millions of acres of Alaska wild lands. Scowcroft went on to become the first executive director of the California Certified Organic Farmers.

. . .

This brings us toward the end of the 1970s. Brower was about to celebrate his sixty-seventh birthday and was thinking it was time to turn over the reins of

Friends of the Earth to someone else. Friends of the Earth had grown to more than twenty thousand members—very small compared to some other organizations but able to get attention in the press and make waves in Washington, in large part owing to the force of Brower's personality and his drive and outspokenness, as well as to FOE's talented and energetic staff.

The conversion of the conservation movement into the environmental movement was well under way. To traditional concerns over wilderness and wildlife had been added energy, pollution, genetic engineering, public health, organic farming, and to some extent, disarmament and social equity. Ronald Reagan was about to be elected president and would launch an all-out attack on environmental laws, regulations, and institutions. Friends of the Earth and its colleague organizations would be sorely tested.

THIRTEEN

A Resumption of Hostilities

Scientists already suspect that our rapid expenditure of fossil
fuels is raising the temperature of the air. Suppose it melts the ice
caps at the poles, as is likely. Then we have several problems—the
relocation of every coastal city on earth. Either that or a real
flood-control project for the Corps of Engineers—a 100-foot sea
wall all around the continent, and a system of locks from the
ports leading up to the oceans.

In July 1979, on the tenth anniversary of the founding of Friends of the
Earth, David Brower retired as president of the organization and handed it
over to Edwin Matthews, the young lawyer he'd tapped ten years earlier to
launch FOE's international efforts. Matthews had begun in France and had
then established sister groups in Great Britain, Sweden, and elsewhere, ultimately cofounding Friends of the Earth International, the umbrella organization under which independent FOE groups would hatch ideas and strategies. He also shared Brower's passion for publishing internationally. He
seemed a perfect successor.

Matthews took the reins as unpaid president of Friends of the Earth in
mid-1979. There was a ceremony at the Fort Mason Officers' Club in San
Francisco. Brower gave Matthews an ancient river-polished stone from Glen
Canyon and said he hoped the younger man would someday return the stone
to where it came from once the reservoir was drained—an event still waiting
to happen.

Matthews had moved from Paris to San Francisco to assume the FOE
presidency in the United States upon Brower's putative retirement. He
remembers Anne Brower saying, "This will be the end of a beautiful friendship."[1] She was right.

Paul Ehrlich, Ralph Nader, John Gofman, and David Brower lambasting nuclear power before an
audience of reporters and pro-nuclear scientists and engineers, San Francisco Hilton, mid-1970s.
Photograph by Lennie Epand.

When Brower resigned as president, he persuaded the board to create a new position, chairman, and appoint him to fill it. He was more than aware of the phenomenon known as "founder's syndrome," wherein the founder of an organization finds it impossible to let go when it's time to move on. Brower tried to let go, but couldn't keep quiet when he saw things going wrong, at least from his perspective. The honeymoon period between the new president and chairman was very short. Brower and Matthews clashed over personnel, administrative policy, and—predictably—finances.

Matthews would later recall, "In my whole experience with him I never found myself in a situation where David said, 'I don't agree with what you're doing, Edwin. I disagree. And here are the reasons you shouldn't do it.' On any number of issues he would agree, then turn around and the next day or week or month I'd hear from somebody else that he disagreed."[2]

Matthews described two situations, which, to his mind, showed a flaw in Brower. FOE was going through a difficult time financially, as it always was, and Matthews thought it would be a good idea to adjust the payroll to pay the best employees more and penalize those who weren't working as hard or producing as well: "I remember going through the salary roster when annual raises came up and suggesting some adjustments." Matthews took a list of FOE employees to the Brower house in the Berkeley hills (he was living in San Francisco). "We went through every name. He nodded. Never said anything. Within days he was going to Sinbad's [then Brower's favorite San Francisco lunch and after-work-drinks spot on the waterfront] with people who hadn't been awarded the top raises and sympathizing with them and fueling dissent, undermining what I'd proposed."

Matthews took pains to say that he was not trying to impose his will but rather was trying to bring some order into what was a delicate situation. He said, "Maybe what I'd proposed was a mistake; that isn't the issue. The issue is why would he sit quietly and agree. We are emotional creatures but we must make rational decisions based on facts." Matthews argued that in his position, he was required to distance himself from how he felt about people: "You may have to fire someone you have great affection for, or hire someone you dislike, who will be beautifully effective for what you need."[3]

The second situation that Matthews felt typified Brower involved what turned out to be the last book in the Earth's Wild Places series of photo-illustrated books, *Wake of the Whale*.[4] The book was scheduled for publication not long after Matthews took over. He sat down with Brower to learn the plans for printing and promotion: "David was ready to give the print order to Mondadori [an Italian printer]. He wanted to order 40,000 copies. I said, 'Do we have a distribution plan? How many copies are we going to sell? What's the chance of selling them?'"

Brower argued that if they ordered fewer copies, it would cost more per copy, so the prudent decision would be to order more rather than fewer. Matthews argued that an order for 10,000 to 15,000 books was the more prudent course, because they could always go back for more. "David said nothing. We sent a print order for 10,000. David phoned Mondadori without telling anybody and raised the print order to 40,000."

According to Matthews, FOE sold 2,000 to 3,000 copies to its members via direct mail. But that was far from the total. According to Joe Kane in *Outside* magazine,[5] the Book of the Month Club took 17,500 copies of *Wake*, E. P. Dutton took 8,500, and a British publisher a further 7,500. Brower, in his autobiography, calls *Wake* "FOE's most successful exhibit format book, having been featured on the cover of *Life*."[6]

David Chatfield gave an explanation for the elevated print order: a substantial fraction of the run was printed with photographs but no text, anticipating foreign-language editions. Chatfield reported that foreign publishers were definitely interested in such editions but wanted to scrap Ken Brower's text and hire their own authors. Dave Brower refused to do that.[7] Matthews remembers that 10,000 to 15,000 sets of sheets were eventually pulped.

Matthews would reflect on these experiences with Brower and observe, "His unwillingness to deal with process in any form was the origin of the conflicts I had with David."[8] Brower's unwillingness to deal with process is an observation that is hardly unique to Ed Matthews. Brower acknowledged as much with his line that "process is that which gets between you and where you want to be." He felt it slowed things down and did not guarantee a desirable result. But resistance to process, to authority, could, and did, get Brower into trouble more than once—far more than once.

Conflict over staff raises, the whale book, and other matters increasingly strained the relationship between Brower and Matthews. On April 14, 1980, Brower wrote a memo to Matthews: "Dear Edwin: What I need to say is disappointing to both of us, and presumptuous. It presumes that I have an obligation to judge. And what is disappointing is that in my judgment you should not be nominated for President of FOE at its forthcoming annual meeting. For reasons neither of us could foresee, our best laid plans have gone awry." He pointed out that the FOE executive committee had been troubled by Matthews's not being able to devote as much time to FOE as he—and they—had hoped; Matthews was running the Coudert Brothers small San Francisco office full-time. "FOE needs a full-time Chief Operating Officer. Other demands on your time have made it impossible for you to acquire the knowledge about FOE's operation or its leaders' roles in the American conservation movement that is essential to effective leadership of FOE. . . . I am sure you must know how troubling it is for me to write this letter."[9]

The letter blindsided Matthews. Brower had not discussed its contents with him. He was wounded and bitter, but he remained on the board of directors in order, he would later say, to serve the organization. "I suppose my reaction was one of determination because I believed in the organization and its cause, and as painful as it was, I wasn't going to just go away. There was process to respect." Matthews insisted that tough decisions had to be made if the organization was to survive, and he felt loyalty to what had been a big part of his life. "Right decisions had to be made. And the last thing I was going to do was quit the board and go away." He added that it was very painful for him to go to meetings once he had been ousted, but he felt an obligation to do so. "Involvement after that was not for myself," he said. "It was for the organization."[10]

Matthews's presidency of Friends of the Earth had lasted less than a year. Still, more than thirty years after his ouster at Brower's insistence, Matthews has complimentary words to say about his old friend and foe: "The most wonderful thing about him was walking with him in nature and he'd see things. A young tree growing from an old log. Life renewing. Life we're all part of. He was most eloquent about that."[11] On the other hand, "It took me years to appreciate his limitations. I met him in 1963 and dealt with him a lot from 1969 to 1979, when I went to San Francisco. I can't remember ever disagreeing with him in that period about anything."

Matthews has a complicated view of what made Brower tick, based on close observation and a friendship that went badly sour: "His reaction to authority became in my dealing with him a huge problem between us, because he wouldn't accept a decision made by somebody else. In a way his whole life was fighting the world. So when the world tells him it doesn't like this or that, almost with relish he struck back, but not in an open way."[12]

Matthews is not alone in noting Brower's resistance to authority; Brower even makes reference to it himself here and there, often in a humorous, self-deprecating manner. But it's a mistake to assume that Brower could never be talked out of a bad idea, says Gary Soucie, whom Brower hired to represent the Sierra Club in New York and later to serve as the first executive director of Friends of the Earth. Soucie suggests that Brower was more amenable to having an idea challenged by a peer or a subordinate, however, than by a person in authority.[13]

After dismissing Matthews as president in 1980, the board moved swiftly to replace him. With Brower's blessing they chose Rafe Pomerance, then head of the Washington, DC, office and a widely respected lobbyist and political operative, with special expertise in the Clean Air Act. At the time of his appointment, Pomerance was in Nairobi, Kenya, at a meeting of the Environment Liaison Centre, a self-appointed watchdog organization keeping an eye on—and assisting whenever possible—the United Nations Environment Programme, which had grown out of the 1972 Stockholm conference. Pomerance would stay in Washington, DC, and run things from there; FOE's administration, accounting, and fund-raising departments, its book-publishing program, and its journal, *Not Man Apart*, would remain in San Francisco.

Pomerance said later that had he understood what he was getting into, he would not have accepted the promotion. But he did accept, and he remained FOE president for the next four years.[14] Reflecting back thirty years later, he said, "Anyone in their right mind would not take a job to be CEO with Dave as the founding chairman. In addition I didn't have experience for such a job. I had never run an organization of this size."[15]

Immediately there were problems. Pomerance recalls, "The first thing that happened that told me how things were going to go was that we [the FOE board] went immediately through this hellish meeting where we had to cut the budget, fire people." Once more, there was a serious fiscal problem, and one of the board's decisions was to eliminate an issue of *Not Man Apart*. Pomerance remembered, "I arrived in Cape Cod for my vacation shortly after the meeting and the first thing I hear is that Brower has ordered the publication of this issue that was supposed to have been cut. Now I'm in charge of the organization, right? I was thrown for a loop, and that began four years of the good, the bad, and the very, very difficult."[16]

Trouble was already brewing by then within FOE, and though Brower had no intention of leaving the organization, there were forces beginning to think of having the organization leave him.

Pomerance and Brower had an uneasy relationship at best, but one positive development that grew out of their association was the beginning of

FOE's awareness of climate change. Pomerance, through his efforts on behalf of clean air, had become acquainted with scientists who were trying to spread news of studies indicating that the growing concentration of carbon dioxide and other pollutants in the atmosphere was beginning to cause disruptions of various kinds. Brower encouraged this activity on the part of Pomerance and others, since he no longer visited Washington often and rarely testified before Congress. Pomerance would occasionally visit San Francisco for meetings with board and staff, but with Pomerance's deep connections to Washington, there was a shift of emphasis for Friends of the Earth toward lobbying and political work, and away from many of Brower's favored activities—publishing in particular.

By the 1980s, Ballantine Books had stopped publishing mass-market environmental battle tracts, so FOE had set up its own book-publishing operation on a much smaller scale than what the Ballantine arrangement had made possible. While a number of modestly successful titles appeared starting in the late seventies, they were break-even affairs as best. Citing fiscal reasons, Pomerance would eventually persuade FOE's executive committee to end the book program in 1983, over the loud but futile objections of Brower.

CONSERVATION AND NATIONAL SECURITY

Although Brower may not have been rubbing elbows with power brokers in Washington very often anymore, he was still considered a leader of great influence. During this time, Brower became deeply concerned about the relationship between natural resource conservation and national security. Always the maverick, he was one of the first to speak about this issue, which is a primary concern of the U.S. Defense Department today. It began in 1981, when Brower was invited to give the twenty-second Horace Albright lecture at the University of California at Berkeley, his alma mater had he not dropped out in his sophomore year. The lecture was given in honor of Albright, the cofounder and second director of the National Park Service, who graduated from the university a few weeks before Brower had been born a few blocks away. The sponsor of the lecture series was the Department of Forestry and Resource Management of the College of Natural Resources. Brower had been nominated for the prestigious honor several times previously but had been vetoed by foresters in the department annoyed by his battles with the

Forest Service and the timber industry. But the climate had changed, by 1981, and Brower was invited to speak.[17]

His topic was conservation and national security. This was a change in subject and emphasis for Brower. Although his talk combined many themes from his stump speech, he argued for the first time that taking care of natural resources must be an urgent priority for national security. He was especially concerned over saber rattling by the new Reagan administration and had some pungent observations about economic growth.

He minced few words: "There is no greater threat to national security, or to the global security to which our own is inextricably tied, than the present rampant discounting of the future—the economists' greatest sin. It fuels the insane contest now being exacerbated by the superpowers." He then repeated a favorite observation from his friend and colleague and the 1976 Albright lecturer, ecologist Ray Dasmann of the University of California at Santa Cruz: "We are already fighting World War III and I am sorry to say we are winning it. It is the war against the earth."

He called for a conservation education plan. "The objective would be to inform the public as promptly and thoroughly as possible about ecosystems and peaceful stability.... The reinterpreters would need to avoid economic and natural-resource clichés and would be prohibited from saying *interface, elitist, input, output, parameter, paradigm, prioritize,* or *holistic.*"

Then, eschewing humor, he cut loose: "The 'vigorous growing economy' all our leaders keep exhorting us to produce is not possible on an earth of fixed size, and continuing attempts to produce it are *the* basic threat to peace." He asked, "Can the economy withstand peace? The concomitant question is, Can limited resources withstand a constantly expanding expenditure? The answer to the first question is and must be yes, and to the second question, no. Both answers are painfully obvious but universally avoided. There is no better cause than to face them squarely and learn to live with them." He added, "It doesn't take much imagination to demonstrate that unending growth will do our children and theirs out of the heritage they deserve—and that we can survive without that unending growth and *only* without it."

He then asked an almost rhetorical question: "Do you know any conservation group that is giving this serious consideration? I don't think you do. It is one of the taboos." And he broadened his observation: "I do not think you can find an agency in government yet willing to question growth. But some growth is bad—for instance, malignant growth.... I believe there is malignancy in our economy, and that all conservation will fail unless it is checked."

Returning to the importance of peace, he invoked another favored quote, from his friend the anthropologist Loren Eiseley: "The need is not really for more brains, the need is now for a gentler, a more tolerant people than those who won for us against the ice, the tiger, and the bear. The hand that hefted the ax, out of some old blind allegiance to the past, fondles the machine gun as lovingly. It is a habit man will have to break to survive, but the roots go very deep."[18]

Brower took off after the new president: "President Reagan has sidelined outstanding Republican conservationists, irritated Wall Street, alarmed our friends abroad, frightened the Third World nations by deepening the inequity of our relations with them, and could be driving our supposed adversary [the Soviet Union], with whom we have never fought, to desperation. . . . Let it be added that he has issued a splendid statement in favor of saving whales. For that act we are grateful. Not for the others."

He turned to another common feature of his talks, something that today would probably be called an interactive lecture (though *interactive* would no doubt have long ago joined Brower's list of banished clichés). He asked members of the audience to imagine that they were president of the United States and come up with a list of projects to spend a trillion dollars on to enhance national security and send the list to him. His own list would start with reforesting derelict land, followed closely by investments in sustainable agriculture. He ended with another of his favorite quotes, this one from Adlai Stevenson:

> We travel together, passengers on a little space craft, dependent upon its vulnerable reserves of air and soil, all committed for our safety to its security and peace, preserved from annihilation only by the work, the care and, I will say, the love we give our fragile craft. We cannot maintain it half comfortable, half miserable; half confident, half despairing; half slave to the ancient enemies of mankind, half free in a liberation of resources undreamed of until this day. No craft, no crew, can travel safely with such vast contradictions. On their resolution depends the survival of us all.

In retrospect, Brower would suggest a tiny bit of revising—the "liberation of resources" troubled him a little; he suggested that love was "the one resource that will be exhausted only if we forget to use it."[19]

The link between national security and conservation was beginning to interest others in the environmental movement and the government. Daniel Ellsberg, the former military analyst who had leaked the Pentagon Papers to the *New York Times*, spoke eloquently of the relationship between the environment and national security. Brower's friend Steve Rauh, whose interview with Linus Pauling had led to Brower's being nominated for the Nobel Peace Prize in 1978, had once interviewed Ellsberg. Rauh suggested the two might profit from meeting each other.

This suggestion led to a series of conferences called "On the Fate of the Earth," the title borrowed from Jonathan Schell's popular book. The first, held at the Cathedral of Saint John the Divine in New York City in 1982, drew a thousand people—activists, organizers, scientists, politicians, and journalists—to the surprise and delight of Brower and the other organizers. Brower was chairman of the conference and spoke first. He greeted the attendees by announcing, "The Fate of the Earth Conference was initiated to remind all governments that conservation, education, and health are as important as military might in securing national defense." He outlined an ambitious agenda: "In this conference, we will be looking at the interdependence of conservation and security in a sustainable society. We will be searching for an economically feasible route to such a society—one that does not overtax the environment, ultimately destroying itself in a final quarrel over the allotment of vanishing resources."[20] He went on to call for the cessation of the nuclear arms race and eventually its reversal. The conference lasted three days and presented a rather extraordinary group of people, including the Nobel laureates Linus Pauling and George Wald, Congressman Ron Dellums, retired admiral Gene La Rocque, Amory Lovins, and Paul Ehrlich, among many others. Pete Seeger, Odetta, and the Paul Winter Consort provided music.

The second installment, five days' worth this time, was held in Washington, DC, in 1984. Only five hundred people turned out for this one, but in Brower's estimation "the program was, if anything, even stronger than the first."[21] The third conference was held in Ottawa, Canada, in 1986, and again a thousand people attended. The fourth took an extra year to organize, as it was held in Managua, Nicaragua, in the midst of earthquakes, hurricanes, and Contras. Twelve hundred people attended, and this time financial assistance came from Canada, Norway, Sweden, the European Economic Community, and the Soviet Union. At the suggestion of Pat Ellsberg, the wife of Daniel, the title was changed to make it more upbeat: The Conference on the Fate and Hope of the Earth. It is impossible to measure the impact of these conferences, but it was substantial.

In fact, Brower was addicted to conferences, beginning with the Sierra Club's wilderness conferences in the late 1940s. He organized dozens and attended hundreds. And he would insist that as important as the formal sessions were, and the good thinking and writing that went into preparation of the presentations, maybe more important were the conversations that took place in hallways and bars. The conferences he organized always had plenty of time for socializing.

UPHEAVALS AT FOE

Right around the time Rafe Pomerance convinced the executive committee to shut down FOE's book-publishing program, to Brower's disappointment, the journal *Not Man Apart* became the next subject of heated internal debate. In 1983 several members of the NMA staff mounted a campaign to change the name of the publication. Readers had complained from time to time that it was sexist and confusing. Angela Gennino, an editor on the journal, gathered complaint letters received over the years and asked the FOE executive committee to consider changing the name.

The committee debated the matter and then asked the NMA staff to take the question to the members via an informal poll following a debate to be published in the journal. Angela Gennino, Sandra Kaiser, Robert Schaeffer, and John Knox, all on the *Not Man Apart* staff, signed the pro-change argument. They said, "The name—*Not Man Apart*—creates two problems, one semantic and one political." The semantic problem was the ambiguity of the phrase and the fact that it starts with a negative word; the political problem was that *man* excluded half the potential audience. David Brower, FOE's California representative Connie Parrish, and I signed the anti-change argument. We wrote—or rather, Brower wrote and we signed—the argument that read in part, "Taking 'man' out of the Bible . . . or out of Robinson Jeffers, is carrying things too far. . . . It is encouraging an assault on reasonable grammar."[22]

Readers were invited to comment and, if they voted for a change, to suggest new names. More than 250 letters poured into the office, an order of magnitude more than had ever been received on a single topic. A few extracts:

"Please change the name of your newsletter from *Not Man Apart* to something else that cannot be in any way said to be exclusionary of women."

"Let us retain the name. I am a female with a female child. The spirit of Jeffers's words is dear to me. I am a traditionalist, biologist, evolutionist, humanist, spiritualist, radical peace-loving woman."

"Who could rally round or be inspired by 'Not' anything?"

"Why quibble over the name? There are urgent issues to work on. FOE and NMA are well known. Let's not confuse the public with new names."

"I say yes, change the name. I'm a school teacher and recently read a research study where children were asked to draw a picture of 'mankind.' Only one child out of 80 drew a picture of a woman."

"The objections raised against the name *Not Man Apart* seem to be excellent reasons for keeping it "

"*Not Man Apart* is known and respected by environmentalists and non-environmentalists alike. Its reputation is no accident and the title is no mistake. I vote we keep it."

"I say absolutely the name must be changed. It begins with a negative, which is a major no-no in sloganeering."

"The flap over the name is one of the silliest bits of irrationality I have come across."[23]

The letters ran about three to two in favor of retaining the name.

At the next meeting of the FOE executive committee, the matter was again debated and the views of the membership examined. Angela Gennino argued for the change—the name is sexist and drives away potential readers—and told me she saw some of the seven committee members present nodding along with her. Then Dave Brower made his case for keeping the name: tradition, history, poetry. He made it clear that this was important to him. When it came time to vote, the tally was one to change, five to keep, and one abstention. Gennino was angry. "I was right," she said, "but I couldn't overcome Brower's eloquence and his influence on the directors. I had tried to shake the foundation of what FOE was. It was still Dave's organization."[24]

But not for too much longer. Rafe Pomerance, meanwhile, inspired by the aggressively anti-environment proposals put forward by the new Reagan administration and in particular by the secretary of the interior, James G. Watt, suggested working up some full-page newspaper ads to try to build opposition to the initiatives. They enlisted Jerry Mander, author of the Grand Canyon ads and by then chief copywriter for the Public Media Center, a nonprofit San Francisco ad agency run by Herbert Chao Gunther, who would shortly join the FOE board. They eventually published five such ads in the *New York Times* and elsewhere, cosigned by Brower and Pomerance—two of them head-on attacks on the administration (for attempting to sell large tracts of public lands to private concerns) and the president ("Ronald Reagan Is the Real James Watt") to bring some public heat to bear on the administration. Pomerance argues that the ads succeeded in shortening the tenure of Secretary Watt and EPA administrator Anne Gorsuch and helped back the Reagan administration off some of its most radical anti-environmental crusades.[25] It was about this time that FOE and the Sierra Club created their political action committees and jumped into several key races. Pomerance remembers that the FOE PAC helped turn out seven hundred volunteers to work, successfully, for the election of Senator Jeff Bingaman of New Mexico, who defeated anti-environmental Senator Harrison Schmitt.

FOE joined the Sierra Club in mounting a nationwide petition seeking the ouster or resignation of Watt, and in a short period the two groups had collected more than a million signatures, a far more difficult task then than it is now in the Internet age. Rafe Pomerance and Sierra Club president Joe Fontaine presented the petitions to Representative Tip O'Neill (D-Mass.) and Senator Alan Cranston (D-Calif.) on the Capitol steps. Not long after that, with the 1984 election bearing down, Watt resigned.

The public anger over Watt and his proposals had caused the membership rolls of many environmental groups to surge. FOE's was no exception, but it remained small (39,000 at its peak) and finances remained shaky. Pomerance produced numbers demonstrating that FOE had a far larger staff-to-membership ratio than other groups and advocated reducing staff to shore up the budget. This, to Brower's mind, was conceding defeat or at least acknowledging weakness, and he resisted mightily.

Fearing for their jobs, distrustful of FOE management, and unhappy about a shifting emphasis to Washington, DC, lobbying and policy-making, the San Francisco staff decided to explore unionizing. "Finally people got so pissed off that they organized a union," Pomerance remembered.[26] They contacted Mary Ann Massenburg, the local representative of District 65 of the United Auto Workers, who had helped the employees at *Mother Jones* magazine organize.

Brower was not directly involved with the unionization effort, but he tacitly supported it. Most directors, even the pro-Brower ones, were not pleased by the move. Insofar as the unionizing effort was a backlash against Pomerance, Robert Chlopak (founder and leader of the FOE political action committee), and the rest of the management team, Brower was content to watch the drama play out. Or, as the journalist Joe Kane put it in *Outside* magazine, "The move was seen both as a vote of no-confidence in the FOE management and as a vote of support for Brower."[27]

The organizers on the FOE San Francisco staff petitioned for a union vote. The FOE board refused. The staff went to the National Labor Relations Board, which decreed that a vote could and must be held. A vote was held in April 1984, and it was unanimous—in favor of affiliating with District 65. This involved only the San Francisco staff, not staff in FOE's other offices. The staff in Washington, DC, was staunchly opposed to the union; the field staff was bemused. Still FOE resisted, dragging its feet on negotiating a contract.

In the spring of 1984, the board agreed to Pomerance's plan to cut back the staff by about 30 percent, undertake a massive reorganization, and stabilize finances. Brower, who staunchly opposed the layoffs, which he feared would cripple the organization, quietly wrote, designed, and paid to place a full-page advertisement in the July-August issue of *Not Man Apart*, appealing for donations to "Save the Team." The donations were to be sent to Brower's discretionary fund, out of the control of FOE management. This was in direct defiance of CEO Pomerance and the board of directors. Mechanicals were shipped off to the printer. Before members' copies were delivered to the post office, a bundle of the papers was delivered to the office in San Francisco. Executive director Jeff Knight opened the bundle and was leafing through a copy when he came upon the ad. He immediately telephoned Pomerance in Washington, DC, and described the situation. Pomerance ordered him to phone the printer and have the papers impounded before they could be sent to the post office. The layoffs, meanwhile, had been carried out.

Pomerance called yet another emergency meeting of the board for July 2, 1984. Dave had turned seventy-two the day before. On July 1, Pomerance abruptly resigned, a move he had been considering for some time. The FOE executive committee endorsed Pomerance's order to seize the newspapers and decreed that the issues be shredded and that the journal be reissued with a page explaining what had just happened.

In an uncanny replay of Brower's experience at the Sierra Club, the FOE board passed a resolution at the meeting that was clearly aimed directly at Brower: "It is the stated policy of Friends of the Earth that neither the Chairman nor any director should involve him or herself in implementing Friends of the Earth policy, except at the direction of the Board or Executive Committee or at the request of the CEO." In case there was any doubt whom they were referring to, the resolution went on to state, "Neither the Chairman nor Board Members are to engage in any actions which contradict, undermine or challenge the authority or discretion of management in implementing board decisions."[28] Brower pronounced this a loyalty oath and said he wouldn't abide by it, as did his remaining board allies at the meeting. Thereupon the board voted nine to two to remove Brower as chairman and throw him off the board—the board of an organization he had created from whole cloth.

The *New York Times* carried news of Brower's ouster on its front page. Other papers across the country also reported the news. Rafe Pomerance made it clear that this was as much about Brower the leader as it was about one issue of the journal. He told the reporter Joe Kane, "Dave Brower is no longer important in national environmental issues on a day-to-day level. . . . He is no longer a media figure. The media watches Washington, D.C. That's where the game is played."[29]

It is true that Brower was no longer in the trenches as he had been for the Dinosaur battle, Grand Canyon, the SST, the Alaska pipeline, and nuclear power. "No longer a media figure" is arguable, as a never-ending string of interviews aired and published across the country would attest. "Washington, DC—that's where the game is played" is precisely the attitude that prompted the unionization effort in San Francisco. Still, Brower was outnumbered and on the defensive, in danger of losing control of another organization.

At the meeting Bob Chlopak had been named acting CEO, and Daniel Luten, a retired chemist, geography professor, and longtime friend and ally of Brower, whose relationship with Brower had become rather strained, was elected president. Luten had chaired the meeting and abstained from the vote to oust Brower. He later told Harold Gilliam of the *San Francisco Chronicle*, "I was really startled when the board went as far as it did and fired Dave. The denouement was classical—a confrontation between strength and weakness. In history, the weak peasants revolt and execute the strong king. We've always had a weak board. A strong board would have been able to work out a rapprochement."[30]

Brower pronounced the whole meeting illegal, as it had been called too hastily, without proper notice according to the organization's bylaws, and not even half the directors were in attendance. Days later he filed suit, and the board quickly rescinded its action, having been advised by David Andrews, an attorney serving on the board, that its meeting had indeed been illegal.

If the foregoing years and months had been tumultuous, the following two years would be even more so. Chlopak was a hard-driving political hand who had created the FOE political action committee, which had endorsed and worked for the election of candidates since 1981, including a futile endorsement of Walter Mondale's challenge to the incumbent Ronald Reagan in 1984. The endorsement—issued during the primary campaign—had enraged many staffers and not a few FOE members, who would rather have seen the endorsement go to Gary Hart, George McGovern, Alan Cranston, or Jesse Jackson.

Staff members in San Francisco were highly suspicious of Chlopak, who was no friend of the union. Tensions mounted, and after several months Chlopak resigned along with the executive director, Jeff Knight. Brower thereupon resumed the post of CEO as a search was undertaken for the next president.

In January 1985, after scouring the country for a new leader, the board chose Karl F. Wendelowski, a businessman who had had experience in Antarctica at a scientific field station and in the Northeast with the Appalachian Mountain Club. Wendelowski was the first choice of all but one member of the board, and hopes were high that he could right the ship.

Wendelowski studied FOE's plight until June—mounting debt, low staff morale, falling membership—and suggested that maybe *he* should resign. Brower and other board members implored him to stay. He agreed. In September he presented to the board a plan to rescue FOE: close the San Francisco office and retrench in Washington, DC. This was greeted with vigorous denunciations by Brower, his allies on the board, and the San Francisco staff.

Then came a board meeting in November that was to become notorious. Staff and pro-Brower directors gathered on a Saturday morning in the FOE office in San Francisco awaiting the arrival of the anti-Brower directors. One of the latter, the treasurer Bob Galen, appeared, counted noses, and abruptly left. Herb Gunther, pro-Brower, followed Galen down to the street and saw him get into a car with three other anti-Brower directors. Geoffrey Webb, a Washington, DC, staff member, was at the wheel. It turned out that the plane carrying Wes Jackson, an anti-Brower director, had been delayed, and without his vote, the antis didn't have a majority, so they decided to boycott the meeting, denying a quorum, until their last member could arrive. Jackson eventually did arrive—the pro-Brower directors having twiddled their thumbs for two hours, fuming. Finally the meeting was called to order and the resolution to close the San Francisco office and lay off the San Francisco staff, not coincidentally busting the union, was approved. The vote was eight to seven.

The losing directors demanded an emergency meeting of the full membership. The majority on the board refused, saying there was no requirement in the bylaws that would force them to acquiesce and, to boot, they filed suit against Brower to stop him from making more trouble. He countersued, seeking use of the organization's mailing list to inform members of what was going on.

The special meeting never happened, but a poll of the members—forced by another *Brower v. FOE* lawsuit—was conducted by mail seeking ratification or the undoing of the office realignment and recall of the eight directors who had pushed it through. The recall failed and the move to Washington was approved by the narrowest of margins: 5,613 ballots were cast; the difference between yeas and nays was 180 votes.[31] The wrangling continued for several more months, but the office closure and staff layoffs had been carried out by early 1986 and FOE's worldly possessions moved east.

Randy Hayes, founder of the Rainforest Action Network and a close ally of Brower's, suggested that much of the blame for the collapse of Friends of the Earth and the ouster of Brower was in some ways Brower's own fault: "Dave had flaws, naturally. One that struck me was his way of picking members of his own boards of directors." Hayes said that Brower seemed to choose board members based on a sense of camaraderie—whether they cared about the right things, whether they were fun to hang out with. "I know specifically that it was true at Friends of the Earth."[32]

Brower finally resigned from the FOE board of directors effective September 21, 1986, telling the *Los Angeles Times*, "It just got hopeless. I thought I might as well not burden them any further."[33] It was another ugly battle with no winners.

Brower set out, with several refugees from the San Francisco office, to build yet another organization: Earth Island Institute. Herb Gunther, who remained on the board with Brower until September, was not unhappy with the outcome of the FOE referendum, believing that the biggest asset was David Brower and his reputation rather than the name Friends of the Earth and the battered organization. Gunther and others determined to build Earth Island into a powerful force.

Approximately three years later, Friends of the Earth, which had become a Washington, DC–centered policy organization, merged with the Environmental Policy Center and Institute, the organization founded by the people who bolted from the FOE staff in Washington in 1972, closing a circle. In 2012, Friends of the Earth rented a field office in the David Brower

Center in Berkeley, where Earth Island Institute has its headquarters, closing another.

• • •

Brower had now been ejected from the Sierra Club and Friends of the Earth. In each case, he led a tiny organization to prominence and then, when it became a known quantity with a measure of influence, it became too important to fail in the eyes of its directors. In the eyes of those holding the balance of power in each organization, the very flamboyance and inventiveness that had driven the organizations to prominence—the legacy of David Brower—threatened the organizations' very existence. Despite this pattern, Brower, at the age of seventy-four, still felt he had much to give, so he turned his energy to Earth Island Institute.

PART FOUR

Evangelist

FOURTEEN

Back to the Sierra Club

> I don't believe in purity. Being too pure is about the same as being too practical. Practical people have made all their decisions. They have lost their ability to listen, and are determined to repeat the errors of their ancestors.

David Brower and a few others founded Earth Island Institute (EII) in 1982 in much the same way and, importantly, with a purpose similar to Brower's creation of the Sierra Club Foundation in 1960 and the John Muir Institute in 1968: as a lifeboat in case one were ever needed. Some of his staunchest allies on the FOE staff—David Phillips, John Knox, Brad Erickson, and Karen Gosling—went straight to work for EII on a deferred-salary basis once FOE closed its San Francisco office.

Gosling remembers that they secured space on a balcony above a vegetarian restaurant on Columbus Avenue in San Francisco, space that had formerly housed the Ecology Center.[1] Four people—Gosling, Brower, Knox, and Erickson—shared a single desk. Dave Phillips got busy saving whales and dolphins. Randy Hayes of the Rainforest Action Network set up shop there as well. Dave Henson and Josh Karliner began building the Environmental Project on Central America in the same space. The buzz started early.

EARTH ISLAND INSTITUTE

The model for Earth Island was quite different from either the Sierra Club or Friends of the Earth and was fashioned to advance Brower's ideas as widely as possible by encouraging people with energy and good ideas. The plan was to set up an umbrella organization, a home for people with ideas for projects in need of support. The institute would have its own programs—led off by

David Brower, probably early 1990s. Photograph courtesy Brower family.

Phillips's Marine Mammal Project, which would quickly make noise in a successful effort to reduce the astronomical number of dolphins killed incidentally by tuna trawlers. But it would also be a home for smaller organizations, called "projects," which it would assist with administration and fundraising, on the theory that most two- or four-person organizations can hardly afford to employ fund-raisers, administrators, and accountants. Brower had been recruiting and inspiring mainly young people for years, and Earth Island would be a place for them to affiliate, get assistance with organizational niceties, perhaps learn a bit at the knee of the master, and then, as in the case of the Rainforest Action Network and others, outgrow Earth Island and light out on their own. The key, Brower said, was to "find the right people, talk them into it, and give them their head. If things start going south instead of north, lend a compass."[2]

Brower described the Institute's mission during a party to celebrate the tenth anniversary of the Nature Company, whose founder, Tom Wrubel, was a childhood friend: "The institute will publish, do research, hold seminars, create exhibits, be environmentally ecumenical, and seek to complement what conservation conscience has already achieved." He added that there would be Earth Island Centers scattered here and there, where people could meet and find information and allies.[3] This echoed a dream for Friends of the Earth that never was realized.

That was in 1983, while Brower was still on the board of Friends of the Earth. Three years later, after he finally dropped off the board voluntarily, the *San Francisco Examiner* reported: "Berkeley's David Brower, having lost control of two of America's most powerful environmental groups, has begun pouring his energy into a new San Francisco-based organization with global goals. . . . The Earth Island Institute now has 3,500 members (dues are $25 a year), many of them formerly with Friends of the Earth, Brower said."[4] As of this writing, there have been 135 official projects on the institute roster, about half of which are still active. Of the others, some folded and some branched off on their own.

Brower played little part in the administration of the institute and did not get involved much in lobbying or other legislative activities, but he did champion several conservation campaigns launched under the auspices of EII, including saving Siberia's Lake Baikal, the world's biggest lake and home to freshwater seals and other unique features. Brower first became fascinated with the lake in the mid-1960s during a trip abroad. He wanted to publish an Exhibit Format volume on the lake with Eliot Porter as photographer, and he suggested that the lake should be included on the United Nations' list of World Heritage sites. The Soviet Union wasn't interested, but after it crumbled, the emergent Russian government understood that the lake was in trouble from dirty industry and overzealous logging and sought outside help. Brower was invited to visit and eventually made five trips there. He recruited people to work on the lake's behalf and helped inspire the Baikal Watch group under Earth Island Institute's umbrella. In 1996, Lake Baikal was added to the World Heritage list.

Despite being in his twilight years (he was nearly eighty), David was no less passionate about the causes and beliefs that were important to him, and he traveled exhaustively to speak about them at rallies, seminars, and conferences all over the world. A memo of activities for this period shows appearances in Leningrad, Eugene, San Rafael, Santa Barbara, Los Angeles, Kyoto, and "Earth Day talks in California, Colorado, Michigan, New York, Ohio, Massachusetts, Wisconsin, and Missouri,"[5] Boulder, Lake Baikal, Estes Park, Portland, New York, St. Louis, Seattle, Cleveland, Los Angeles, Washington, DC, and many more in San Francisco and Berkeley.

BACK ON THE BOARD

In an ironic but fitting twist, a fair amount of the work he did during the last few years of his career was on behalf of the Sierra Club—where he'd first begun his long journey. In 1982, after more than a decade of healing and some attrition among the old guard, the Sierra Club board elected Brower an honorary vice president. It had already given him its highest award, named for John Muir, in 1977. Others honored as ceremonial vice presidents in 1982 were Horace Albright, a former director of the club and second head of the National Park Service; Lewis Clark, former director; Polly Dyer, former director and member of Brower's unsuccessful slate of candidates in the club's 1969 board election; Al Forsyth, longtime club activist and cofounder of Friends of the Earth; Pat Goldsworthy, former director and cofounder of the North Cascades Conservation Council; George Marshall, former director; Will Siri, former director; and Ansel Adams, former director. Adams refused to accept the honor, because Brower was on the list. Still mad.

Later that year, some unhappy Sierra Club members approached Dave Brower and urged him to allow his name be put in nomination for a spot on the club's board via a petition. These members felt that the club was becoming ossified, too willing to compromise, unwilling to take controversial positions, too bureaucratic, too big. Brower felt the same way and agreed to run. In a display of reconciliation, both Ansel Adams and Dick Leonard signed his petition. Brower later wrote, "Dick asked, 'Will you behave?' I said 'No.' He signed anyway."[6] What changed Adams's mind is not known. Perhaps having Brower as an active director rather than an honorary one seemed less risky.

Brower's candidacy was not universally welcomed, however. Les Reid, an old Sierra Club friend, expressed reservations. Brower wrote back, thanking Reid for letting him know that not all old friends approved of his attempt to return to the board. He explained, "I find that the important thing to be loyal to is the idea those organizations are supposed to support. I have been able to do that almost all of the time for the nearly fifty years I have been a member of the Sierra Club." He then pointed out where the club, to his mind, had gone astray—at Diablo Canyon and elsewhere. "But the main thing is the idea. And I have spent most of my waking hours working for the same things the club is working for, trying always to give credit to the organization in the lead, whether the club, FOE, NRDC, or someone else. Anyhow, I am running for the Sierra Club Board, and would certainly appreciate support from the Reids. Keep the condors flying!"[7]

He was elected easily. He began to try to get the club to work on disarmament, with mixed success. The organization endorsed the second Fate of the Earth conference but was unwilling to include disarmament activities in its formal list of priorities. Brower ran for reelection in 1986 and won again, only to become disillusioned and resign in 1988, a year before his term was over. He was immediately made an honorary vice president—again.

One of his principal criticisms of the club was that it was becoming too eager to compromise. One glaring example of that, to his mind, was in the struggle to save the native forests of the Pacific Northwest, then being logged at a prodigious rate. The Sierra Club Legal Defense Fund—an independent spin-off from the club—had filed suit to win Endangered Species Act protection for the northern spotted owl, whose rapid decline indicated that the primeval forests themselves were in declining health. The club had argued against the suit and tried, unsuccessfully, to persuade its sister organization not to file it, fearing a backlash that might dismantle the Endangered Species Act. Brower agreed with the decision to sue. This provoked a lively debate between him and Michael Fischer, then executive director of the club. Fischer opined that the Sierra Club Legal Defense Fund shouldn't be engaging in this reckless litigation and shouldn't be using the Sierra Club name. Brower retorted that the too-cautious Sierra Club shouldn't be using the Sierra Club name.

About this time, Tim Hermach was the head of the Many Rivers group of the Sierra Club in Eugene, Oregon. He clashed constantly with people in club headquarters in San Francisco, whom he considered sellouts. After one particularly nasty confrontation, Hermach phoned Brower and enumerated his complaints about the club brass. This prompted Brower to write a widely circulated letter to the club's conservation director, Doug Scott. He wrote, "My thesis is that compromise is often necessary but that it ought not originate with the Sierra Club." He suggested that the proper role for the club and groups like it was to hold fast to what they believed was right, fight for it, and find allies and push all possible arguments that supported their position. If they couldn't manage to win, so be it. Let someone else propose a compromise. "We thereupon work hard to coax it our way. We become a nucleus around which the strongest force can build and function."[8]

Brower listed places saved by the club's refusal to compromise—Dinosaur and Grand Canyon—and some places lost through compromise, including Glen Canyon. He added, "There is massive scenic vandalism along the Tioga road, perpetrated by the decision makers of the National Park Service, because the club compromised. We could have stopped that destruction. There is a highway to Copper Creek in Kings Canyon for the same reason. It could have remained entirely a wilderness national park if the board had stood firm. The board had good reason to, but didn't." He pointed out that, because it wanted "to play Alaska state politics," the Sierra Club had refused to join a lawsuit that stopped construction of the trans-Alaska pipeline for several years and forced many safety features to be incorporated. He summed up: "The club is so eager to appear reasonable that it goes soft, undercuts the strong grassroots efforts of chapters, groups, and other organizations—as if the new professionalization and prioritization requires rampant tenderization."

AUTOBIOGRAPHIES

Not only did Brower put countless tens of thousands of words in print via letters such as this, as well as articles, op-eds, advertisements, and other missives on one topic or another, he also finally invested his literary energy in writing a memoir of his life's work. *For Earth's Sake: The Life and Times of David Brower*, was published in 1990 by Gibbs Smith of Salt Lake City. It is unconventional to say the least. It is organized by theme rather than chronology, and original narrative is heavily larded with reprinted forewords, editorials, letters, obituaries, and other documents.

A reviewer for the *New York Times* liked it. Roger Swain wrote, "The real mother lode for any of us prospecting the origins of today's environmentalism is first-person narrative; in autobiographies we have the greatest chance of striking it rich.... At its worst, an autobiography is an exercise in self-glorification. In the pages of this long overdue book, though, readers will find not fool's gold, but the real stuff."[9] And he observed of the author, "What distinguishes the man in this volume, though, is not so much the impassioned championing of wilderness as the compassion with which he treats opponents and the criticisms he reserves for himself. He is quick to recount his failings as a father too often away from home . . . and to honor the patience and support of his wife, Anne Hus Brower."

A far less complimentary review appeared in, of all places, *Sierra* (the new name of the *Sierra Club Bulletin*), written by one of Brower's good friends and collaborators, the historian Roderick Nash of the University of California at Santa Barbara. "A Hero's Story, Poorly Told," the headline proclaimed. The review began, "David Brower is a great man, but this is not a great book. The problem is that Brower does not write books. His literary specialty is the humorous aphorism, the graceful foreword, the borrowed quotation. He has the ad writer's knack for concentration, a talent that has helped save wild places for half a century, but that does not create original, 500-page books." Nash objected to the description of the book as an autobiography, saying it was actually an anthology. "Brower's mountaineering and World War II exploits make for exciting reading, just as they did when the bulk of the material was published in the 1930s and '40s." Nash called Brower's reprinting of his congressional testimony during the Dinosaur campaign an "easy out." He would have preferred a fresh commentary, informed by the passage of years. "David Brower is a hero to me. He indeed wears the mantle of [John] Muir. For that reason I choose to think of David Brower, not as an author—for this volume would earn him only a passing grade—but as a man of extraordinary idealism, energy, and charisma, whose life and times I would rate straight-A."[10]

This prompted a riposte from Brower: "What Makes Rod Gnash?" (The magazine changed the title to "And There's the Bell," referring to Brower's "the bell rings for new rounds in the same old bouts.") He wrote, "Yes, I did anthologize, thinking it would be useful to reveal how early or late I came up with brilliant ideas and how they grew or withered. " He pointed out that most of the anthologized material had long been inaccessible. "There is good reason, I believe, not to leave it in limbo, but to make it readily and usefully retrievable." He argued that there are lessons to be learned from his battles with the Forest Service, the timber industry, the Bureau of Reclamation, and other miscreants. "Most of these struggles were Sierra Club struggles of an earlier era, now being relived and therefore, I believe, worth referring to as the bell rings for new rounds in the same old bouts." Nash had lamented the absence of Brower's account of his internal battles in the Sierra Club and Friends of the Earth. Brower replied, "The Sierra Club and FOE strife did hurt, and would have turned me gray if I hadn't already been so. I prefer to dwell on reconciliation (which has happened), not on getting even, whether or not it would be more fun. As Rod Nash suspects, and as I have confessed, it isn't good to spend one's remaining days looking backward."[11]

Sales of the book were disappointing; Brower ascribed that to the Nash review—he had counted on strong sales to members of the Sierra Club. *For Earth's Sake* was followed by a second volume, titled *Work in Progress*. It has a little more original material but also contains many reprints. The two volumes contain a wealth of information, oddly organized or disorganized. Many people had tried to help get Brower's story in order starting in the early seventies, if not earlier. Publishers were interested in Brower's grand statement about the environment and how it should be treated. He had signed contracts for memoirs, but more urgent responsibilities had always intervened until *For Earth's Sake*.

Finally, a young journalist named Steve Chapple approached Brower. Both men were in Rio de Janeiro at the United Nations Earth Summit in 1992, Chapple to report for the *Los Angeles Times Magazine*, Brower to recruit and inspire. Chapple attended several of Brower's talks and thought, "This should be distilled into a book." He tried the idea on Brower, who liked it and felt some kinship with Chapple, who had grown up wandering the Beartooth Mountains in Montana, much as Brower had spent vast amounts of time in the Sierra Nevada. HarperCollins, which had published Chapple's *Kayaking the Full Moon*, agreed to publish it. Alfred Heller, Thomas Winnett, and the Foundation for Deep Ecology chipped in modest financial support.

Brower spent several weeks in Bozeman, Chapple's home at the time. He would show up promptly at 8:00 A.M. every day, and the two would outline and write. "We didn't fight," Chapple said.[12] Later, Chapple would make several trips to Berkeley to finish the project.

The result was *Let the Mountains Talk, Let the Rivers Run: A Call to Those Who Would Save the Earth*, published in 1995. The title was Chapple's, the subtitle Brower's. The book is compact and tidy, where the earlier autobiographies were anything but. Brower skips lightly through a broad range of issues, ever stretching the boundaries of environmentalism. He leaves out personalities for the most part (these are prominent and valuable in *For Earth's Sake* and *Work in Progress*) and keeps the tone light and witty. The book was printed on kenaf, a fast-growing plant in the hibiscus family that makes fine paper, thus sparing a few trees. Chapple has said *Let the Mountains Talk* "was the first book printed on flowers."

Brower put in a condensed version of his week-of-creation "sermon." Chapple said that an editor at HarperCollins wrote in the margin of the manuscript, "Isn't this a cliché?" To which Brower replied, "Maybe so, but I said it first."[13] Major reviews appeared in *USA Today* and other papers, and sales were brisk. Italian and Japanese-language editions followed. The book, still in print, was taken over, appropriately, by the Sierra Club. It is the best distillation of the Brower philosophy yet in print. Of the experience of writing with Brower, Chapple says, "He had an encyclopedic memory and a great sense of humor. Occasionally I'd suggest checking the precise wording of a poem or quotation he wanted to use. He'd say, 'Don't bother; that's the quote.' He was always right."

On the heels of his memoirs, Earth Island threw a birthday party (as it often did—a fund-raiser, of course) to celebrate Dave Brower's eighty-second. The jazz saxophonist Paul Winter, who had met Brower at a conference at the Grand Canyon and become a friend, admirer, and sometime collaborator, provided the entertainment. The birthday party was at the Officers' Club at the Presidio of San Francisco. As the guests were drifting away at the end of the evening and the waiters were clearing the tables, Winter recalled that "lovely piano music began drifting from the shadows. It was Dave. I had no idea he played the piano. I asked what the tune was he was playing and he said, 'Oh just something I came up with many years ago.'" Winter described the music as reminiscent of Gershwin, "thirties style, like a show tune but not the syrupy kind."[14]

On the plane back to his Connecticut home, Winter thought to himself that Brower's piano repertoire should be recorded. And so the following fall, Brower "improvised for three days" in the recording studio in Winter's barn, including a few duets on standards with Winter on soprano sax. "My engineer and I tried to make a coherent tape out of all the snippets and fragments. It was like trying to assemble an ancient pot from shards. I sent demo tapes to various people asking for money to get it published and distributed, but that didn't work. I'm still trying. It's lovely stuff and deserves to be heard. He was a man of many talents."

Asked if he sees a connection between the appreciation of music and the appreciation of nature, Winter said, "I think they're connected, a great kinship. Music may evoke or reflect nature better than any other medium, even better than prose or poetry or photography. There's something living about music beyond the cortical. We take in music with all our being as we take in nature."

Reminiscing, he added, "In the fall of '65 I was in Kentucky at someone's home. I saw *In Wildness*. I was so stunned by the beauty of that book that I went back to New York City where I was living, packed up, and moved to rural Connecticut. I have been here ever since. Any time I look at that book, it tells me it's home—where I live. That book had more to do with awakening in me a sense of involvement with nature, with the earth, than anything else."

ON THE BOARD AGAIN

Though Brower wasn't much involved firsthand in political and legislative skirmishing by this time, he never lost touch with the critical issues of the day. He trusted the energy and convictions of the Sierra Club's younger guard. On more than one occasion, their appeals to him galvanized him to take a public stance on controversial issues where his influence as an environmental powerhouse still held sway.

The Zero-Cut Campaign

In 1994, for instance, Sierra Club members were presented with an initiative circulated by a group of club members calling themselves the John Muir Sierrans. Their aim was to persuade the Sierra Club to adopt the position that there should be no commercial logging on federal lands: national forests, wildlife refuges, military installations, and areas managed by the Bureau of Land Management. They collected the requisite number of signatures for the proposition "The Sierra Club supports eliminating logging for wood and fiber production on all public forests." There followed a long explanation of how this might be accomplished: stop all logging in roadless areas and other areas with old-growth forests, and in all publicly owned forests when feasible. Legitimate demand could be met, the initiative argued, by reducing demand and using every bit of wood logged from already logged or roaded areas.[15]

Sierra Club management and a majority of the board opposed the initiative, arguing that the prospects of enacting such a ban were minuscule and that adopting such a position would sever whatever access club lobbyists had to officials in government land-management agencies. The board then rewrote the language that would appear on the ballot—much as Will Siri had rewritten the original referendum concerning the Diablo Canyon nuclear power plant. The revision read, "Shall the Sierra Club's existing forest policy be retained as is, and not changed by amendment as proposed by the petition?" Thus, supporters of the zero-cut position would have to vote no on the proposition they had brought forward. The ballot question passed by about three to two, leaving club policy unchanged.

Dave Brower, on the sidelines for the previous six years, was ambivalent about the zero-cut position and stayed neutral during the initiative campaign. He reasoned that if all commercial logging were forbidden on federal lands, it would simply increase pressure on private lands.[16] Shortly he had his mind changed on the subject of zero cut by Chad Hanson, the author of the 1994 petition, a young lawyer who had been horrified by all the clear-cuts he had seen on a hike along the Pacific Crest Trail in Washington and Oregon.

Hanson argued that reasonable demand for timber could be met by utilizing everything that was already logged and by halting exports of raw logs, mostly to Japan. Brower came around to Hanson's way of thinking, and his resolve was solidified when he learned of the games the club board had played with the ballot language. He called the rewrite "as unethical as you can get."[17] In fact, partly because of the zero-cut fiasco, Brower decided to run once more for election to the club board, in 1995, as a supporter of zero cut and the John Muir Sierrans. He won handily.

The next year another zero-cut initiative was qualified for the ballot. This one was streamlined and unlikely to be changed, partly because of its simplicity and partly because the new board was more sympathetic to its intent. It read, "Shall the Sierra Club support protecting all federal publicly owned lands in the United States by advocating an end to all commercial logging on these lands?"[18] It passed by two to one, and it may have helped spur the Clinton Forest Service to begin a process to forbid logging on nearly sixty million acres of otherwise unprotected national forest lands under the Roadless Area Conservation Rule.[19]

Adam Werbach

At the same time that the John Muir Sierrans were challenging the club's status quo, another headline-grabbing event took place. In 1994, the Sierra Club elected the youngest person ever to the board, twenty-three-year-old Adam Werbach. Founder of the Sierra Student Coalition, he was an admirer of David Brower and they became close allies. Soon, Brower began spreading the idea that Werbach might make a good president for the club, inject youthful vigor and new perspectives and shake up the old guard.

Brower nominated Werbach at the Sierra Club's annual meeting in 1996. Werbach, who went on to make a name for himself in sustainable business and write two controversial books on the subject, won by a single vote. The next day a photograph of Werbach and Brower appeared in the *New York Times*. Around midday, Jane Kay of the *San Francisco Examiner* telephoned Werbach: "What did you do to make David Brower resign?" It turned out that Brower, unhappy with a club-approved plan to move a Sierra Club ski hut in Yosemite, had indeed tendered his resignation from the board. According to Werbach, he got hold of Brower "and he unresigned at the end of the day."[20]

Werbach was a big admirer of Brower for several reasons:

> He loved being part of any fight; regardless of the fight, he just wanted to be part of it. One of the things that's really inspiring about him is that there were really lots of peculiarities and warts and challenges to him, and that's actually what made him such a good hero to me. He had the frailties along with the strengths. I think pictures of him that are drawn without the fact that he was really a pain in the ass really miss the point, and I'm sure Anne would have said the same thing!

Anne is not with us to agree or disagree. She was, famously, her husband's sternest critic and his staunchest defender.

Werbach summed up, "I just feel really lucky to have known him. I miss him. I'm amazed how much I constantly refer back to him. Certainly on a weekly basis his name comes up, or something he taught me or inspired me to think about."

Toward the end of 1996, Brower suggested that it was past time for the Sierra Club to take a formal step to atone for the mistake it had made in the 1950s when it approved the compromise that resulted in the construction of the Glen Canyon Dam, the creation of Lake Powell, and the destruction of Glen Canyon itself. Two years before, the new Glen Canyon Institute had sponsored a debate between Brower and Floyd Dominy—the Bureau of Reclamation commissioner who had led the campaign to build dams in the Grand Canyon—over whether the Glen Canyon Dam had outlived whatever usefulness it might have had. "This was the first time talk of draining the reservoir was undertaken," said Rich Ingebretsen, head of the institute.[21]

A year later a second meeting was held in Salt Lake City, and 1,800 participants vowed to seek the draining of the reservoir. Brower was the keynote speaker at the meeting and went away promising to get the Sierra Club to take a similar position. With no prior warning he, Werbach, and Earth First! founder Dave Foreman, who had been elected to the Sierra Club board along with Brower in 1995, offered a resolution for the board's consideration at its meeting on November 16, 1996, to put the club on record in favor of draining the reservoir and restoring the canyon. The resolution passed unanimously.

The club's chapters in Utah and Arizona had not been warned of this maneuver, however, so the board majority decided not to announce the news until they could figure out how to handle it diplomatically internally. Brower wasn't having any of that: he immediately telephoned the *New York Times*, the *Washington Post*, and the Associated Press to release news of the board's decision. Once the news broke, the Sierra Club chapters in Utah and Arizona were roasted in the local newspapers and on radio and television by people who predicted economic ruin if the reservoir were to be drained. Adam Werbach reported that for a time he had to have police protection when he visited Utah in his role as Sierra Club president.

As with disarmament, the club may have taken a position on the matter, but that didn't mean the organization would put much effort into realizing its goal. That would fall to the Glen Canyon Institute, which has been working diligently toward that objective for a decade and a half. As of this writing, a persistent drought is draining the reservoir naturally, and the institute is hard at work trying to ensure that it never refills, even if rainy days return.

Following the success of the John Muir Sierrans, another band of renegades took aim at the club board. Led by Alan Kuper of Ohio, they were devoted to the notion that overpopulation was one of the biggest, if not the biggest, threats to the natural systems of the earth, a position many would agree with. The Sierra Club had long held the position that population growth overall must be halted, but had shied away from the contentious issue of immigration. The insurgents, however, argued passionately that immigration was the key problem. They produced statistics showing that population growth in the United States was fuelled almost entirely by immigration, legal and otherwise. They wanted the Sierra Club to take the position that immigration must be curbed to protect the environment. This was before Proposition 187 roiled California politics.

In 1994, California voters passed Prop 187, a heavy-handed anti-immigration initiative that aimed to prohibit illegal immigrants from attending public schools and partaking of other social services. The Sierra Club had opposed the proposition, which had caused a serious backlash against its promoters; the proposition would be declared unconstitutional in 1999.

The club's opposition to Prop 187 angered Kuper and his allies; they asked the board to take a position that immigration must be reduced. Again, the Sierra Club establishment balked, fearing that adopting a position limiting immigration for environmental reasons would be seen as racist and would complicate alliances it was seeking with various minorities and civil rights organizations. Initially, Brower sided with the insurgents.

He had become concerned about population growth as far back as the 1950s, partly through his association with Daniel Luten, who had delivered a speech titled "How Dense Can People Be?" at the 1959 Wilderness Conference. Eight or nine years later Brower was at home with a rare head cold and turned on the television. He happened upon a program where a young Stanford biologist named Paul Ehrlich was talking about how the population explosion threatened to make every other concern for the planet and human societies academic if it wasn't reversed soon.

Brower telephoned Ehrlich and asked if he'd be willing to write a book on the subject, a popular book for general distribution. No, Ehrlich said, too busy. So Brower phoned his friend Ian Ballantine of Ballantine Books and asked if maybe he could be more persuasive. Ballantine could be. The result was *The Population Bomb*, coauthored by Paul and Anne Ehrlich in the space of a few weeks. (Anne's name was omitted from the credits at Ian Ballantine's insistence; he wanted a single-author book, which supposedly would help sales.) It sold well over a million copies and led to Paul Ehrlich's being a guest on Johnny Carson's *Tonight Show* two dozen times. Brower's experience with the Ehrlichs and the *Bomb* undoubtedly made Brower sympathetic to the arguments of the group trying to force the Sierra Club into adopting immigration limitation as an issue.

The immigration-policy debate raged within the club and outside as well. Civil rights groups were scornful, but some environmental heavyweights weighed in in favor of stricter immigration policies, including the Worldwatch Institute's Lester Brown, former interior secretary Stewart Udall, Canadian author Farley Mowat, former Wisconsin senator and Earth Day founder Gaylord Nelson, former Colorado governor Dick Lamm, biologist E. O. Wilson, former Sierra Club stalwarts Martin Litton and Brock Evans, Sierra Club board member Dave Foreman, and others. Foreman decried how those opposing the measure tarred the proponents with the charge of racism.

Brower's admirers, some of them at least, were troubled by his stance and leaned on him to change his position. Two principal ones were Adam Werbach, then president of the board, and Larry Fahn, a future president. Brower said Werbach told him that "people are lighting up on this whole thing and saying any attempt to control immigration is racist. And he was just having a fit about that, so he was for not doing anything on it. Because of this, I chickened out. I didn't take either position."[22]

Brower softened his stand, stayed neutral, and two anti-immigrant initiatives were defeated. Here's how he explained his thinking: "Overpopulation is one of our biggest problems, overmigration is an important part of it. We can ignore neither, and let's address both. Do we realize that there are a lot of people who'd probably like to come over here and share the loot we stole from them?" He then pulled out one of his mega-statistics: "In the fifty years since World War II, the United States has used up more resources than all the rest of the world in all previous history. And we think that's a good idea, but nobody else does."[23]

Another Resignation

Brower's return to the Sierra Club board had mixed results. He had enjoyed some successes in changing—or adding to—club policies, but more as elder statesman than as a warrior in the trenches.

Bruce Hamilton's perspective is useful. Hamilton had been an editor of *High Country News* in the seventies and then a field representative for the Sierra Club in the Northern Great Plains; in the eighties he moved to San Francisco to become national field director, conservation director, and then deputy executive director for the club. He had close contact with Brower, especially when Brower rejoined the club's board of directors. "Dave, with all the deep respect I have for him," said Hamilton, "was mainly interested in creating passion for big visions and sowing doubt about club policies when he rejoined the board." Hamilton observed that in Brower's early years as executive director, he ran big campaigns—Dinosaur and Grand Canyon: "He was engaged soup to nuts and understood the pressure points. He developed brilliant strategies and worked the press and politicians, gathered data, and directed the campaigns to success." Later, Hamilton suggested, Brower was more content to give speeches. "He wanted to force the club to execute his vision. His vision was broad, bold, and uncompromising. But sometimes all or nothing works and sometimes it doesn't."[24]

Again, frustrated with the club's board for not following his lead, Brower resigned before the end of his term. He had become steadily more impatient with process and with people who refused to go along with his suggestions. His politics drifted ever leftward as he allied himself with Ralph Nader and Daniel Ellsberg and others in the progressive camp.

BROWER AND PRESIDENTIAL POLITICS

Brower's view of politics was rather unusual. When the first attempts were under way to start a third, environmental political party in the United States, he suggested that there needed to be a liberal Green Party and a conservative Green Party, more or less libertarian, since it was vital to attract both liberals and conservatives to the environmental cause. In 1974 he endorsed the idea of a third party for the first time—he suggested it be called the Equity Party—but that idea never went anywhere. This was before the first successful Green Party emerged in Germany and then another in France in the late 1970s. A Values Party had been created in New Zealand even before the Green Parties were organized in Europe. The American Green Party, whose banner Ralph Nader carried for a while, came a little later.

Brower supported Jimmy Carter and endorsed Walter Mondale, Michael Dukakis, and Bill Clinton (in 1992). By 1996, he was thoroughly disillusioned with Clinton (he put a bumper sticker on his car saying, "Free Al Gore"). He wrote an angry op-ed piece in the *Los Angeles Times* headlined "Why I Won't Vote for Clinton," with the subhead "This president has done more harm than Bush and Reagan combined." The article enumerated Clinton's sins, including passage of the "salvage logging" rider, which was causing the destruction of ancient public forests and critical watersheds; the signing of the Panama Declaration, which undermined protection for dolphins, whales, and other marine mammals; the continuation of the use of methyl bromide, a highly toxic pesticide known to damage the earth's ozone layer; and the weakening, if not gutting, of the Endangered Species Act. He added the signing of the North American Free Trade Agreement (NAFTA) and the General Agreement on Tariffs and Trade (GATT), "international trade agreements that represent the biggest sellout of American workers in U.S. history and effectively remove environmental protections passed by Congress"; the lowering of grazing fees on public land despite promises by candidate Clinton to raise those fees; the continued subsidy of the sugar industry in Florida; presidential decrees opening wildlife refuges to hunting and fishing; and increasing dependence on Middle East oil by breaking the promise to not allow the export of Alaskan oil. He then threw his support to the challenger: "I have known Ralph Nader for nearly 30 years, and in that time he has never let me or the environment down."[25]

Clinton, it must be said, became far friendlier to the environment in his second term, but that didn't mollify Brower or make him more enthusiastic about the candidacy in 2000 of Al Gore. He continued to support Ralph Nader and lent his name to a small effort calling itself Environmentalists against Gore, which worked on behalf of Nader in Florida and elsewhere. Tim Hermach, a firebrand Sierra Club member in Oregon, and other dissident Sierra Club members including two directors, Michael Dorsey and Chad Hanson, led the anti-Gore effort. They recruited several hundred environmentalists from across the country unhappy with what they saw as Gore's betrayal of the admirable principles he had espoused in his 1990 book, *Earth in the Balance*. They were angry at what they saw as sellouts in the Everglades, Appalachia, and Alaska, among other places, where the Clinton administration's record was poor in their opinion.

Some of the Environmentalists against Gore were supporters of Nader; others were not. Here's a bit of Brower's reasoning for his stance: "If George W. Bush wins the election, then at least we could expect the national environmental community to really fight for tougher pollution enforcement and genuine protection of our living life-support system." He argued that Gore was inclined to side with clear-cutting timber barons, big sugar, big oil, and real estate speculators rather than with forests and watersheds, parks and wildlife. "We [will] lose those fights because when Al Gore sells out, national environmental groups come to his aid, claiming the problem lies somewhere else. But we all know the buck stops at the White House."[26]

Environmentalists supporting Al Gore took heart from his selection of Senator Joseph Lieberman as his running mate, since the senator's environmental record was excellent. Brower was not impressed: "Al Gore talks tough about protecting the environment, but whenever money and political dealers ask him to, Gore uses his power to hurt the Earth—from encouraging coal companies to strip away mountains and the timber companies to ruin our national forests, to helping the sugar industry steal water from the Everglades and the major oil companies damage our coasts and beaches."[27]

Brower didn't live to see the George W. Bush administration, and one must wonder whether he would have continued to defend his work for Nader and against Gore given what happened over the following eight years—the steadfast attempt to roll back what modest environmental progress had been racked up over the previous decade. It seems unlikely that Brower would have second-guessed himself, though we'll never know.

· · ·

While most people of his age—he was well into his eighties by this time—would have been content to retreat fully into retirement, Brower never waned in his passion. Only his body weakened, but even though travel was more taxing now, he put himself out in the world whenever he could. This tireless dedication to what Carl Sagan once eloquently referred to as our "pale blue dot" didn't go unrecognized. In the spring of 1998, David Brower learned that he was to be one of two recipients of the Asahi Glass Foundation's Blue Planet award, given annually to environmental champions and accompanied by a prize totaling 50 million yen (approximately $420,000 in 1998).

In his acceptance speech, Brower spoke of the great honor—generally reserved for scientists—being bestowed on him. He said that the most valuable natural resources are to be found in the time-tested information in the planet's biota. "We should base human technologies on the design wisdom of nature as we find it, rather than cracking the genetic code to subvert evolution as some would have us do. If we wish to extract the design wisdom and ecosystem services from the natural world, we must preserve intact ecosystems." He summed up, "No other species has soiled its nest on the grand scale that we have and no other species can cause the human race to turn around and take the first of many steps away from the brink of disaster at which we find ourselves today."[28]

Ken Brower accompanied his eighty-six-year-old father on the trip. On the flight over, Ken broached the awkward subject of the monetary prize and wondered if his father had thought of setting any of it aside for his three grandchildren's support and education. "There will be no education on a dead planet," the elder Brower replied. He had the Blue Planet prize money paid directly to the Brower Fund (a project of Earth Island Institute), which deprived the Internal Revenue Service of its slice. As Anne Brower's care and medical bills mounted as she slowly succumbed to Parkinson's disease and old age, and as Dave started bouncing checks, he had to relent from his initial pledge not to accept any of the money personally. He was paid monthly as a consultant to the Brower Fund in the last two years of his life, about $2,000 per month. This was supplemented by a small pension Friends of the Earth had bestowed on him when he left that organization.

More important, he had money to give away in those last years to help establish Glen Canyon Institute, help fund the environment-labor alliance with the United Steelworkers, and support grassroots transportation activists, among other projects. Earth Island, via the Brower Fund, did give seed grants to some up-and-comers who were on the young side, but most of the focus on funding youth came after Dave's death, ultimately in collaboration with the Brower Youth Awards. The youth awards are given each year to a half-dozen or so young people who are doing productive and exciting environmental protection work. They are feted at a gala reception each year in San Francisco. Earth Island Institute is now the anchor tenant in the David Brower Center in Berkeley, where it shares space with many small progressive organizations and plays host to frequent and popular programs of one kind or another. One can only assume Dave would be proud to see what is being done under his roof.

FIFTEEN

The End of the Trail

To me, God and Nature are synonymous, and neither could wait billions of years before man showed up to decide what to look like. I like mystery, the unending search for truth, the truth of beauty. I would have no use for pearly gates and streets of gold if canyon wrens were not admitted.

In the summer of 1996, Dave, Anne, and their second son, Bob, were in Lone Pine, in the Owens Valley on the east side of the Sierra Nevada, for a reunion of Sierra Club High Trippers. As Ken Brower recalls the story he heard secondhand, the Browers were eating dinner at a restaurant. Dave was in a seat with a view of the Sierra crest, a picket line of peaks he knew better than anybody. Slowly he realized something was wrong, that one of the peaks had been deleted and its neighbors moved closer together, just as proofreaders will delete a mistaken character and close up the space. He was having a stroke. Bob was the first to sense that something bad was happening. They raced to the hospital, and Dave was put into intensive care.

Dave recalled later, "I was very lucky. I couldn't remember the town—I couldn't remember the name of Lone Pine where I was hospitalized. And while I was there I tried to begin to piece together where am I, can I remember any name—I can remember the Sierra, all right, then I got to Mono Lake. I got to Mammoth. But I couldn't get to Big Pine or Lone Pine. I finally got Big Pine, then Lone Pine, but I had to go down through the geographical route."[1] His faculties slowly returned, and he was released from the hospital and went home after a few days.

Ken remembers that one effect of the stroke was that his father, who had been an excellent speller, lost his ability to spell. "He'd make lists of all the words he couldn't remember how to spell, words he'd have to look up. Rather than lament his misfortune, he took it as a learning experience."[2] Dave put it

Barbara Brower and David Brower, 1980. Photograph courtesy Brower family.

this way: "The only thing that I've lost . . . is in spelling. I was a very good speller; now I have a hell of a time with it. . . . But it's recoverable—it's still there." And indeed, his ability to spell returned quite quickly.

But he was a little shaky on his feet. He had a tumor on his bladder and had suffered a mild heart attack that had required installation of a pacemaker in 1994 ("Now maybe I'll be able to keep up with myself," he quipped). He was, after all, well into his eighties. Yet he continued to travel, to give speeches, to evangelize. Although many people of that age instruct their doctors not to perform heroic measures to prolong life if something goes wrong, Brower was all for heroic measures; he had an earth to save.

Mikhail Davis, Brower's last administrative assistant, who accompanied Brower on all his trips after Brower got lost in the Pittsburgh airport in the late 1990s, said that the energy Brower drew from a crowd, most of whom were young, was remarkable. Davis would push Brower through an airport in a wheelchair, help him to a seat on the plane, help him get to an auditorium or outdoor rally. The minute Brower got behind the microphone, he'd straighten up, his voice would gain strength. It was as if twenty years had instantly fallen away. But he wouldn't last forever.

David Brower died from his various afflictions on the afternoon of Sunday, November 5, 2000, at the age, he would have said, of eighty-eight-point-three. Two days later George W. Bush was elected president of the United States, in the famous hanging-chad election ultimately decided by the Supreme Court. Brower had voted—absentee—for Ralph Nader. As a California resident, his vote had no effect on the results of the election—Gore won California easily. Brower's support for Nader in Florida, however, might have helped tip that state into the Bush column and Bush into the White House.

Brower died at home with his family around him. Anne was there, but she was incapacitated by then from Parkinson's disease and other maladies of old age. She didn't speak and was confined to bed or wheelchair. It was not clear how much of what she saw and heard she took in, though when her daughter, Barbara, was with her, Anne's eyes would track Barbara wherever she went. Anne lived another year, with around-the-clock care, at home.

Dave was cremated, and his ashes, along with Anne's, were eventually scattered by their children and grandchildren at what was informally called Brower Bench near Tuolumne Meadows in Yosemite National Park—a quiet, unmarked, off-trail spot the elder Browers visited often in their later years. "I hope whoever gets my ashes next," Dave once said, "has as much fun with them as I've had."[3]

Brower's death was reported by newspapers across the land. Earth Island Institute bought a two-page spread in the *New York Times* to commemorate his passing and his lifelong crusade to save the planet from destruction at the hands of what Anne termed "greedlock." A December memorial service at Berkeley High School, which lists Brower as a member of its hall of fame, drew close to two thousand people. Speakers included Martin Litton, Amory Lovins, Barbara Brower, Kenneth Brower, Robert Brower, Joseph Brower, Huey Johnson, Stephanie Mills, Ray Anderson, Paul Hawken, Bill McKibben, Julia Butterfly, Adam Werbach, and Eric Kessler. All vowed to carry on Brower's work. Johnson, a close Brower friend, founder of the Trust for Public Land and former resources secretary for the state of California, announced that he would try to persuade the appropriate authority to name a Sierra peak after Brower, a campaign yet to succeed. Musical numbers were performed by saxophonist Paul Winter and folk singer and songwriter Katie Lee. Katy Olsen, Dave's granddaughter, Jan Olsen, his son-in-law, and I sang a song titled "Friend of the Earth."[4] Tributes poured in from near and far—from Bill Clinton and Bruce Babbitt and Stewart Udall, and from other politicians and environmental stalwarts.

In 2009 the David Brower Center opened in Berkeley, across the street from the university Brower dropped out of eighty years earlier. The center houses Earth Island Institute, Friends of the Earth, and many small environmental and social justice organizations, plus an art gallery, a theater, and a restaurant. The institute gives annual Brower Youth Awards to young activists. Brower's centennial was celebrated in 2012 with an exhibit featuring Brower's photo books, lectures, panel discussions, and a birthday party with many old friends in attendance, munching on Brower-style waffles. The Bancroft Library, on the UC Berkeley campus, where the Brower papers are housed, produced an exhibit as well.

REMEMBERING DAVE

Herb Gunther, head of the Public Media Center and a former member of the Friends of the Earth board of directors, paints a remembrance in grand strokes: "He was ultimately a philosopher about everything: technology, civil rights—all the strands came together in Brower. He never had the arrogance to write a manifesto. He was the reincarnation of a founding father. Calling him an environmentalist would be selling him short." For Gunther, democracy needs activists. "Citizenship means activism. Commercial values destroy that. The counterweight was what Brower was preaching. Brower inspired, he led. He was a beacon for saving democracy. There's no hope for the environment without democracy."[5]

Jim Moorman, the first executive director of the Sierra Club Legal Defense Fund, identified another facet of Brower's complicated personality: "Charisma is like, but different from, sex appeal. When you have it, you get the benefits of many doubts. People just instantly like you and want to know you, and he had it in spades. He probably didn't even quite understand it himself, but he must have known that people were starting to hang around him like flies on flypaper." Moorman observed that charisma, generally assumed to be a big plus for a political leader, is also "a dangerous thing. If someone with charisma that you get to know doesn't do what you want, the disappointment can be greater than you expect." He suggested that this is one of the reasons for Brower's downfall at the Sierra Club. "I thought the level of heat in the argument between Dave and some of his colleagues when he got fired [from the Sierra Club] was higher than the facts merited. So it has to have been the fact that they were all really close, like a family. It was a huge tragedy when Dave left the Sierra Club. The world is a better place for Dave's having been one of its creatures. We need more Daves."[6]

John McPhee, who spent most of a year with Brower in 1969 and 1970 putting together *Encounters with the Archdruid*, wrote a short remembrance for *Sierra* after Brower's death: "He was feisty, heaven knew. And arrogant, possibly. And relentless, certainly. And above all effective—for he began his mission when ecology connoted the root and shoot relationships of communal plants, and he, as much or more than anyone in the midcentury, expanded its reach and inherent power until it became the environmental movement. Others in time would learn more than he knew and advance the argument in a stabilizing way, but they would always be following him."[7]

Perhaps Dave Pesonen, who as a young man had vanquished the planned nuclear power plant at Bodega Head on the California coast, summed up best: "He started the environmental movement. He created it. He was not a manager. He was a visionary. He had the sense to know it wasn't enough for him to enjoy his vision. It had to be shared. . . . He understood how to deliver a message. And he inspired people. He inspired people because his vision was out there, all the time. You couldn't be around him very long without being infected by it. He wore it on his sleeve."[8]

David Brower left behind a rich legacy measured in acres, in timeless books, and in thousands of inspired people. He joined the Sierra Club when that organization had almost withdrawn from the fray, having lost its founder, John Muir, and the battle for Hetch Hetchy. Conservation found its way into Brower's blood at high altitude, and he began to get active during the effort to create Kings Canyon National Park in the late 1930s.

After World War II, Brower became more and more active within the club, and at the end of 1952, he became the organization's first executive director. In that role, he began to develop as a national leader, working closely with Howard Zahniser of the Wilderness Society and others in organizations that now share the workload with organizations founded in the ferment that produced the first Earth Day in 1970— the Natural Resources Defense Council, Greenpeace, the Environmental Defense Fund, Earthjustice, and one he created himself, Friends of the Earth, plus dozens that have come since.

Brower's main role in the Sierra Club and afterward was as nature's publicist. He was a passionate devotee of the printed word and of the photograph. His books drew people into the movement by the thousands. They influenced politicians and other decision makers. And the newspaper advertisements he ran on behalf of the Grand Canyon and myriad other places stopped many an ill-considered proposal. He probably stuck with the big books a little too long— commercial publishers and nonprofit groups alike drifted away from that art form eventually—but their impact in their day is hard to overstate.

Brower's two principal experiences—in the Sierra Club and Friends of the Earth—have many similarities. The club, of course, was well-established when Brower took over, but it was a modest institution with around seven thousand members, a somewhat staid journal, and a vigorous outings program. By the time Brower was forced out, the membership had increased tenfold, an award-winning book program had been created, and the Grand Canyon had been saved. Now, the flamboyant acts that had resulted in the phenomenal growth in the organization's size and influence made cautious members of the board of directors very nervous. The institution had become venerable and valuable, and anything that threatened its continued existence must be reined in.

A similar pattern emerged at Friends of the Earth. Brower started that organization from nothing; there was no value there to preserve. But again through innovation and determination, Brower and his allies built an organization that won battles, attracted supporters, and began to be worth preserving. Cautious people worried that the Brower style threatened the organization's long-range prospects, and he was again shown the door. But before that happened, FOE helped expand the concerns of the evolving environmental movement to include pollution of air and water, energy production in its various forms, agriculture, public health, and many other topics outside the purview of the traditional conservation groups, which were mainly concerned with wild lands and wildlife. And the new movement tried, with occasional successes, to make common cause with organizations devoted to civil rights, organized labor, and gender equality. On the last one Brower was a late convert, at least as regards language. He resisted changing the name of the Friends of the Earth journal, *Not Man Apart*; he once wrote a memo asking if we should begin talking about "hupersonity"; and when someone suggested that his title should be chair (of Friends of the Earth), he replied, "I am not a piece of furniture." But he eventually came around.

In tangible, measurable achievements, first come the places that he helped spare from ruination of one stripe or another. Among their number are Echo Park in Dinosaur National Monument, a free-flowing river in the Grand Canyon, Redwood National Park at Redwood Creek, North Cascades National Park, Point Reyes National Seashore, Mineral King in Sequoia National Park, and the more than one hundred million acres preserved in nearly eight hundred wilderness areas scattered across the land. He did not save these places by himself, far from it. But he was key to their preservation—preservation that will last only if this and future generations demand it.

Next come the books, the dozens that he edited and wrote forewords for, published by the University of California Press, the Sierra Club, and Friends of the Earth.[9] As mentioned repeatedly throughout this book, Brower's books—especially the Exhibit Format series—opened the eyes of thousands of people and encouraged hundreds to get involved in the cause through various organizations. Though the world has moved on to digital art forms and modes of communication, in Brower's time books were king, and his innovations helped shape the awareness of a generation.

On the issues, time will tell, but for now we can say this: of the positions he took before many others did, many are now, if not exactly mainstream, at least held seriously by serious people and are gaining adherents swiftly, such as the idea that fossil fuels—coal, oil, gas, tar sands, shale, the lot—should be left in the ground, untapped and unburned, to lessen future damage to our badly wounded climate. Similarly, after the catastrophes at Chernobyl and Fukushima among others, the nuclear experiment appears doomed, even though many argue that it is the only feasible solution to the climate crisis. Brower would argue that the effects of radiation, not to mention the possibility of nuclear weapons' being used, make nuclear power too dangerous to gamble on and that, ultimately, the best course is to live off income—sunshine—rather than capital. The use of solar power is growing rapidly; whether fast enough to rescue the climate remains to be seen. And Brower talked for decades about how humans have been heating up the atmosphere for centuries and should pay closer attention to the effects and do something about them.

Earlier this chapter quoted Herb Gunther as saying that Brower "never had the arrogance to write a manifesto." One could argue that *Let the Mountains Talk* has a bit of the manifesto about it, but Gunther makes a good point. Rod Nash criticized *For Earth's Sake* for not having more reflection and analysis, and people have asked what Brower thought about Deep Ecology, for example, or other philosophical frameworks scholars build to explain various facets of the complicated subject that is the environment and the movement that has arisen to try to protect it.

Brower was too impatient for navel-gazing and theorizing in abstractions. There was always some emergency deadline bearing down that didn't leave time for deep reflection. He was quick to support any idea or proposal that had promise, whether it was practical or not. How it fit into an intellectual framework was of no interest to Brower.

I would argue that his determination, his drive, and his ability to inspire others, especially young people, were what made him such an important figure in the latter part of the twentieth century. He had a special ability to convince people that everyone matters, everyone can make a difference. Apathy was anathema. And I would echo an observation made by many along the way—namely that had he been more diplomatic, more willing to follow procedures, more accommodating to other people's positions, he might have accomplished far more than he did.

It has been argued that Brower was an elitist, a position I have a difficult time understanding. He was from a poor family and had to earn his way from the beginning. Nothing was handed to him; he cut his own hair! He certainly could be disdainful of ideas he thought foolish or wrong, and he was a tenacious battler, but he didn't think that an idea or suggestion should be accepted simply because it originated with him. It is true that through his years at the Sierra Club and many of those at Friends of the Earth, he operated in a male-dominated world, but that's the way it was, and he slowly changed with the times. He also understood that the message must be distributed to all minorities and ethnic groups for a whole variety of reasons, not least of which is that unless everyone joins the crusade, it is doomed to failure. And he was eager to learn what other cultures, other societies, could teach.

One modern trend that would undoubtedly have driven him to distraction (or worse) is the attitude of some toward the idea (and the fact) of wilderness. To Brower, wilderness preservation was the bedrock, the most important activity a person could participate in, the first responsibility of the movement. Today, some argue that wilderness is passé, an outmoded romantic ideal, that a sustainable economy and a renewable energy regime are what one should worry about and work toward, that human activity has tainted every corner of the planet and that there is no real, pure wilderness left. This would have frustrated Brower, no doubt.

His point, now nearly lost in the cacophony, was that wilderness and evolution produced human beings and every other creature on earth. Our understanding of how wilderness works, how it evolved, is still rudimentary, and we fiddle with it at our peril.

He would point out that every person on earth is the product of a system born in wilderness, that every living person can track his or her roots back to the very first organisms—and that the string of life from the beginning to the present has worked perfectly. To meddle with that is a definition of madness.

ACKNOWLEDGMENTS

I am grateful to all who consented to share with me their memories of Dave Brower and their insights, critical and otherwise. If one had an axe to grind, an agenda to promote, or a score to settle, he or she could find ample ammunition in the archives and the dozens of books that touch on Brower's life one way or another to come to whatever conclusion he or she wanted. I have no such motive.

I worked closely with Brower for most of my professional life, and he made my career possible and rewarding—also, more than occasionally frustrating. Still, I undertook this project believing that, though he had shortcomings, Brower was an extremely important and influential figure in the latter half of the last century, a key player in the growth and evolution of the environmental movement, from whom much can be learned, good and bad, and whose teachings, if that's the right word, should be part of our political discourse now more than ever.

Specifically, I wish to thank Mark Harvey, who reviewed the entire manuscript at the request of the publisher and made many useful suggestions (also saved me from an embarrassing error or two), Walt Patterson, who likewise gave the whole manuscript a careful review, and David Chatfield, Jeff Ingram, Edwin Matthews, Mike McCloskey, John McPhee, Rafe Pomerance, and Gary Soucie for careful review of parts of the manuscript. I offer fervent thanks for their help to John Adams, George Alderson, Phil Berry, Brent Blackwelder, Barbara Brower, Joe Brower, Ken Brower, Joe Browder, Steve Chapple, Mikhail Davis, Ed Dobson, Louise Dunlap, Marion Edey, Brock Evans, Larry Fahn, Dave Foreman, Bunny Gabel, Dan Gabel, Angela Gennino, Karen Gosling, Herb Gunther, Rich Ingebretsen, Bruce Hamilton, Joan Hamilton, Chad Hanson, Jim Harding, Randy Hayes, Huey Johnson, Joe Kane, Jeff Knight, John Knox, Brice Lalonde, Martin Litton, Juliette

Majot, Jerry Mander, Patricia Matthews, Brenda Moorman, Jim Moorman, Dick Norgaard, Owen Olpin, Connie Parrish, David Perlman, Dave Pesonen, David Phillips, Robert Schaeffer, Doug Scott, David Sive, Gar Smith, Adam Werbach, Al Wellikoff, and Ed Zahniser.

I also wish to thank Ellen Byrne, the Sierra Club librarian in San Francisco, for letting me camp in her jam-packed library and pore through oral histories, old copies of the *Sierra Club Bulletin*, and other materials. My thanks as well to Ellen Manchester and the rest of the crew at Earth Island Institute at the David Brower Center in Berkeley, who let me swim through boxes of documents and photographs.

Thanks also to my good friend and recovering lawyer Joe Brecher (you may call him Biff), who made the photographs print-worthy with his professional scanner and his facility with Photoshop.

And thanks to my daughter, Katy Turner, for yeowoman service transcribing many of the interviews.

Thanks too to the wonderful staff at the Bancroft Library at the University of California at Berkeley, where the Brower papers are housed. Dave rarely threw away anything on paper, and when he started passing along his archive to the Bancroft, it was a chaotic nightmare: Dave couldn't find anything there and no one else could, either. But through the generosity of Brian and Jennifer Maxwell and the careful organization of Tanya Hollis and Alison E. Bridger, the archive is as well arranged and catalogued as one could hope. The total, for those who keep score, is approximately 173 linear feet of boxes and cartons of varying sizes, containing letters, postcards, memos, journals, photographs, manuscripts, advertisements, videotapes, Christmas cards, party invitations, and more.

Many thanks to Jacqueline Volin, a dear friend, former colleague at the Sierra Club Legal Defense Fund and UC Press alumna, who helped immensely my labored attempts to navigate the mysterious thickets of the UC Press style book.

And while we're at the press, heartfelt thanks to Kim Robinson, Merrik Bush-Pirkle, Rachel Berchten, and Barbara Armentrout, my editors, for making the manuscript far better than it would otherwise have been. All four are tactful, skilled, and a delight to work with. Securing final approval for publication was no easy task; Kim made it happen, and Merrik and Barbara helped immensely with final revisions and reorganizations, and I'm very grateful. Thanks also to Anne Ferguson at the press, who made sense of the list of Brower books in the appendix.

Finally, my thanks to Mary Catherine Jorgensen, my wife of thirty-six years and counting, mother of Katy and Bret, our two children, and grandmother of our granddaughter, Alice. She had to listen nightly to my anguished recitation of the death throes of Friends of the Earth in the mid-1980s, a struggle that seemed as if it might never end. More recently, she has carefully reviewed the manuscript and made many valuable observations and suggestions. This project has preoccupied me for going on six years, and Mary's support and patience have made it possible.

—Tom Turner, Berkeley, March 2015

Books Published under the
Editorial Direction of David R. Brower

FOR THE UNIVERSITY OF CALIFORNIA PRESS

Manual of Ski Mountaineering, edited by David Brower and compiled under the auspices of the National Ski Association of America, 1st ed., 1942; 2nd ed., 1946

100 Years in Yosemite, by Carl P. Russell, 1947 (http://www.yosemite.ca.us/library /one_hundred_years_in_yosemite/)

Yosemite Bibliography, by Francis P. Farquhar, 1948

Marin Flora, by John Thomas Howell, 1949

Up and Down California in 1860–1864: The Journal of William H. Brewer, by William H. Brewer (1st ed. edited by Francis P. Farquhar, 1930), 2nd ed., 1949

The Incomparable Valley, by François Matthes, edited by Fritiof Fryxell, 1950

Sequoia National Park: A Geological Album, by François Matthes, edited by Fritiof Fryxell, 1950

Birds and Mammals of the Sierra Nevada, by Lowell Sumner and Joseph S. Dixon, 1953

FOR THE SIERRA CLUB

Exhibit Format series

This Is the American Earth, by Ansel Adams and Nancy Newhall, 1960 (no.1)

Words of the Earth, by Cedric Wright, foreword by Ansel Adams, edited by Nancy Newhall, 1960 (no. 2)

These We Inherit: The Parklands of America, by Ansel Adams, 1962 (no. 3)

"In Wildness Is the Preservation of the World," photographs by Eliot Porter, text from Henry David Thoreau, introduction by Joseph Wood Krutch, 1962 (no. 4)

The Place No One Knew: Glen Canyon on the Colorado, by Eliot Porter, edited by David Brower, 1963 (no. 5)

The Last Redwoods: Photographs and Story of a Vanishing Scenic Resource, by Philip Hyde and François Leydet, foreword by Stewart L. Udall, 1964 (no. 6)

Ansel Adams, Vol. I: *The Eloquent Light*, by Nancy Wynne Newhall, 1964 (no. 7)

Time and the River Flowing: Grand Canyon, by François Leydet, edited by David Brower, 1964 (no. 8)

Gentle Wilderness: The Sierra Nevada, photographs by Richard Kauffman, text from John Muir (condensed from *My First Summer in the Sierra*), edited by David Brower, 1964 (no. 9)

Not Man Apart: Photographs of the Big Sur Coast, lines by Robinson Jeffers, photographs by Ansel Adams and others, 1965 (no. 10)

The Wild Cascades: Forgotten Parkland, by Harvey Manning; photographs by Ansel Adams, Philip Hyde, David Simons, Bob and Ira Spring, John Warth, and others; lines from Theodore Roethke; foreword by William O. Douglas, 1965 (no. 11)

Everest: The West Ridge, by Thomas F. Hornbein; photographs from the American Mount Everest Expedition and by its leader, Norman Dyhrenfurth; introduction by William Siri; edited by David Brower, 1965 (no. 12)

Summer Island: Penobscot Country, by Eliot Porter, edited by David Brower, 1966 (no. 13)

Navajo Wildlands: "As Long as the Rivers Shall Run," photographs by Philip Hyde; text by Stephen C. Jett, with selections from Willa Cather and others; foreword by David Brower; edited by Kenneth Brower, 1967 (no. 14)

Kauai and the Park Country of Hawai'i, by Robert Wenkam, foreword by David Brower, edited by Kenneth Brower, 1967 (no. 15)

Glacier Bay: The Land and the Silence, photographs and text by Dave Bohn, edited by David Brower, 1967 (no. 16)

Baja California and the Geography of Hope, photographs by Eliot Porter; text by Joseph Wood Krutch, with lines from Octavio Paz; foreword by David Brower; edited by Kenneth Brower, 1967 (no. 17)

Central Park Country: A Tune within Us, photographs by Nancy and Retta Johnston, text by Mireille Johnston, introduction by Marianne Moore; edited, with foreword, by David Brower, 1968 (no. 18)

Galapagos: The Flow of Wildness, photographs by Eliot Porter, introduction by Loren Eiseley, foreword by David Brower, edited by Kenneth Brower. Vol. 1: *Discovery*, with selections from Herman Melville and others. Vol. 2: *Prospect*, introduction by John P. Milton, text by Eliot Porter and Kenneth Brower, 1968 (nos. 19–20)

Historical and regional studies

John Muir's Studies in the Sierra, foreword by John Buwalda, edited by William Colby, 1960

Ramblings through the High Sierra, by Joseph LeConte (reprinted from *A Journal of Ramblings*, 1875), 1960

François Matthes and the Marks of Time: Yosemite and the High Sierra, edited by Fritiof Fryxell, 1962

Island in Time: The Point Reyes Peninsula, photographs by Philip Hyde, text by Harold Gilliam, foreword by Stewart Udall, 1962

The Peninsula: A Story of the Olympic Country, by Don Moser, 1962

Wilderness and Recreation: A Report on Resources, Values, and Problems, report to the Outdoor Recreation Resources Review Commission by the Wildland Research Center, University of California, 1962

John Muir and the Sierra Club: The Battle for Yosemite, by Holway Jones, 1965

Wilderness Conference books

The Meaning of Wilderness to Science, proceedings of 6th Wilderness Conference, Daniel B. Beard and other contributors, edited by David Brower, 1960

Wilderness: America's Living Heritage, proceedings of 7th Wilderness Conference, Ansel Adams and other contributors, edited by David Brower, 1961

Tomorrow's Wilderness, proceedings of 8th Wilderness Conference, Ansel Adams and other contributors, foreword by Howard Zahniser, edited by François Leydet, 1963

Wildlands in Our Civilization, John Collier and participants in the discussions of the first five biennial Wilderness Conferences, 1949–1957; edited, with contributions, by David Brower, 1964

Wilderness in a Changing World, proceedings of 9th Wilderness Conference, Clinton P. Anderson and other contributors, foreword by Peggy Wayburn, edited by Bruce Kilgore, 1966

Voices for the Wilderness, from Sierra Club Wilderness Conferences, edited by William Schwartz, 1969

Wilderness exploration guides

Going Light, with Backpack or Burro, by Lewis F. Clark and other contributors, edited by David Brower, 1952, 1968

Illustrated Guide to Yosemite, by Virginia Best Adams and Ansel Adams, 1952, 1963

A Climber's Guide to the High Sierra: Routes and Records for California Peaks from Bond Pass to Army Pass and for Rock Climbs in Yosemite Valley and Kings Canyon, edited by Hervey H. Voge, 1954

Belaying the Leader: An Omnibus on Climbing Safety, by Richard M. Leonard, 1956

Starr's Guide to the John Muir Trail, by Walter Starr, Jr., revised editions, 1956, 1959, 1967

The Mammoth Lakes Sierra: A Handbook for Roadside and Trail, by Genny Schumacher and others, illustrated by Dean and Susan Rinehart and others, 1959

A Climber's Guide to Glacier National Park, by J. Gordon Edwards, 1960

Exploring Glaciers with a Camera, by A. E. Harrison, 1960

Deepest Valley: Guide to Owens Valley and Its Mountain Lakes, Roadsides, and Trails, by Paul Bateman and other contributors, edited by Genny Schumacher, 1962

Manual of Ski Mountaineering, 3rd ed., edited by David Brower, 1962

A Climber's Guide to Yosemite Valley, by Steve Roper, drawings by Al MacDonald, 1964

A Climber's Guide to the Teton Range, by Leigh Ortenberger, illustrated by Eldon N. Dye, 1965

Other Sierra Club publications

Nature Next Door: Interpretive Notes on the Film and on Nature Areas for Education, by Robert C. Stebbins, 1962

On the Loose, by Terry Russell and Renny Russell, 1967

Almost Ancestors: The First Californians, by Theodora Kroeber and Robert F. Heizer, edited by F. David Hales, 1968

The Sierra Club Wilderness Handbook, edited by David Brower, 1968 (Ballantine Books)

The Population Bomb, by Paul Ehrlich, 1969 (hardback by Sierra Club; paperback by Ballantine Books)

Aldabra Alone, by Tony Beamish, foreword by Julian Huxley, 1970

Grand Canyon of the Living Colorado, photographs and a journal by Ernest Braun; contributions by Colin Fletcher and others, with excerpts from the narration of the Sierra Club film *The Grand Canyon* by David Brower, Jeffrey Ingram, and Martin Litton; edited by Roderick Nash, 1970

Ascent (a mountaineering periodical)

FOR FRIENDS OF THE EARTH

The Earth's Wild Places series

Maui: The Last Hawaiian Place, by Robert Wenkam, with Kipahulu sketches by Kenneth Brower, introduction by Charles Lindbergh, foreword by David Brower, edited by Kenneth Brower, 1970 (no. 1)

Return to the Alps, by Max Knight; photographs by Gerhard Klammet; edited, with a foreword and selections from Alpine literature, by David R. Brower, 1970 (no. 2)

Earth and the Great Weather: The Brooks Range, by Kenneth Brower, photographs by Pete Martin and others, selections from Lois Crisler and others, introduction by John P. Milton, foreword by David Brower, 1971 (no. 3)

The Primal Alliance: Earth and Ocean, photographs of Big Sur coast by Richard Kauffman, selections from *The Atlantic Shore* by John Hay, foreword by David R. Brower, edited by Kenneth Brower, 1971 (no. 4)

Eryri: The Mountains of Longing, by Amory Lovins; photographs by Philip Evans; introduction by Sir Charles Evans; edited, with a foreword, by David R. Brower, 1971 (no. 5)

A Sense of Place: The Artist and the American Land, by Alan Gussow, introduction by Richard Wilbur, foreword by David R. Brower, 1972 (no. 6)

Guale: The Golden Coast of Georgia, photographs by James Valentine, text by Robert Hanie, edited by Kenneth Brower, 1974 (no. 7)

Micronesia: Island Wilderness, photographs and introduction by Robert Wenkam; text selected by Kenneth Brower from the writings of Paul Gauguin, Ernest Hemingway, Somerset Maugham, and others; prefatory statements by David R. Brower and Raymond F. Dasmann, 1975 (no. 8)

New England's White Mountains: At Home in the Wild, by Brooks Atkinson and W. Kent Olson; photographs by Philip H. Evans, Amory B. Lovins, and George DeWolfe; foreword by David R. Brower; edited by Stephen Lyons, 1978 (no. 9)

Wake of the Whale, photographs by William R. Curtsinger, text by Kenneth Brower, 1979 (no. 10)

Headlands, photographs by Richard Kauffman; with foreword and selections from Robinson Jeffers by David R. Brower, 1975 and 1976. (A limited edition of 800 copies was printed by Richard Kauffman in 1975 and 1976 for Friends of the Earth. Most of the photographs are from *The Primal Alliance: Earth and Ocean* and here printed from new, enlarged plates.)

Celebrating the Earth series

Only a Little Planet, photographs by Martin Schweitzer, lines by Lawrence Collins, edited by David R. Brower, 1972 (no. 1)

Song of the Earth Spirit, by Susanne Anderson; edited, with a foreword, by David R. Brower, 1973 (no. 2)

Of All Things Most Yielding, photographs by John Chang McCurdy, selections from Oriental literature by Marc Lappé; edited, with a foreword, by David R. Brower, 1973 (no. 3)

Resource books on energy

An Assessment of the Emergency Core Cooling System's Rulemaking Hearings [on spine: *ECCS Hearings*], by Daniel Ford and Henry Kendall, Union of Concerned Scientists, 1974 [FOE Energy Papers]

Non-Nuclear Futures: The Case for an Ethical Energy Strategy, by Amory Lovins ("Nuclear Power: Technical Bases for Ethical Concern") and John Price ("Dynamic Energy Analysis and Nuclear Power"), 1975 [FOE Energy Papers]

World Energy Strategies: Facts, Issues, and Options, by Amory Lovins 1975 [FOE Energy Papers]

Progress as if Survival Mattered: A Handbook for a Conserver Society, edited by Hugh
  Nash, introduction by David R. Brower, 1977; revised and expanded edition, 1981
Soft Energy Paths: Toward a Durable Peace, by Amory Lovins, 1977 [FOE Energy
  Papers]
*Sun! A Handbook for the Solar Decade: The Official Book of the First International
  Sun Day*, by Stephen Lyons, foreword by David R. Brower, published in coopera-
  tion with Solar Action, 1978
The Energy Controversy, by Amory Lovins and his critics, edited by Hugh Nash,
  1979
Frozen Fire: Where Will It Happen Next? by Lee Niedringhaus Davis, 1979
The Energy and Environment Checklist: An Annotated Bibliography of Resources,
  prepared by Betty Warren 1980

Friends of the Earth/Ballantine books

Defoliation: What Are Our Herbicides Doing to Us? by Thomas Whiteside, foreword
  by George Wald, 1970
*The Environmental Handbook: Prepared for the First National Environmental
  Teach-In*, Garrett DeBell, editor, 1970
Nuclear Dilemma, by Gene Bryerton, foreword by David R. Inglis, 1970
*SST and Sonic Boom Handbook: A Documented Sourcebook on the Supersonic Trans-
  port Planes (SSTs) Now Being Developed and the Sonic Booms They Would Pro-
  duce*, by William A. Shurcliff 1970
User's Guide to the Protection of the Environment, by Paul Swatek, 1970
Voter's Guide to Environmental Politics before, during, and after the Election, Garrett
  DeBell, editor, 1970
*Environmental Law Handbook: The Legal Remedies in Existence Now to Stop Gov-
  ernment and Industry from Destroying Our Environment*, by Norman J. Landau
  and Paul D. Rheingold, 1971
How to Be a Survivor, by Paul R. Ehrlich and Richard L. Harriman, 1971
Teaching for Survival, by Mark Terry, foreword by Garrett Hardin, 1971

Other Friends of the Earth publications

Cry Crisis! Rehearsal in Alaska, by Harvey Manning, with chapters by Kenneth
  Brower; foreword by David R. Brower, edited by Hugh Nash, 1974
New Roots for Agriculture, by Wes Jackson, 1980 (published in cooperation with the
  Land Institute)

NOTES

ABBREVIATIONS

Brower oral history 1   David Brower, *David R. Brower: Environmental Activist, Publicist, and Prophet,* an oral history conducted in 1974–1978 by Susan Schrepfer, Sierra Club History Series (Regional Oral History Office, Bancroft Library, University of California, Berkeley, 1980), https://archive.org/details/environmentalactoobrowrich.

Brower oral history 2   David Brower, *David Ross Brower: Reflections on the Sierra Club, Friends of the Earth, and Earth Island Institute,* an oral history conducted in 1999 by Ann Lage, Sierra Club History Series (Regional Oral History Office, Bancroft Library, University of California, Berkeley, 2012), http://digitalassets.lib.berkeley.edu/roho/ucb/text/brower_david.pdf.

Brower papers   David Ross Brower Papers, Bancroft Library, University of California, Berkeley, BANC MSS 79/9 c.

Brower Sierra Club correspondence   David Ross Brower, Correspondence, 1936–1969, Sierra Club Office of the Executive Director Records, Bancroft Library, University of California, Berkeley, BANC MSS 2002/230 c.

Encounters with the Archdruid   John McPhee, *Encounters with the Archdruid* (New York: Farrar, Straus and Giroux, 1971).

For Earth's Sake   David R. Brower, *For Earth's Sake: The Life and Times of David Brower* (Layton, UT: Gibbs Smith, 1990).

In the Thick of It	J. Michael McCloskey, *In the Thick of It: My Life in the Sierra Club*, (Washington, DC: Island Press, 2005).
Let the Mountains Talk	David R. Brower, with Steve Chapple, *Let the Mountains Talk, Let the Rivers Run: A Call to Those Who Would Save the Earth* (San Francisco: HarperCollins West, 1995).
Sierra Club Board minutes	Sierra Club Board of Directors meeting minutes, 1892–1995, BANC film 2945, Online Archive of California, http://www.oac.cdlib.org/findaid /ark:/13030/hb9290139g/.
Wildness Within	Kenneth Brower, *The Wildness Within: Remembering David Brower* (Berkeley, CA: Heyday, 2012).
Work in Progress	David Brower, *Work in Progress* (Layton, UT: Gibbs Smith, 1991).

PROLOGUE

1. "Clair Tappaan Lodge," Sierra Club, www.sierraclub.org/outings/lodges/ctl/.

2. *The Redwoods*, produced by Trevor Greenwood and Mark Jonathan Harris for the Sierra Club, 1967.

3. Sierra Club Board minutes, September 15, 1968, Brower papers, Series 4.2.1, carton 20, folder 2. Available at Online Archive of California, http://www.oac .cdlib.org/ark:/28722/bk0007b7k7g/?order=26&brand=oac4, Items 25–27.

CHAPTER ONE

Epigraph: David Brower, *Let the Mountains Talk*, 174.

1. California State Data Center, "Historical Census Populations of Counties and Incorporated Cities in California, 1850–2010," California Department of Finance, August 2011, www.dof.ca.gov/research/demographic/state_census_data _center/historical_census_1850–2010/view/php.

2. *For Earth's Sake*, 135. These are Dave's figures. His brother Joe says rents began at five dollars a month (Joseph Brower, "Early Haste Street—the 20's and 30's" [unpublished memoir, 2009], in author's papers.)

3. Riya Bhattacharjee, "Commission Landmarks Brower House," *Berkeley Daily Planet*, August 14–20, 2008, 3.

4. *For Earth's Sake*, 135.

5. Ibid., 2.

6. David Brower, typed diary, page headed "1925," Brower papers, box 14, folder 1.

7. *Encounters with the Archdruid*, 27.

8. Brower oral history 1, 3.

9. *For Earth's Sake*, 16.

10. David Brower, untitled interview manuscript, September 12, 1997, Brower papers, carton 18, folder 64.

11. Joseph Brower, interview with the author, April 19, 2010, Santa Rosa, CA.

12. *For Earth's Sake*, 19.

13. Brower oral history 1, 11.

14. *For Earth's Sake*, 25.

15. David Brower, handwritten journal, 1931, 6–7, Brower papers, box 14, folder 7.

16. Ibid., 19.

17. Echo Lake is pinched nearly in two near its center, giving the impression of being two lakes, although it is a single body of water. The channel connecting the upper and lower parts of the lake is wide enough to accommodate small boats, which ferry hikers to the trailhead at the north end of the lake.

18. David Brower to Ross Brower, July 24, 1932, Brower papers, box 2, folder 1.

19. Joseph Brower, interview, April 19, 2010.

20. Many, if not most, histories call Yellowstone National Park, created in 1872, the world's first national park. Brower and the Sierra Club stoutly dispute that claim and argue that the Yosemite Reserve, set aside in 1864 for perpetual protection, was the first national park even though it wasn't given the name. Its protection was given to California originally. This is more than an esoteric debate, as argued brilliantly by Professor Hans Huth in "Yosemite: The Story of an Idea," *Sierra Club Bulletin* 33, no. 3 (March 1948): 47.

21. John Muir, "A Wind Storm in the Forests," *My First Summer in the Sierra* (Boston: Houghton Mifflin; Cambridge: Riverside, 1911), http://vault.sierraclub .org/john_muir_exhibit/writings/my_first_summer_in_the_sierra/.

22. David Brower, journal, 1930, 4, Brower papers, box 14, folder 6.

23. At one point in Brower oral history 1, Brower says, "I was shy and still am, but I overcome it superficially," 7.

24. *For Earth's Sake*, 28.

25. Ibid.

26. David Brower, "Backyard Interlude," Brower papers, carton 4, folder 68.

27. Ibid.

CHAPTER TWO

Epigraph: David Brower, *Let the Mountains Talk*, 24.

1. Brower oral history 1, 31.

2. David Brower, "They Said It Couldn't Be Climbed," *Saturday Evening Post*, February 1940.

3. Bestor Robinson, "The First Ascent of Shiprock," *Sierra Club Bulletin* 25, no. 1 (February 1940): 1.

4. Brower oral history 1, 33.

5. *For Earth's Sake*, 40–57.

6. Ibid., 57.

7. David Brower to Ross Brower, October 1, 1935, Brower papers, box 2, folder 7.

8. David Brower to Jack Tarr, October 30, 1936, Brower papers, box 10, folder 3.

9. David Brower to Ross Brower, October 1, 1935, Brower papers.

10. National Parked, "Yosemite Visitation Statistics," www.nationalparked .com/US/Yosemite/Visitation_History.php.

11. *Work in Progress*, 10.

12. *For Earth's Sake*, 190.

13. David Brower, "Yosemite Valley Notes," Brower papers, carton 119, folder 2.

14. Ibid.

15. Ibid. Brower would go on to edit two books by Matthes (*The Incomparable Valley*, with Fritiof Fryxell [Berkeley: University of California Press, 1950] and *Sequoia Album*, also with Fryxell [Berkeley: University of California Press, 1950]) and publish one about him (Fritiof Fryxell, *François Matthes and the Marks of Time* [San Francisco: Sierra Club, 1962]).

16. David Brower to Dear Dad and Mother, August 21, 1935, Brower papers, box 2, folder 1.

17. Ibid.

18. David Brower to Dear Mother and Dad, August 22, 1935, Brower papers, box 2, folder 1. C.C.C. stands for Civilian Conservation Corps, a Depression-era federal program that put people to work on various conservation projects.

19. Ibid.

20. David Brower to Dear Dad and Mother, October 29, 1935, Brower papers, box 2, folder 1.

21. David Brower to Dear Mother, January 8, 1936, Brower papers, box 2, folder 2.

CHAPTER THREE

Epigraph: David Brower, *Let the Mountains Talk*, 27.

1. Francis P. Farquhar, *History of the Sierra Nevada* (Berkeley: University of California Press, 1965), among other books.

2. Walter A. "Pete" Starr, a young lawyer and mountaineer, finished the manuscript of the *Guide* shortly before he died in a solo climbing accident in the Sierra in 1933.

3. Brower oral history 1, 39.

4. Handwritten "Plan," n.d., Brower papers, carton 119, folder 8.

5. *For Earth's Sake*, 64.

6. T.H. Watkins, *Righteous Pilgrim: The Life and Times of Harold L. Ickes, 1874–1952* (New York: Henry Holt, 1990), 571–72.

7. Ibid., 572.

8. Brower oral history 1, 45.

9. Kenneth Brower, "Climbing the Spiral Staircase," *California Magazine*, Spring 2013.

10. Phillip Berry, interview with the author, September 13, 2011, Lafayette, CA.

11. David Brower, "Tripping High—1939," *Sierra Club Bulletin* 25, no. 1 (January 1940): 8. In this article he also wrote, "I could never understand what the swimmers found in icy Sierra streams," which may have telegraphed what appears to have been a fear of water.

12. Brower oral history 1, 30.

13. *For Earth's Sake*, 317.

14. *Work in Progress*, 45.

15. Some vintage Brower footage showing his understanding of the medium is included in the Kelly Duane film *Monumental: David Brower's Fight for Wild America*, First Run Features, 2004, www.firstrunfeatures.com.

CHAPTER FOUR

Epigraph: David Brower, letter to the Wilderness Society Council, October 23, 1959, quoted in Mark Harvey, *Wilderness Forever: Howard Zahniser and the Path to the Wilderness Act* (Seattle: University of Washington Press, 2005), 214.

1. Peter Shelton, *Climb to Conquer: The Untold Story of World War II's 10th Mountain Division Ski Troops* (New York: Scribner, 2003), 24.

2. Peter Shelton, *Climb to Conquer*, 13.

3. Charles Minot Dole, press notice, October 25, 1941, Brower papers, box 4, folder 21.

4. Kenneth Brower, "Climbing the Spiral Staircase," *California Magazine*, Spring 2013.

5. Joel Hildebrand to Charles M. Dole, March 27, 1942, Brower papers, carton 118, folder 1.

6. David Brower to "Appropriate Military Authority," May 27, 1942, Brower papers, carton 118, folder 1.

7. David Brower, ed., *Manual of Ski Mountaineering* (Berkeley: University of California Press, 1942).

8. David Brower to "Appropriate Military Authority," November 24, 1942, Brower papers, carton 118, folder 1.

9. Ibid.

10. *For Earth's Sake*, 87.

11. David Brower to Alan Hedden, October 29, 1942, Brower papers, box 6, folder 1.

12. Ibid.

13. David Brower to Ross Brower, November 24, 1942, Brower papers, box 2, folder 7.

14. David Brower to Dick and Doris Leonard, November 9, 1942, Brower papers, box 7, folder 1.

15. David Brower to Ross Brower, November 24, 1942.

16. David Brower to Ross Brower, November 30, 1942.

17. Doris Leonard to David Brower, December 4, 1942, Brower papers, box 7, folder 3.

18. *For Earth's Sake*, 89.

19. Barbara Bedayn to David Brower, April 8, 1943, Brower papers, box 10, folder 4.

20. David Brower to his parents and siblings, February 7, 1943, Brower papers, box 2, folder 11.

21. David Brower to Frank French, February 21, 1943, Brower papers, box 4, folder 32.

22. John de Graaf, *For Earth's Sake: The Life and Times of David Brower* (Seattle: KCTS, 1989), distributed by Bullfrog Films, www.bullfrogfilms.com.

23. Kenneth Brower, "Climbing the Spiral Staircase."

24. *For Earth's Sake*, 95.

25. Sgt. William C. Hosking to the author, February 17, 2012. Brower makes no mention of bridge in his papers or his autobiography.

26. David Brower, *Remount Blue: The Combat Story of the 3d Battalion, 86th Mountain Infantry* (Berkeley: Self-published, 1948), 1. Digitized manuscript at Hathi Trust Digital Library, http://hdl.handle.net/2027/mdp.39015027912396.

27. William C. Hosking, "What We Did in Italy" (unpublished manuscript, 2002), in the author's papers. © William C. Hosking.

28. Ibid.

29. Ibid.

30. David Brower, *Remount Blue*, 2.

31. We won't dwell overlong on this part of the story, which is well covered in David Brower, *Remount Blue;* David Brower, *For Earth's Sake;* and Beth and George Gage's film *Fire on the Mountain* (First Run Features, 1995). The Tenth Mountain Division's version, "The Riva Ridge Operation: Report of Lt. Col. Henry J. Hampton," can be found at http://10thmtndivassoc.org/Hampton.pdf.

32. David Brower, "Pursuit in the Alps," *Sierra Club Bulletin* 31, no. 7 (December 1946): 32, http://content.sierraclub.org/brower/alps-ww2-bulletin. The essay also appears in *Remount Blue*.

33. David Brower, "How to Kill a Wilderness," evidently written in 1945 for the *Sierra Club Bulletin* but not listed in any *Bulletin* index. Brower papers, box 4, folder 85; reprinted in *For Earth's Sake*, 125–28.

34. This is a dig at Gifford Pinchot, the first chief forester of the Forest Service, who promoted what he called "wise use," which he defined as managing natural resources for the greatest good for the greatest number for the longest time. As Brower would point out frequently over the years, the longest-time part was too often forgotten.

35. Peter Shelton, *Climb to Conquer*, 241.

36. Ibid., 218.

37. Kenneth Brower, personal communication with the author, February 2, 2013.

CHAPTER FIVE

Epigraph: David Brower, *Let the Mountains Talk*, 16.

1. David Brower to Professor Alden H. Miller, November 6, 1946, Brower papers, carton 119, folder 8.

2. August Frugé, *A Publisher's Career with the University of California Press, the Sierra Club, and the California Native Plant Society*, an oral history conducted by Suzanne B. Riess (Bancroft Library, University of California, Berkeley, 2001).

3. Bernard De Voto, "The West against Itself," *Sierra Club Bulletin* 32 (April 1951): 36 (originally in *Harper's*); Howard Zahniser, "How Much Wilderness Can We Afford to Lose?" *Sierra Club Bulletin* 32 (April 1951): 5; and Robert B. Marshall, "The Problems of the Wilderness," *Sierra Club Bulletin* 32 (April 1951): 43 (originally in *Scientific Monthly*, February 1930).

4. Hans Huth, "Yosemite: The Story of an Idea," *Sierra Club Bulletin* 33, no. 3 (March 1948): 47.

5. David Brower, ed., *Manual of Ski Mountaineering* (University of California Press, 1942).

6. David Brower, "San Gorgonio Auction, Going, Going, —," *Sierra Club Bulletin* 32 (January 1947): 3.

7. "San Gorgonio: Another Viewpoint," *Sierra Club Bulletin* 32 (January 1947): 12.

8. *For Earth's Sake*, 438.

9. Richard M. Leonard, "Report on San Gorgonio Hearing," *Sierra Club Bulletin* 32 (February 1947): 13.

10. Richard M. Leonard, "Text of San Gorgonio Announcement," *Sierra Club Bulletin* 32 (July 1947): 3.

11. David Brower and Richard Felter, "Surveying California's Ski Terrain," *Sierra Club Bulletin* 33 (March 1947): 97.

12. Ibid.

13. Sierra Club Board minutes, August 31, 1947, in Michael P. Cohen, *The History of the Sierra Club, 1892–1970* (San Francisco: Sierra Club Books, 1988), 88. The Mineral King discussion is also available in the typescript of the minutes in Online Archive of California, http://www.oac.cdlib.org/ark:/28/22/bk0o0779m2v/?order=95&brand=oac4, Items 93–94.

14. Harold D. Bradley and David R. Brower, "Roads in the National Parks," *Sierra Club Bulletin* 34 (June 1949): 31.

15. Richard M. Leonard, "Olympic National Park Seriously Threatened," *Sierra Club Bulletin* 32 (June 1947): 3; David Brower, "The Olympic National Park," *Sierra Club Bulletin* 32 (June 1947): 15; David Brower, "What Price Lumber?" with Lowell

NOTES TO PAGES 49–61 · 265

Sumner, "A Bird's Eye View of the Threat to Olympic National Park" (aerial photographs), *Sierra Club Bulletin* 32 (June 1947): 17.

16. David Brower, "The Olympic National Park."

17. Lowell Sumner, "A Bird's Eye View."

18. David R. Brower, ed., *The Meaning of Wilderness to Science* (San Francisco: Sierra Club, 1960), vi.

19. Ansel Adams with Nancy Newhall, *This Is the American Earth* (San Francisco: Sierra Club, 1960), 62.

20. See the appendix for a list of the Wilderness Conference books.

21. *For Earth's Sake*, 274.

22. Michael Cohen, *History of the Sierra Club*, 124–25; Roderick Nash, *Wilderness and the American Mind* (New Haven, CT: Yale University Press, 2001).

CHAPTER SIX

Epigraph: David Brower, speech to the Izaak Walton League, May 14, 1957, Brower papers, carton 9, folder 1.

1. Harold E. Crowe, "For the January Record, Announcement from the President," *Sierra Club Bulletin* 38, no. 1 (January 1953): 1.

2. Francis Farquhar, "Francis P. Farquhar, Sierra Club Mountaineer and Editor," an oral history conducted by Ann and Ray Lage, in *Sierra Club Reminiscences I, 1900s–1960s*, Sierra Club History Series (Bancroft Library, University of California, Berkeley, 1974), 2–60.

3. David Brower, "The Sierra Club: National, Regional, or State?" memo to the board of directors of the Sierra Club, October 17, 1953, Brower papers, carton 9, folder 4.

4. Sierra Club Board minutes, October 17, 1953.

5. Mark W. T. Harvey, *A Symbol of Wilderness: Echo Park and the American Conservation Movement* (Seattle: University of Washington Press, 2000), 8.

6. Jon M. Cosco, *Echo Park: Struggle for Preservation* (Boulder, CO: Johnson Books, 1995), 25.

7. Ibid., 16.

8. *For Earth's Sake*, 221.

9. Jon Cosco, *Echo Park*, 16.

10. Howard Zahniser to David Brower, April 2, 1953, Brower Sierra Club correspondence, box 9, folder 10.

11. David Brower to Howard Zahniser, April 8, 1953, Brower Sierra Club correspondence, box 9, folder 10.

12. Ed Zahniser, telephone interview with the author, June 11, 2012.

13. Congress creates national parks. Presidents, under the authority of the Antiquities Act of 1906, create national monuments. Many national parks began as national monuments and were converted to parks by acts of Congress.

14. David Perlman, "Sierra Club Challenge: Renewed Fight against Echo Park Dam Pledged," *San Francisco Chronicle*, January 4, 1955.

15. Kenneth Brower, interview with the author, January 25, 2013.

16. For the fine points of the debates and the calculations, see Mark Harvey, *Symbol of Wilderness;* Jon Cosco, *Echo Park;* and David Brower, *For Earth's Sake, Work in Progress, Let the Mountains Talk;* and Brower oral history 1, 46, 52, 111–37, 156–57, 208, 276.

17. *For Earth's Sake*, 328.

18. Ibid., 338.

19. David Perlman, interview with the author, March 4, 2011, San Francisco. At the time of our interview, Perlman was about to mark his sixtieth continuous year with the *San Francisco Chronicle*.

20. John Oakes, introduction to Brower oral history 1, viii.

21. *For Earth's Sake*, 438.

22. Eggert donated his time; the club paid for film, duplication, and distribution.

23. David Brower, photographer and narrator, *Two Yosemites*, produced by the Sierra Club, May 1955, https://archive.org/details/cubanc_000041; Brower oral history 1, 128.

24. Wallace Stegner, ed., *This Is Dinosaur: Echo Park Country and Its Magic Rivers*, rev. ed. (Lanham, MD: Roberts Rinehart, 1985), vi.

25. United States v. Harriss, 347 U.S. 612 (1954).

26. Cited in Russell Martin, *A Story That Stands like a Dam: Glen Canyon and the Struggle for the Soul of the West* (New York: Henry Holt, 1989), 71.

27. Charles Eggert to David Brower, September 8, 1955, Brower Sierra Club correspondence, box 3, folder 4

28. David Brower quoted in Jon Cosco, *Echo Park*, 109.

29. Michael McCloskey, interview with the author, March 21, 2012, San Francisco.

30. Richard Norgaard, interview with the author, September 8, 2011, Berkeley, CA.

31. *Encounters with the Archdruid*, 231–32.

32. Brower oral history 1, 142.

33. Jon Cosco, *Echo Park*, xv.

CHAPTER SEVEN

Epigraph: David Brower, quoted in David Sheff, "Occupation: Saving the Earth," *Interview*, February 1990. Sheff asked Brower if he considered himself a radical, and Brower answered, "Absolutely not."

1. The Sierra Club published the proceedings of the Wilderness Conferences; see appendix for those published under Brower.

2. *For Earth's Sake*, 226.

3. The organization is now called the National Parks Conservation Association.

4. This quip is attributed variously to Howard Zahniser, David Brower, or Mrs. Malaprop.

5. Wallace Stegner, *Beyond the Hundredth Meridian: John Wesley Powell and the Second Opening of the West* (Boston: Houghton Mifflin, 1954).

6. *Wildness Within*, 64–65.

7. David Brower, "'Mission 65' Is Proposed by Reviewer of Park Service's New Brochure on Wilderness, Calls Attention to Changes in Publication from Earlier Version and Urges Wilderness Bill Support," *National Parks Magazine*, January–March 1958, 3.

8. Brower would soon hire Kilgore to edit the *Sierra Club Bulletin*.

9. Conrad L. Wirth to Bruce M. Kilgore, February 18, 1958, Brower papers, carton 5, folder 7.

10. Horace Albright to Fred Packard, February 27, 1958, Brower papers, carton 5, folder 7. Joseph Carithers was a founder of the Arizona state park system and worked at various times for the National Park Service (interview with Joseph Carithers by John R. Moore, 1994, "Interview no. 851," Institute of Oral History, University of Texas at El Paso; http://digitalcommons.utep.edu/cgi/viewcontent.cgi?article=1863&context=interviews).

11. Sierra Club Board of Directors resolution adopted December 5, 1959, reproduced in Brower oral history 1, 322.

12. Brower oral history 1, 43.

13. Mike McCloskey, interview with the author, March 21, 2012, San Francisco.

14. Newton Drury to David Brower, Brower papers, carton 5, folder 9.

CHAPTER EIGHT

Epigraph: David Brower, *Work in Progress*, 34.

1. David Brower to Ansel Adams, September 27, 1956, Brower Sierra Club correspondence, box 1, folder 2.

2. *Work in Progress*, 12–13. The *i* in *Is* was capitalized for the book's title but not the exhibit's.

3. *Work in Progress*, 15.

4. Ibid., 13–14.

5. Ibid.

6. See the appendix for a list of the Exhibit Format books that Brower initiated.

7. *Work in Progress*, 23.

8. Ibid., 24.

9. Martin Litton, interview with the author, November 11, 2011, Portola Valley, CA.

10. Martin Litton, interview with Mark Kitchell for the 2012 film *A Fierce Green Fire*.

11. Brower oral history 1, 210.

12. David Brower to Ansel Adams, August 16, 1962, Brower Sierra Club correspondence, box 1, folder 3.

13. Ansel Adams to David Brower, August 31, 1962, Brower Sierra Club correspondence, box 1, folder 3.

14. Kenneth Brower, interview with the author, January 25, 2013, Berkeley.

15. August Frugé, memo to Sierra Club Publications Committee, August 9, 1963, quoted in August Frugé, *A Publisher's Career with the University of California Press, the Sierra Club, and the California Native Plant Society*, an oral history conducted by Suzanne B. Riess (Bancroft Library, University of California, Berkeley, 2001), 86.

16. William Hogan, "Award to Sierra Club for Spectacular Publishing," *San Francisco Chronicle*, May 2, 1965.

17. Brower oral history 1, 211.

18. *In the Thick of It*, 86.

CHAPTER NINE

Epigraph: David Brower, "Water and Esthetics in the Lower Colorado River Basin," *Grand Canyon Round-Up* (San Francisco: Sierra Club, 1966), Brower papers, carton 5, folder 20.

1. *In the Thick of It*, 86–87.

2. A Sierra Club lawsuit did reach the Supreme Court in the early 1970s, a case involving the proposed ski resort at Mineral King. The high court ruled that the club hadn't proved that it deserved to bring the case in the first place but invited it to try again. Justice Douglas wrote a ringing dissent that argued that the club deserved its day in court. The club rewrote its complaint and satisfied the standing requirement suggested by the Supreme Court. Mineral King was saved.

3. William O. Douglas to David Brower, February 21, 1962, Brower Sierra Club correspondence, box 2, folder 17. The numerous letters from Douglas indicate that he was not shy about badgering the Forest Service and members of Congress when he felt they were falling down on the job, an unusual activity for a Supreme Court justice.

4. For good summaries of this history, see Thomas Wellock, "The Battle for Bodega Bay: The Sierra Club and Nuclear Power, 1958–1964," *California History* 4, no. 2 (Summer 1992): 192–211; and Susan Schrepfer, "The Nuclear Crucible: Diablo Canyon and the Transformation of the Sierra Club, 1965–1985," *California History* 4, no. 2 (Summer 1992): 212–37. David Pesonen's version can be found in Kenneth Brower, *The Wildness Within: Remembering David Brower* (Berkeley, CA: Heyday, 2012), 55–77.

5. David Pesonen quoted in Kenneth Brower, *Wildness Within*, 71.

6. Ibid.

7. Philip Berry, interview with the author, September 13, 2011, Lafayette, CA.

8. David Pesonen quoted in Kenneth Brower, *Wildness Within*, 71.

9. Brower oral history 1, 160. Brower hated the expression "coffee table book," but here he seems to admit that his books did indeed wind up on coffee tables now and again.

10. This and much more is beautifully chronicled in Susan Schrepfer's *The Fight to Save the Redwoods: A History of Environmental Reform, 1917–1978* (Madison: University of Wisconsin Press, 1983).

11. David Sive, "David Sive, Pioneering Environmental Lawyer, Atlantic Chapter Leader, 1961–1982," an oral history conducted by Ann Lage, in *Sierra Club Leaders II: 1960s–1970s*, Sierra Club History Series (Bancroft Library, University of California, Berkeley, 1982), 13.

12. For a comprehensive discussion of the Mineral King litigation, see Tom Turner, *Wild by Law: The Sierra Club Legal Defense Fund and the Places It Has Saved* (San Francisco: Sierra Club Books, 1990), chapter 1; and John Harper, *Mineral King: Public Concern with Government Policy* (Arcata, CA: Pacifica, 1982).

13. David R. Brower, Nathan Clark, Charles Hessey, and John Handley, photography, *Wilderness Alps of Stehekin;* narrated by David Brower; organ music by Clair Leonard; by special arrangement with Charles Eggert, produced by the Sierra Club, 1957, http://youtu.be/Jc_EOcj6ZYw.

14. Hal Wingo, "Knight Errant to Nature's Rescue," *Life*, May 27, 1966.

15. David Brower to Hal Wingo, May 27, 1966, Brower papers, carton 120, folder 13.

16. David Brower to Allan Kitchal, May 27, 1966, Brower papers, carton 120, folder 13.

17. Jeff Ingram, interview with the author, April 1, 2012, Berkeley, CA.

18. Jeff Ingram archives; copy of Brower's note sent to the author.

19. Jeff Ingram, interview, April 1, 2012.

20. Brock Evans, interview with the author, May 7, 2012, Washington, DC.

21. Alan Carlin, at the time of this writing—early 2013—was a prominent critic of scientists concerned about global warming. He was working on a memoir and declined to be interviewed for this book.

22. Susan Senecah, "The Environmental Discourse of David Brower: Using Advocacy Advertising to Save Grand Canyon," PhD diss., University of Minnesota, 1992, 141.

23. And why hate beloved Smokey? Says Brower, "I thought Smokey the Bear was a pious-looking bear who had no understanding of the importance of fire in the construction of a forest." Brower oral history 1, 164.

24. Mander has been teased about his name all his life and insists that his parents, immigrants from Eastern Europe, knew nothing of the word *gerrymander*. "It's been good," he says in *Wildness Within*, 97. "It makes me easy to remember."

25. Jerry Mander, interview with the author, May 8, 2011, San Francisco.

26. Dan Dreyfus, quoted in Mark Reisner, *Cadillac Desert: The American West and Its Disappearing Water* (New York: Viking, 1986), 297.

27. Susan Senecah, *Environmental Discourse of David Brower*, 150.

28. Mike McCloskey, interview with the author, March 21, 2012, San Francisco.

29. David Brower to Ernest T. Wyatt, Jr., March 13, 1975: The IRS moved against the Sierra Club "with the admitted help of Mo Udall—'That was my biggest mistake in the Grand Canyon battle,' he told me later." Brower papers, carton 75, folder 20.

30. Byron Eugene Pearson, "People above Scenery: The Struggle over the Grand Canyon Dams, 1963–68," PhD diss., 1998, Department of History, University of Arizona, 209, cited in Donald Carson and James Johnson, *Mo: The Life and Times of Morris K. Udall* (Tucson: University of Arizona Press, 2001), 282.

31. *In the Thick of It*, 146. The source for this is not cited in McCloskey's book, and when asked in an interview where he got the story, he couldn't remember.

32. Stewart L. Udall, *The Quiet Crisis and the Next Generation* (Layton, UT: Gibbs Smith, 1988), 210. Udall does not say who in the White House issued the order, if in fact that's what happened.

33. Morris K. Udall, *Too Funny to Be President* (New York: Henry Holt, 1988), 55.

34. Jeff Ingram interview, April 1, 2012.

35. Morris Udall, *Too Funny to Be President*, 56.

36. The Sistine Chapel ad ran in a half-dozen newspapers and magazines during the period from August through September 1966, and once again on April 16, 1967. The series of Grand Canyon ads are digitized on the Sierra Club website, http://content.sierraclub.org/brower/grand-canyon-ads.

37. Morris Udall, *Too Funny to Be President*, 56.

38. Jeff Ingram interview, April 1, 2012.

39. Morris Udall, *Too Funny to Be President*, 60.

40. Roderick Nash, ed., *Grand Canyon of the Living Colorado* (San Francisco: Sierra Club, 1970), 87.

41. Donald Worster, *Rivers of Empire: Water, Aridity, and the Growth of the American West* (New York: Oxford University Press, 1985), 276.

42. Jeff Ingram interview, April 1, 2012.

CHAPTER TEN

Epigraph: Joe Kane, "Best Friend of the Earth," *San Francisco Focus*, October 1984.

1. The letters between David Brower and Ansel Adams are in Brower Sierra Club correspondence, box 1.

2. David Brower to Ansel Adams, October 31, 1968, Brower Sierra Club correspondence, box 1, folder 4.

3. *Encounters with the Archdruid*, 216.

4. Phillip Berry, interview with the author, September 13, 2011, Lafayette, CA.

5. Ibid.

6. Susan Schrepfer, "The Nuclear Crucible: Diablo Canyon and the Transformation of the Sierra Club," *California History*, Summer 1992.

7. Sierra Club Board minutes, May 7–8, 1966, item 20.

8. Martin Litton to Shermer Sibley, June 10, 1966, Brower papers, carton 124, folder 19.

9. George Marshall to Martin Litton, June 25, 1966, Brower papers, carton 124, folder 19.

10. The council is made up of one representative from each of the Sierra Club's chapters.

11. At a party commemorating Brower's hundredth birthday (July 1, 2012), Litton introduced himself to the crowd as "the person who got Dave Brower thrown out of the Sierra Club, by persuading him to oppose the Diablo Canyon power plants." Author's notes.

12. Richard Sill, "Open Letter to Directors Fred Eissler and Martin Litton," February 7, 1967, Brower papers, carton 124, folder 20.

13. David Brower to Richard Sill, February 13, 1967, Brower papers, carton 124, folder 20.

14. *Sierra Club Bulletin* (February 1967): 3.

15. William E. Siri, *Reflections on the Sierra Club, the Environment, and Mountaineering, 1950s–1970s*, an oral history conducted by Ann Lage, Sierra Club History Series (Bancroft Library, University of California, Berkeley, 1979), 109.

16. Ibid.

17. Phillip Berry interview, September 13, 2011.

18. Hugh Nash memo to Will Siri, cc: Board of Directors and Executive Director, February 16, 1967, Brower papers, carton 124, folder 20.

19. William Siri, *Reflections on the Sierra Club*, 112.

20. Sierra Club Board minutes, September 15, 1968, Brower papers, carton 4, folder 7.

21. It would be the second referendum on Diablo.

22. Richard Sill to Edgar Wayburn, September 21, 1968, Brower papers, carton 4, folder 7.

23. Anne Brower, "Scribblings Found on the Floor at the Palace after the Sierra Club Directors Had Met in San Francisco, December 15, 1968," Brower papers, carton 20, folder 30. It is unsigned, but Anne Brower acknowledged authorship, and the sheet shows slight editing in David Brower's hand. A second limerick, relevant to the Diablo back-and-forth, reads thusly:

> And the varying stances of Berry
> Find his colleagues required to be wary.
> The superior range
> Of his chop and his change
> Is predictable, true, but not very.

24. James Moorman to Sierra Club Board of Directors, January 28, 1969, Brower papers, carton 20, folder 1.

25. *Work in Progress*, 97.

26. Edgar Wayburn to David Brower January 28, 1969, Brower papers, carton 20, folder 20.

27. Edgar Wayburn, with Alison Alsup, *Your Land and Mine: Evolution of a Conservationist* (San Francisco: Sierra Club Books, 2004), 119–20.

28. Phillip Berry to David Brower, January 30, 1969, Brower papers, carton 20, folder 19.

29. Jerry Mander, interview with the author, March 3, 2011, San Francisco.

30. Gary Soucie, interview with the author, October 11, 2011, Williamstown, MA. Hickel was dismissed as interior secretary after criticizing the Nixon administration's response to Vietnam War protestors and the tragedy at Kent State.

31. Sierra Club Board minutes, February 8–9, 1969.

32. Michael Cohen, *The History of the Sierra Club 1892–1970* (San Francisco: Sierra Club Books, 1988), 395–434. Cohen attributes the expression to Ed Wayburn, but it doesn't appear in Wayburn's memoir.

33. Cicely M. Christy, letter to the editor, *Yodeler*, October 1968.

34. James McCracken, letter to the editor, *Yodeler*, October 1968. McCracken would go on to be one of Brower's harshest critics.

35. Anne Brower to Dick Leonard, September 30, 1968, Brower papers, carton 19, folder 44.

36. Dick Leonard to Anne Brower, October 1, 1968, Brower papers, carton 19, folder 44.

37. Anne Brower to Dick Leonard, October 8, 1968, Brower papers, carton 19, folder 44.

38. Hugh Nash, memo to David Brower, Brower papers, carton 20, folder 20.

39. Hugh Nash, "Suspension of Sierra Club Bulletin Editor," March 7, 1969, Brower papers, carton 20, folder 26.

40. Wallace Stegner, "Views of Brower Foes in Sierra Club," *Palo Alto Times*, February 11, 1969.

41. David Brower, "Viewpoint: What's Eating the Sierra Club?" handwritten note, February 26, 1969, Brower papers, carton 20, folder 20.

42. Anne Brower to Marjorie Jones, February 28, 1968, Brower papers, carton 20, folder 14.

43. Ansel Adams to California attorney general, February 10, 1969, Brower papers, carton 21, folder 1.

44. Arthur Godfrey to David Brower, March 30, 1969, Brower Sierra Club correspondence, box 3, folder 14.

45. Anne Brower to Dear Joe and Gayle, March 7, 1969, Brower papers, carton 120, folder 17.

46. Anne Brower to Dear Joe and Gayle, March 20, 1969, Brower papers, carton 120, folder 17.

47. Minutes, Sierra Club Board of Directors meeting, May 3, 1969; also Brower papers, box 9, folder 73.

48. Ibid.

49. Ibid.

50. *In the Thick of It*, 89.

51. Mike McCloskey, interview with the author, March 21, 2012, San Francisco.

52. Phillip Berry interview, September 13, 2011.

53. Martin Litton, "Sierra Club Director and Uncompromising Preservationist, 1950s–1970s," an oral history conducted by Ann Lage, with an introduction by David Brower, in *Sierra Club Leaders: 1950s–1970s*, Sierra Club History Series (Bancroft Library, University of California, Berkeley, 1982), 89–211.

CHAPTER ELEVEN

Epigraph: David Brower, statement to the Subcommittee on Conservation of the Democratic Western States Conference, Fairmont Hotel, San Francisco, January 23, 1960, Brower papers, box 9, folder 28.

1. John McPhee, telephone interview with the author, June 12, 2012.

2. Peter Hessler, "John McPhee: The Art of Nonfiction no. 3," *Paris Review*, no. 192, Spring 2010.

3. John McPhee interview, June 12, 2012.

4. Kenneth Brower, memo "To DRB From KDB," June 18, 1968, Brower papers, box 2, folder 4.

5. Theodore Roosevelt, "Speech at Grand Canyon, Arizona," May 6, 1903, *Presidential Addresses and State Papers, February 19, 1902 to May 13, 1903* (New York: Review of Reviews, 1910), 369–72.

6. *Encounters with the Archdruid*, 103.

7. Brower papers, carton 120, folder 17. Ansel was very fond of capital letters and exclamation points.

8. Ibid.

9. Philip S. Bernays to Editor, *New Yorker*, June 6, 1971, Brower Sierra Club correspondence, box 1, folder 17.

10. Alvin Beam, "The Archdruid: Nature Militant," [Cleveland] *Plain Dealer*, August 1, 1971.

11. Ibid.

12. *Encounters with the Archdruid*, 103.

13. "Polluted Rhetoric," *Wall Street Journal*, May 8, 1971.

14. *Encounters with the Archdruid*, 137.

15. David Brower to John McPhee, undated (but certainly mid-1971), Brower papers, carton 59, folder 13. The ad had been prepared by Jerry Mander and placed by the North Cascades Conservation Council.

16. *For Earth's Sake*, 363.

17. Brower oral history 1, 6.

18. David Brower to John McPhee, undated (but certainly mid-1971).

19. John McPhee to David Brower, handwritten, undated letter on *New Yorker* stationery, Brower papers, carton 62, folder 22.

20. Ogilvy, a Sierra Club activist, referred to the Population Institute as Popeye. Aitken, a physics professor at Stanford, had been chairman of the ABC Committee, the group that supported the unsuccessful Brower slate in the Sierra Club board election of 1969. Milton was an ecologist with the Conservation Foundation. Fraser Darling was a British ecologist and author, and Dasmann was a professor at the University of California at Santa Cruz.

21. David Chatfield, interview with the author, April 3, 2013, Berkeley, CA.

22. Marion Edey to David Brower, May 7, 1969, in the author's papers, provided by George Alderson.

23. Ibid.

24. Marion Edey, interview with the author, May 8, 2012, Washington, DC.

25. Lawrence F. Davies, "Naturalists Get a Political Arm," *New York Times*, September 17, 1969.

26. Marion Edey, personal communication with the author, September 2013.

27. Letter from David Brower to Nick Arguimbau, June 16, 1980, in the author's papers.

28. William Murray, "The Porn Capital of America," *New York Times Magazine*, January 3, 1971.

29. Gary Soucie, memo to Friends of the Earth directors and the staff of *Not Man Apart*, January 7, 1971, in the author's papers.

CHAPTER TWELVE

Epigraph: David Brower, Brower oral history 2, 168.

1. Tom Wolfe, *Radical Chic and Mau-Mauing the Flak Catchers* (New York: Farrar, Straus and Giroux, 1970), 47–49.

2. Edwin Matthews, interview with the author, September 27, 2011, Washington Depot, CT.

3. Brent Blackwelder, interview with the author, May 8, 2012, Washington, DC.

4. Brower oral history 1, 306.

5. Jamie Heard, "Friends of the Earth Give Environmental Interests an Activist Voice," *National Journal*, August 8, 1970.

6. Peter A. Coates, *The Trans-Alaska Pipeline Controversy: Technology, Conservation, and the Frontier* (Bethlehem, PA: Lehigh University Press, 1991), 164: "In January 1968, Atlantic Richfield repeated its pioneering success on the Kenai with the first commercial strike on the state-leased lands in the Arctic."

7. James Moorman, interview with the author, May 9, 2012, Washington, DC.

8. A fascinating discussion of this whole affair is in Peter Coates, *Trans-Alaska Pipeline Controversy*.

9. James Moorman interview, May 9, 2012.

10. David Brower, "Who Needs the Alaska Pipeline?" *New York Times*, February 5, 1971.

11. Steve Haycox, "Modern Alaska: Oil Discovery and Development in Alaska," *Alaska History and Cultural Studies*, Alaska Humanities Forum, n.d., www.akhistorycourse.org/articles/article.php?artID=140.

12. Colorado River Storage Project Act of 1956, 43 U.S.C. §§ 620–620o (1956). Reprinted in *Not Man Apart*, January 1971, 10; available on U.S. Bureau of Reclamation website, www.usbr.gov/lc/region/g1000/pdfiles/crspuc.pdf.

13. Owen Olpin, telephone interview with the author, September 6, 2012.

14. Ibid.

15. "China Declares," *Stockholm Conference ECO*, June 10, 1972.

16. *For Earth's Sake*, 470.

17. Brower oral history 1, 302.

18. Steve Rauh, telephone interview with the author, March 18, 2013.

19. *For Earth's Sake*, 474.

20. The moratorium remains in effect nearly thirty years later, though Japan continues to take a few whales under a self-issued scientific permit.

21. *Work in Progress*, 173–74.

22. *Wildness Within*, 189.

23. Ibid., 190. By *representational*, the author of the answer seems to have meant that there are no humans in the pictures.

24. Ibid., 201.

25. Brower, the sophomore dropout, had received at least a half-dozen honorary degrees by this time, but never referred to himself as Doctor.

26. Representative Ronald V. Dellums, letter to the Norwegian Nobel Foundation, January 20, 1978, in author's papers.

27. *Let the Mountains Talk*, 146.

28. David Phillips quoted in *Wildness Within*, 167.

29. Gary A. Soucie, interview with the author, October 11, 2011, Williamstown, MA.

30. George Alderson, interview with the author, May 7, 2012, Washington, DC. In addition to the Wilderness Society, Alderson went on to work for the Defenders of Wildlife, the Bureau of Land Management, and the Environmental Protection Agency.

31. Bestor Robinson, "Bestor Robinson: Thoughts on Conservation and the Sierra Club," an oral history conducted by Susan R. Schrepfer, in *Sierra Club Reminiscences I, 1900s–1960s*, Sierra Club History Series (Bancroft Library, University of California, Berkeley, 1974), 139–208.

32. Mike McCloskey, interview with the author, March 21, 2012, San Francisco.

33. Fletcher was the author of *The Man Who Walked through Time*, an account of a trek through the Grand Canyon.

34. Gary A. Soucie interview, October 11, 2011.

35. Ibid.

36. Juliette Majot, interview with the author, May 8, 2013, Berkeley, CA.

37. Mary Lou Vandeventer, interview with the author, January 7, 2013, Berkeley, CA.

38. Dave B to Mary Lou, April 4, 1975, Brower papers, carton 59, folder 10. Here is a sample of Souvenir:

THE QUICK BROWN FOX JUMPS OVER THE LAZY DOG. the quick brown fox jumps over the lazy dog. 0123456789

39. Liebe Cavalieri, "New Strains of Life or Death," *Not Man Apart*, January 1977.

CHAPTER THIRTEEN

Epigraph: David Brower, speech to conference sponsored by Izaak Walton League of America, March 1957, Brower papers, carton 9, folder 16.

1. Edwin Matthews, interview with the author, September 27, 2011, Washington Depot, CT.
2. Ibid.
3. Ibid.
4. Kenneth Brower and William Curtsinger, photographer, *Wake of the Whale* (San Francisco: Friends of the Earth, 1980).
5. Joe Kane, "The Friends of David Brower," *Outside*, December 1984.
6. *For Earth's Sake*, 175.
7. David Chatfield, interview with the author, April 3, 2013, Berkeley, CA.
8. Edwin Matthews, interview, September 27, 2011.
9. David Brower to Edwin Matthews, memo, April 14, 1980, in author's papers.
10. Edwin Matthews interview, September 27, 2011.
11. Ibid.
12. Ibid.
13. Gary A. Soucie, interview with the author, October 11, 2011, Williamstown, MA.
14. Rafe Pomerance, interview with the author, May 8, 2012, Washington, DC.
15. Ibid.
16. Ibid.
17. The lecture is included in *Work in Progress*, 233–46.
18. Loren Eiseley, *The Immense Journey* (New York: Random House, 1957).
19. *Work in Progress*, 246.
20. David Brower, opening speech at first biennial On the Fate of the Earth conference: Conservation and Security in a Sustainable Society, New York City, 1982 (Berkeley, CA: Earth Island Institute, 1983), 4.
21. *Work in Progress*, 266.
22. "What's in a Name?" *Not Man Apart* 13, no. 9 (October 1983): 2.
23. "The Great NMA Name Debate," *Not Man Apart* 13, no. 11 (December 1983): 25.
24. Angela Gennino, interview with the author, May 8, 2013, Berkeley.

25. Rafe Pomerance interview, May 8, 2012.

26. Ibid.

27. Joe Kane, "Friends of David Brower."

28. Friends of the Earth Board of Directors minutes, July 1, 1984, Brower papers, carton 75, folder 37.

29. Joe Kane, "Best Friend of the Earth," *San Francisco Focus*, October 1984.

30. Harold Gilliam, "Temblor at Friends of the Earth," *San Francisco Chronicle*, July 22, 1984.

31. Stuart Ingis, "Inside of a Public Interest Group," senior thesis, Hamilton College, 1993, 48.

32. *Wildness Within*, 245.

33. Larry B. Stammer, "Founder Quits Friends of the Earth, Says Situation 'Just Got Hopeless,'" *Los Angeles Times*, October 11, 1986.

CHAPTER FOURTEEN

Epigraph: David Brower, *Let the Mountains Talk*, 180.

1. Karen Gosling, interview with the author, January 7, 2013, Berkeley, CA.

2. "The World's First Earth Island Center Opens: Remarks by David Brower, President of Earth Island Institute," Berkeley, CA, November 11, 1983, in the author's papers.

3. Ibid.

4. Eric Brazil, "New Venture for David Brower," *San Francisco Examiner*, October 12, 1986.

5. "Highlights of David R. Brower's Activities 1990–91," in the author's papers. How he could have given Earth Day talks in eight states is not explained—possibly by satellite television.

6. Brower oral history 2, 71.

7. David Brower to Les Reid, December 23, 1982, in the author's papers.

8. *For Earth's Sake*, 436–43.

9. Roger B. Swain, *New York Times Book Review*, 1990, Brower papers carton 121, box 14.

10. Roderick Frazier Nash, "A Hero's Story, Poorly Told," *Sierra*, July–August 1990.

11. David Brower, "And There's the Bell," *Sierra*, November–December 1990.

12. Steve Chapple, telephone interview with the author, July 22, 2013.

13. Ibid. See chapter 12 for a condensed version of the "sermon."

14. Paul Winter, telephone interview with the author, March 15, 2013. Winter had performed at the first Fate of the Earth conference in New York in 1982.

15. Jim Bensman (Sierra Club member from Illinois) to David Brower, June 8, 1993, in author's papers.

16. Brower oral history 2, 158.

17. Ibid.

18. Douglas Bevington, *The Rebirth of Environmentalism: Grassroots Activism from the Spotted Owl to the Polar Bear* (Washington, DC: Island Press, 2009), 135.

19. This is examined in detail in Tom Turner, *Roadless Rules: The Struggle for the Last Wild Forests* (Washington, DC: Island Press, 2009).

20. Adam Werbach, interview with the author, December 11, 2012, San Francisco, CA.

21. Rich Ingebretsen, e-mail interview with the author, June 8, 2013.

22. Brower oral history 2, 181.

23. Ibid.

24. Bruce Hamilton, interview with the author, September 5, 2011, San Francisco, CA.

25. David Brower, "Why I Won't Vote for Clinton," *Los Angeles Times*, July 22, 1996.

26. Julie Nolen, "Sierra Club Announces Support for Gore Campaign," *Daily Texan*, July 25, 2000.

27. Jonathan Weisman, "Fiery Talk on Ecology Continues to Dog Gore, Environmental Policies Too Weak, Say Activists," *Baltimore Sun*, September 17, 2000.

28. David Brower, "On the Blue Planet: CPR for Business and the Planet," Blue Planet Award acceptance speech, Tokyo, October 30, 1998, Earth Island Institute reprint.

CHAPTER FIFTEEN

Epigraph: David Brower, *Let the Mountains Talk*, 176.

1. Brower oral history 2, 69.

2. Kenneth Brower, interview with the author, January 25, 2013, Berkeley, CA.

3. *Earth Island Journal*, Spring 2001, a collection of quotes by and about Brower in tribute to his career. The line was inspired by a favorite quote from Loren Eiseley: "We are compounded from dust and the light of a star."

4. "Friend of the Earth" was written by David Gancher, who had worked at FOE in the early 1970s, and his brother Carl. It was not a tribute to Brower per se, the chorus is "Anyone who is a friend of the earth, a friend of the earth, is a friend of mine."

5. Herbert Chao Gunther, interview with the author, November 9, 2012, San Francisco.

6. James Moorman, interview with the author, May 9, 2012, Washington, DC.

7. John McPhee, "Farewell to the Archdruid," *Sierra*, January–February 2001.

8. *Wildness Within*, 76–77.

9. Brower's books are listed in the appendix.

BIBLIOGRAPHY

ARCHIVES AND ORAL HISTORIES

Brower, David Ross. Correspondence, 1936–1969. Sierra Club Office of the Executive Director Records, BANC MSS 2002/230 c, Subseries 1.1. Bancroft Library, University of California, Berkeley.

———. *David R. Brower: Environmental Activist, Publicist, and Prophet*, an oral history conducted in 1974–1978 by Susan Schrepfer. Sierra Club History Series. Regional Oral History Office, Bancroft Library, University of California, Berkeley, 1980. https://archive.org/details/environmentalactoobrowrich.

———. David Ross Brower Papers, BANC MSS 79/9 c. Bancroft Library, University of California, Berkeley.

———. *David Ross Brower: Reflections on the Sierra Club, Friends of the Earth, and Earth Island Institute*, an oral history conducted in 1999 by Ann Lage, Sierra Club History Series. Regional Oral History Office, Bancroft Library, University of California, Berkeley, 2012. http://digitalassets.lib.berkeley.edu/roho/ucb/text/brower_david.pdf.

Farquhar, Francis. "Francis P. Farquhar, Sierra Club Mountaineer and Editor," an oral history conducted in 1974 by Ann and Ray Lage, Sierra Club History Committee, San Francisco. In *Sierra Club Reminiscences I, 1900s–1960s*, Sierra Club History Series, Regional Oral History Office, Bancroft Library, University of California, Berkeley, 1974, 2–60. http://digitalassets.lib.berkeley.edu/roho/ucb/text/sc_reminiscences1.pdf.

Frugé, August. *A Publisher's Career with the University of California Press, the Sierra Club, and the California Native Plant Society*, an oral history conducted in 1997–1998 by Suzanne B. Riess. Regional Oral History Office, Bancroft Library, University of California, Berkeley, 2001, http://content.cdlib.org/ark:/13030/kt596nb0t2/.

Litton, Martin. "Sierra Club Director and Uncompromising Preservationist, 1950s–1970s," an oral history conducted in 1980–1981 by Ann Lage, with an introduction by David Brower, in *Sierra Club Leaders: 1950s–1970s*. Sierra Club History

Series. Regional Oral History Office, Bancroft Library, University of California, Berkeley, 1982, 89–211. https://archive.org/details/sierraclubleaders01lagerich.

Robinson, Bestor. "Bestor Robinson: Thoughts on Conservation and the Sierra Club," an oral history conducted in 1974 by Susan R. Schrepfer, Sierra Club History Committee, San Francisco. In *Sierra Club Reminiscences I, 1900s–1960s,* Sierra Club History Series, Regional Oral History Office, Bancroft Library, University of California, Berkeley, 1974, 139–208. http://digitalassets.lib.berkeley.edu/roho/ucb/text/sc_reminiscences1.pdf.

Siri, William E. *Reflections on the Sierra Club, the Environment, and Mountaineering, 1950s–1970s,* an oral history conducted in 1979 by Ann Lage. Sierra Club History Series, Regional Oral History Office, Bancroft Library, University of California, Berkeley, 1979. https://archive.org/details/reflectsierraclub00siririch.

Sive, David. "David Sive: Pioneering Environmental Lawyer, Atlantic Chapter Leader, 1961–1982," an oral history conducted in 1982 by Ann Lage. In *Sierra Club Leaders II: 1960s–1970s,* Sierra Club History Series, Regional Oral History Office, Bancroft Library, University of California, Berkeley, 1982, 272–333, https://archive.org/details/sierraclubleaders02lagerich.

Turner, Tom. "Tom Turner: A Perspective on David Brower and the Sierra Club, 1968–1969," an oral history conducted in 1974 by Susan Schrepfer, Sierra Club History Committee, San Francisco. In *Sierra Club Nationwide II,* Sierra Club Oral History Project, Regional Oral History Office, Bancroft Library, University of California, Berkeley, 1984, 231–68, http://digitalassets.lib.berkeley.edu/roho/ucb/text/sierra_club_nationwide2.pdf.

BOOKS AND ARTICLES

Adams, Ansel. *Yosemite.* Boston: Little, Brown, 1995.

Adams, Ansel, with Mary Street Alinder. *Ansel Adams: An Autobiography.* Boston: Little, Brown, 1985.

Adams, Ansel, with Nancy Newhall. *This Is the American Earth.* San Francisco: Sierra Club, 1960.

Adams, John H., Patricia Adams, and George Black. *A Force for Nature: The Story of NRDC and the Fight to Save Our Planet.* San Francisco: Chronicle Books, 2010.

Alinder, Mary Street. *Ansel Adams: A Biography.* New York: Henry Holt, 1996.

Baker, Richard Allan. *Conservation Politics: The Senate Career of Clinton P. Anderson.* Albuquerque: University of New Mexico Press, 1982.

Beam, Alvin. "The Archdruid: Nature Militant," [Cleveland] *Plain Dealer,* August 1, 1971.

Bevington, Douglas. *The Rebirth of Environmentalism: Grassroots Activism from the Spotted Owl to the Polar Bear.* Washington, DC: Island Press, 2009.

Bhattacharjee, Riya. "Commission Landmarks Brower House." *Berkeley Daily Planet,* August 14–20, 2008.

Bradley Harold D., and David R. Brower. "Roads in the National Parks." *Sierra Club Bulletin* 34 (June 1949).

Brazil, Eric. "New Venture for David Brower." *San Francisco Examiner*, October 12, 1986.

Brower, David R. "And There's the Bell." *Sierra*, November–December 1990.

———. *For Earth's Sake: The Life and Times of David Brower.* Layton, UT: Gibbs Smith, 1990.

———, ed. *Going Light with Backpack or Burro.* San Francisco: Sierra Club, 1951.

———, ed. *Manual of Ski Mountaineering.* 2nd ed. Berkeley: University of California Press, 1946. (1st ed., 1942, compiled under the auspices of the National Ski Association of America)

———, ed. *The Meaning of Wilderness to Science.* San Francisco: Sierra Club, 1959.

———. "'Mission 65' Is Proposed by Reviewer of Park Service's New Brochure on Wilderness, Calls Attention to Changes in Publication from Earlier Version and Urges Wilderness Bill Support," *National Parks Magazine*, January–March 1958, 3.

———. "The Olympic National Park." *Sierra Club Bulletin* 32 (June 1947).

———. "Pursuit in the Alps." *Sierra Club Bulletin* 31, no. 7 (December 1946). http://content.sierraclub.org/brower/alps-ww2-bulletin.

———, compiler and ed. *Remount Blue: The Combat Story of the 3d Battalion, 86th Mountain Infantry.* Berkeley: Self-published, 1948; Uncommon Valor Press, 2014. Digitized manuscript at Hathi Trust Digital Library, http://hdl.handle .net/2027/mdp.39015027912396.

———. "San Gorgonio Auction, Going, Going, —." *Sierra Club Bulletin* 32 (January 1947).

———. "They Said It Couldn't Be Climbed." *Saturday Evening Post*, February 1940.

———, ed. *Tomorrow's Wilderness.* San Francisco: Sierra Club, 1963.

———. "Tripping High—1939," *Sierra Club Bulletin* 25, no. 1 (January 1940).

———. "Why I Won't Vote for Clinton." *Los Angeles Times*, July 22, 1996.

———, ed. *Wilderness: America's Living Heritage.* San Francisco: Sierra Club, 1961.

———, ed. *Wildlands in Our Civilization.* San Francisco, Sierra Club, 1964.

———. *Work in Progress.* Layton, UT: Gibbs Smith, 1991.

Brower, David R., with Steve Chapple. *Let the Mountains Talk, Let the Rivers Run: A Call to Those Who Would Save the Earth.* San Francisco: HarperCollins West, 1995.

Brower, David, and Richard Felter. "Surveying California's Ski Terrain." *Sierra Club Bulletin* 33 (March 1947).

Brower, David, with Lowell Sumner. "What Price Lumber?" and "A Bird's Eye View of the Threat to Olympic National Park" (aerial photographs). *Sierra Club Bulletin* 32 (June 1947).

Brower, Joseph. "Early Haste Street (The 20's and 30's)." Unpublished memoir, 2009.

Brower, Kenneth. "Climbing the Spiral Staircase." *California Magazine*, Spring 2013.

———. *The Wildness Within: Remembering David Brower.* Berkeley, CA: Heyday, 2012.

Brower, Kenneth, and William Curtsinger, photographer. *Wake of the Whale*. San Francisco: Friends of the Earth, 1980.

Carson, Donald W., and James W. Johnson. *Mo: The Life and Times of Morris K. Udall*. Tucson: University of Arizona Press, 2001.

Cavalieri, Liebe. "New Strains of Life or Death." *Not Man Apart*, January 1977.

"China Declares." *Stockholm Conference ECO*, June 10, 1972.

Coates, Peter. *The Trans-Alaska Pipeline Controversy: Technology, Conservation, and the Frontier*. Bethlehem, PA: Lehigh University Press, 1991.

Cohen, Michael P. *The History of the Sierra Club, 1892–1970*. San Francisco: Sierra Club Books, 1988.

Colorado River Storage Project Act of 1956, 43 U.S.C. §§ 620–620o (1956). Reprinted in *Not Man Apart*, January 1971, 10; available on U.S. Bureau of Reclamation website, www.usbr.gov/lc/region/g1000/pdfiles/crspuc.pdf.

Cosco, Jon M. *Echo Park: Struggle for Preservation*. Foreword by David Brower. Boulder, CO: Johnson Books, 1995.

Crowe, Harold E. "For the January Record, Announcement from the President." *Sierra Club Bulletin* 38, no. 1 (January 1953): 1.

Davies, Lawrence F. "Naturalists Get a Political Arm." *New York Times*, September 17, 1969.

De Voto, Bernard. "The West against Itself." *Sierra Club Bulletin* 32 (April 1951).

Dreier, Peter. *The 100 Greatest Americans of the 20th Century: A Social Justice Hall of Fame*. New York: Nation Books, 2012.

Ehrlich, Paul. *The Population Bomb*. New York: Ballantine Books, 1968.

Eiseley, Loren. *The Immense Journey*. New York: Random House, 1957.

Farquhar, Francis P. *History of the Sierra Nevada*. Berkeley: University of California Press, 1965.

Foreman, Dave. *Confessions of an Eco-Warrior*. New York: Harmony Books, 1991.

Fox, Stephen. *John Muir and His Legacy: The American Conservation Movement*. Boston: Little, Brown, 1981.

Fradken, Philip L. *A River No More: The Colorado River and the West*. Berkeley: University of California Press, 1968.

Frugé, August. *A Skeptic among Scholars*. Berkeley: University of California Press, 1993.

Gilliam, Ann. *Voices for the Earth: A Treasury of the Sierra Club Bulletin*. San Francisco: Sierra Club Books, 1979.

Gilliam, Harold. "Temblor at Friends of the Earth." *San Francisco Chronicle*, July 22, 1984.

Gore, Al. *Earth in the Balance: Ecology and the Human Spirit*. New York: Houghton Mifflin, 1992.

Graham, Kevin, and Gary Chandler. *Environmental Heroes: Success Stories of People at Work for the Earth*. Boulder, CO: Pruett, 1996.

"The Great NMA Name Debate." *Not Man Apart* 13, no. 11 (December 1983): 25.

Harper, John L. *Mineral King: Public Concern with Government Policy*. Arcata, CA: Pacifica, 1982.

Harrison, Steve. *Changing the World Is the Only Fit Work for a Grown Man: An Eyewitness Account of the Life and Times of Howard Luck Gossage, 1960s America's Most Innovative, Influential and Irreverent Advertising Genius.* London: Adworld Press, 2012.

Hart, John, and Nancy Kittle. *Legacy: Portraits of Fifty Bay Area Environmental Elders.* San Francisco: Sierra Club Books, 2006.

Harvey, Mark W. T. *A Symbol of Wilderness: Echo Park and the American Conservation Movement.* Seattle: University of Washington Press, 2000.

———. *Wilderness Forever: Howard Zahniser and the Path to the Wilderness Act.* Seattle: University of Washington Press, 2005.

———, ed. *The Wilderness Writings of Howard Zahniser.* Seattle: University of Washington Press, 2014.

Haycox, Steve. "Modern Alaska: Oil Discovery and Development in Alaska." *Alaska History and Cultural Studies*, Alaska Humanities Forum, n.d. www.akhistorycourse.org/articles/article.php?artID=140.

Hays, Samuel P. *Beauty, Health, and Permanence: Environmental Politics in the United States, 1955–1985.* New York: Cambridge University Press, 1993.

Heard, Jamie. "Friends of the Earth Give Environmental Interests an Activist Voice." *National Journal*, August 8, 1970.

Hessler, Peter. "John McPhee: The Art of Nonfiction no. 3." *Paris Review*, no. 192, Spring 2010.

Hogan, William. "Award to Sierra Club for Spectacular Publishing." *San Francisco Chronicle*, May 2, 1965.

Huth, Hans. "Yosemite: The Story of an Idea." *Sierra Club Bulletin* 33, no. 3 (March 1948).

Ingis, Stuart. "Friends of the Earth: Inside of a Public Interest Group." Senior thesis, Hamilton College, 1993.

Ingram, Jeff. *Hijacking a River.* Flagstaff, AZ: Vishnu Temple Press, 2003.

Jenkins, McKay. *The Last Ridge: The Epic Story of the U.S. Army's 10th Mountain Division and the Assault on Hitler's Europe.* New York: Random House, 2003.

Jones, Chris. *Climbing in North America.* Seattle: The Mountaineers, 1997.

Kane, Joe. "Best Friend of the Earth." *San Francisco Focus*, October 1984.

———. "The Friends of David Brower," *Outside*, December 1984.

Kelly, Amy S., ed. *The Second Biennial Conference on the Fate of the Earth: Peace on and with the Earth for All Its Children.* San Francisco: Earth Island Institute, 1985.

Kimball, H. Stewart. *History of the Sierra Club Outing Committee, 1901–1972.* San Francisco: Sierra Club Outing Committee, 1990.

Leonard, Richard M. "Olympic National Park Seriously Threatened." *Sierra Club Bulletin* 32 (June 1947).

———. "Report on San Gorgonio Hearing." *Sierra Club Bulletin* 32 (February 1947).

———. "Text of San Gorgonio Announcement." *Sierra Club Bulletin* 32 (July 1947).

Marshall, Robert B. "The Problems of the Wilderness." *Sierra Club Bulletin* 32 (April 1951).

Martin, Russell. *A Story That Stands like a Dam: Glen Canyon and the Struggle for the Soul of the West*. New York: Henry Holt, 1989.

Matthiessen, Peter. *Baikal: Sacred Sea of Siberia*. San Francisco: Sierra Club, 1992.

McCloskey, J. Michael. *In the Thick of It: My Life in the Sierra Club*. Washington, DC: Island Press, 2005.

McKibben, Bill, ed. *American Earth: Environmental Writing since Thoreau*. New York: Library of America, 2008.

———. *The Bill McKibben Reader: Pieces from an Active Life*. New York: Henry Holt, 2008.

McPhee, John. *Coming into the Country*. New York: Farrar, Straus and Giroux, 1977.

———. *Encounters with the Archdruid*. New York: Farrar, Straus and Giroux, 1971.

———. "Farewell to the Archdruid." *Sierra*, January–February 2001.

Merchant, Caroline. *The Columbia Guide to American Environmental History*. New York: Columbia University Press, 2013.

Miles, John C. *Guardians of the Parks: A History of the National Parks and Conservation Association*. New York: Taylor & Francis, 1995.

Muir, John. *My First Summer in the Sierra*. Boston: Houghton Mifflin; Cambridge: Riverside, 1911. http://vault.sierraclub.org/john_muir_exhibit/writings/my _first_summer_in_the_sierra/.

Murray, William. "The Porn Capital of America." *New York Times Magazine*, January 3, 1971.

Nash, Roderick, ed. *Grand Canyon of the Living Colorado*. San Francisco: Sierra Club, 1970.

———. "A Hero's Story, Poorly Told." *Sierra*, July–August 1990.

———. *Wilderness and the American Mind*. New Haven, CT: Yale University Press, 1967.

Nolen, Julie. "Sierra Club Announces Support for Gore Campaign." *Daily Texan*, July 25, 2000.

Pearson, Byron. *Still the River Runs Free: Congress, the Sierra Club, and the Fight to Save Grand Canyon*. Tucson: University of Arizona Press, 2002.

Perlman, David. "Sierra Club Challenge: Renewed Fight against Echo Park Dam Pledged." *San Francisco Chronicle*, January 4, 1955.

Pettitt, George A. *Berkeley: The Town and Gown of It*. Berkeley, CA: Howell-North Books, 1973.

"Polluted Rhetoric." *Wall Street Journal*, May 8, 1971.

Powell, James Lawrence. *Dead Pool: Lake Powell, Global Warming, and the Future of Water in the West*. Berkeley: University of California Press, 2008.

Reisner, Mark. *Cadillac Desert: The American West and Its Disappearing Water*. New York: Viking, 1986.

Richardson, Elmo. *Dams, Parks and Politics: Resources and Development in the Truman-Eisenhower Era*. Lexington: University Press of Kentucky, 1973.

Robinson, Bestor. "The First Ascent of Shiprock." *Sierra Club Bulletin* 25, no. 1 (February 1940).

Rome, Adam. *The Genius of Earth Day: How a 1970 Teach-In Unexpectedly Made the First Green Generation.* New York: Hill & Wang, 2013.

Roth, Dennis M. *The Wilderness Movement and the National Forests: 1964–1980.* Washington, DC: United States Department of Agriculture Forest Service, 1984.

"San Gorgonio: Another Viewpoint." *Sierra Club Bulletin* 32 (January 1947).

Schell, Jonathan. *The Fate of the Earth.* New York: Alfred Knopf, 1982.

Schrepfer, Susan. *The Fight to Save the Redwoods: A History of Environmental Reform, 1917–1978.* Madison, WI: University of Wisconsin Press, 1983.

———. "The Nuclear Crucible: Diablo Canyon and the Transformation of the Sierra Club, 1965–1985." *California History* 4, no. 2 (Summer 1992): 212–37.

Scott, Doug. *The Enduring Wilderness.* Golden, CO: Fulcrum, 2004.

Sellars, Richard West. *Preserving Nature in the National Parks: A History.* New Haven, CT: Yale University Press, 1997.

Senecah, Susan Louise. "The Environmental Discourse of David Brower: Using Advocacy Advertising to Save Grand Canyon." PhD diss., University of Minnesota, 1992.

Shabecoff, Philip. *A Fierce Green Fire: The American Environmental Movement.* Washington, DC: Island Press, 2003.

Sheff, David. "Occupation: Saving the Earth," *Interview,* February 1990.

Shelton, Peter. *Climb to Conquer: The Untold Story of World War II's 10th Mountain Division Ski Troops.* New York: Scribner, 2003.

Smith, Frank E. *The Politics of Conservation.* New York: Pantheon Books, 1966.

Snyder, Susan. *Beyond Words: Two Hundred Years of Illustrated Diaries.* Berkeley, CA: Heyday, 2011.

Stammer, Larry B. "Founder Quits Friends of the Earth, Says Situation 'Just Got Hopeless.'" *Los Angeles Times,* October 11, 1986.

Starr, Walter A., Jr. *Starr's Guide to the John Muir Trail.* San Francisco: Sierra Club, 1934.

Stegner, Wallace. *Beyond the Hundredth Meridian: John Wesley Powell and the Second Opening of the West.* Boston: Houghton Mifflin, 1954.

———, ed. *This Is Dinosaur: Echo Park Country and Its Magic Rivers.* New York: Alfred A. Knopf, 1955. (Revised edition, Lanham, MD: Roberts Rinehart, 1985.)

———. "Views of Brower Foes in Sierra Club." *Palo Alto Times,* February 11, 1969.

Strong, Douglas. *Dreamers and Defenders: American Conservationists.* Lincoln. University of Nebraska Press, 1988.

Taylor, Joseph E., III. *Pilgrims of the Vertical: Yosemite Rock Climbers and Nature at Risk.* Cambridge, MA: Harvard University Press, 2010.

Terkel, Studs. *Coming of Age: The Story of Our Century by Those Who Lived It.* New York: New Press, 1995.

Turner, Tom. *Friends of the Earth: The First Sixteen Years.* San Francisco: Earth Island Institute, 1986.

———. *Roadless Rules: The Struggle for the Last Wild Forests.* Washington, DC: Island Press, 2009.

————. *Sierra Club: One Hundred Years of Protecting Nature.* New York: Harry Abrams, 1991.

————. *Wild by Law: The Sierra Club Legal Defense Fund and the Places It Has Saved.* San Francisco: Sierra Club Books, 1990.

Udall, Morris K. *Too Funny to Be President.* New York: Henry Holt, 1988.

Udall, Stewart L. *The Quiet Crisis and the Next Generation.* Layton, UT: Gibbs Smith, 1988.

Voge, Hervey, ed. *A Climber's Guide to the High Sierra.* San Francisco: Sierra Club, 1954.

Watkins, T. H. *Righteous Pilgrim: The Life and Times of Harold L. Ickes, 1874–1952.* New York: Henry Holt, 1990.

Wayburn, Edgar, with Alison Allsup. *Your Land and Mine: Evolution of a Conservationist.* San Francisco: Sierra Club Books, 2004.

Weisman, Jonathan. "Fiery Talk on Ecology Continues to Dog Gore, Environmental Policies Too Weak, Say Activists," *Baltimore Sun*, September 17, 2000.

Wellock, Thomas. "The Battle for Bodega Bay: The Sierra Club and Nuclear Power, 1958–1964." *California History* 4, no. 2 (Summer 1992): 192–211.

"What's in a Name?" *Not Man Apart* 13, no. 9 (October 1983): 2.

Wilkinson, Charles. *Blood Struggle: The Rise of Modern Indian Nations.* New York: Norton, 2005.

————. *Fire on the Plateau: Conflict and Endurance in the American Southwest.* Washington, DC: Island Press, 1999.

Wingo, Hal. "Knight Errant to Nature's Rescue." *Life*, May 27, 1966.

Wirth, Conrad. *Parks, Politics, and the People.* Norman: University of Oklahoma Press, 1980.

Wolfe, Tom. *Radical Chic and Mau-Mauing the Flak Catchers.* New York: Farrar, Straus and Giroux, 1970.

Worster, Donald. *Rivers of Empire: Water, Aridity, and the Growth of the American West.* New York: Oxford University Press, 1985.

Zahniser, Howard. "How Much Wilderness Can We Afford to Lose?" *Sierra Club Bulletin* 32 (April 1951).

Zelko, Frank, *Make It a Green Peace! The Rise of Countercultural Environmentalism.* New York: Oxford University Press, 2013.

FILMS

Brower, David R., photographer and narrator. *Two Yosemites.* Produced by the Sierra Club, May 1955. https://archive.org/details/cubanc_000041?start=704.5.

Brower, David R., Nathan Clark, Charles Hessey, and John Handley, photography. *Wilderness Alps of Stehekin.* Narrated by David Brower; organ music by Clair Leonard. By special arrangement with Charles Eggert, produced by the Sierra Club, 1957. http://youtu.be/Jc_EOcj6ZYw.

Brower, David R., and Richard M. Leonard. *Sky-Land Trails of the Kings: A Story of Happy Days in the Kings Canyon National Park.* Titles by Torcom Bedayan. Produced by the Sierra Club, 1940. Distributed by the Bancroft Library, University of California, Berkeley, https://archive.org/details/cubanc_000178.

de Graaf, John. *For Earth's Sake: The Life and Times of David Brower.* Seattle: KCTS, 1989. Distributed by Bullfrog Films, www.bullfrogfilms.com.

Duane, Kelly. *Monumental: David Brower's Fight for Wild America.* First Run Features, 2004. Distributed by First Run Features, www.firstrunfeatures.com.

Gage, Beth, and George Gage. *Fire on the Mountain: The U.S. Army Tenth Mountain Division.* First Run Features, 1995. Distributed by First Run Features, www.firstrunfeatures.com.

Kitchell, Mark. *A Fierce Green Fire: The Battle for a Living Planet,* 2012. Distributed by First Run Features, www.firstrunfeatures.com.

INDEX

Page numbers in italics refer to photographs and captions.

Berry, Phillip: and the Bodega nuclear
plant fight, 109; and Brower's
leadership and activities, 132, 137, 138,
141, 151; and Diablo Canyon, 136, 137,
272n23; as High Trip staff, 34, *52*
Bingaman, Jeff, 212
Blackwelder, Brent, 176, 195
Blake, Arthur, 24
Blue Planet award, 237–38
Bodega Head nuclear plant proposal,
107–10, 128–29
Boeing SST, 175–78
Bohemian Club, 32
bowhead whaling, 186–87
BP (British Petroleum), 178
Bradley, Harold, 61
Bradley, Richard, 70
Brand, Stewart, 162
Brandborg, Stewart, 180
Brant, Irving, 31–32
Bridge Canyon dam proposal. *See* Grand
Canyon dam proposals
British Airways, 175
British Petroleum (BP), 178
Brooks, Paul, 106, 107, 137, 147
Browder, Joe, 194–95
Brower, Anne, 4, *36, 52,* 226, 231, 241; on
the "American Earth" exhibit, 94; and
the anti-Brower campaign of 1968–
1969, 144–45, 146, 147–48; on the
Dinosaur National Monument
campaign, 70; home and family life,
53–54, 67, 83; ill health and death of,
238, 242; limericks written at Sierra
Club board meetings, 139, 272n23; on
Matthews's assumption of the FOE
presidency, 201; meeting with and
marriage to Brower, 38–39, 42–44;
War Department editing job, 45
Brower, Barbara, 145, *240,* 242, 243
Brower, David
—BACKGROUND AND PERSONAL LIFE,
9–18; Army service, 38, 39–42, 44–49,
53, 191; childhood, 9–11; climbing and
mountaineering experience, 13, 14–18,
21–24, 27, 39–40, 57, 83; early
experiences in the Sierra, 12–17; early
paying jobs, 13–15, 23–27; education

and honorary degrees, 9, 10, 13, 276n25;
home and family life with Anne, 53–54,
67, 83; ill health and death, 241–42;
marriage and children, 38–39, 42–44,
53; personal finances, 27, 33, 132, 238;
photographs, 1920s–1940s, *8, 20, 28, 36;*
photographs, 1950s–1960s, *52, 64, 82,
92, 130, 154, 170;* photographs,
1970s–1990s, *104, 200, 220, 240;*
physical characteristics, 22; piano
playing and compositions, 228–29
—CORRESPONDENCE: with Adams, 94,
99–100, 131–32; with Anne, 42; with
his parents, 14, 23–24, 26–27, 41–42,
44; letters of qualification to the Army,
39–40; with McPhee, 159; while in the
Army, 40–41, 42, 44; with William O.
Douglas, 107, 269n3; from Yosemite,
23–24, 26–27; with Zahniser, 68–69
—ENVIRONMENTAL CAREER AND
ACTIVISM: activist skills, style, and
tactics, 62, 74, 75, 193–94; Army service
and, 48, 49; climate change awareness
and activism, 201, 206, 247; *Encounters
with the Archdruid* and its impact,
155–60; honors and awards, x, 191–92,
223–24, 237–38; lectures and travel,
192–93, 206–8, 223, 228, 237–38, 242;
legacy and influence, 2, 4, 150–51, 243–
48; positions on nuclear energy and
disarmament, 75, 109–10, 188, 191, 209;
public speaking and communication
abilities, 27, 33, 35, 121; talent-spotting
abilities, 108, 120–21, 188, 195; view of
conservation as a national security issue,
206–10; views on compromise, 59, 78,
127, 146, 224–25; wilderness
preservation ethic, 32, 34, 57–58, 60–62,
248. *See also* —AS PUBLISHER/EDITOR/
AUTHOR; Friends of the Earth *entries*;
Sierra Club *entries; specific issues and
campaigns*
—PERSONAL CHARACTERISTICS, x, 4, 5,
121, 231, 243–44, 247–48; fears, 15, 21,
79, 263n11; gregariousness, x, 46;
impatience with authority and process,
5, 41, 110, 131, 203, 204–5, 235; Ingram
on, 121; risk-taking, 17, 21, 27; shyness,

196–97, 261n23; willingness to confront, 15, 21, 58, 88, 89

—PERSONAL RELATIONSHIPS: with Adams, 17, 18, 25, 30, 131–32; friendships forged in the Sierra, 18; with Leonard, 18, 21, 30, 40, 41, 132, 144; with Litton, 74, 187, 188; with Matthews, 174, 201–4; with Sive, 114; with women in the workplace, 196–97; with Zahniser, 56, 68–69

—AS PUBLISHER/EDITOR/AUTHOR, 245, 246; Adams and, 25, 30, 100; autobiographies, 225–27, 247; during his Army service, 41; early articles and projects, 22, 25–27, 29–30, 31, 39, 40; editing and production skills, 54–55, 72–73; film productions, 35, 74–75, 194, 263n15; full list of publications, 253–58; the gender-neutral language issue, 210–11, 246; *National Parks Magazine* article opposing Mission 66, 87–88; op-ed pieces, 180, 236; photography skills, 25, 30; proposed Lake Baikal book, 223–24; publishing mentors, 25, 30, 39; *Sunset* job offer, 74; typeface fastidiousness, 123, 197–98, 277n38; University of California Press employment and publications, 38–39, 54–55, 65, 73, 143, 253. *See also* Friends of the Earth publications; newspaper advertising; Sierra Club publications; *specific campaigns and titles*

—VIEWS AND OPINIONS: on economic growth, 80, 192, 207; on environmental destruction in the Alps, 48; on federal agencies, 12, 32–33, 85, 86–88, 89, 105; on genetic engineering, 198; on nuclear energy and weapons, 75, 109–10, 188, 191, 209; on politics and politicians, 16, 29, 83, 208, 235–37, 242; on purity and practicality, 221; on responsibility for the 1966 IRS action against the Sierra Club, 124; on risk taking, 21; on the Sierra Club board's 1959 gag order, 88, 101; on Smokey the Bear, 123, 270n23; on spirituality, 241; on typography, 123, 197–98; on the value of High Trips, 34; on Wise Use, 48, 264n34. *See also*—

ENVIRONMENTAL CAREER AND ACTIVISM

Brower, Gayle, 148
Brower, Grace Barlow, 10, 11, 27
Brower, John, 79, 145
Brower, Joseph, 148, 243
Brower, Kenneth, 45, 52, 73, 181, 243; and the Blue Planet prize money, 238; on Brower as High Trip leader, 33; on his father's Army honors, 49; on his father's stroke, 241; on his parents' meeting, 39; and McPhee's profile, 156; on production of the first Exhibit Format title, 95; as writer and editor, 98, 139, 156, 203
Brower, Robert, 52, 73, 167, 241, 243
Brower, Ross, 9, 10, 12
Brower Center (Berkeley), 238, 243
Brower Fund, 238
"Brower miles," 34
Brower Youth Awards, 238, 243
Brown, Lester, 234
Bunyard, Peter, 184
Bureau of Reclamation: and Dinosaur National Monument dam proposals, 67–68, 70, 71. *See also* Colorado River Storage Project; Dinosaur National Monument dam proposals; Grand Canyon dam proposals
Burgess, Harry, 156
Bush, George W., 236–37, 242

Caen, Herb, 162
California Certified Organic Farmers (CCOF), 198
California condor captive breeding program, 193–94
California Public Utilities Commission, 108–9
California State Parks, 90
campaign finance laws, 165
Camp Carson, Colorado, 40–42
Camp Hale, Colorado, 42, 44
Camp Swift, Texas, 45
Candler, Sam, 154
CAP (Central Arizona Project), 119, 127, 128. *See also* Grand Canyon dam proposals

Carhart, Arthur, 68, 70
Carithers, Joseph, 88
Carlin, Alan, 122, 145, 270n21
Carson, Rachel, 101, 105–6
Carter, Jimmy, 235
Cathedral in the Desert, 78
Cavalieri, Liebe, 198
CCOF (California Certified Organic Farmers), 198
Cedar Grove, 31, 32
Celebrating the Earth book series, 196, 257
celebrities, conservation campaigns and, 173
Center for Law and Social Policy, 179
Central Arizona Project (CAP), 119, 127, 128. *See also* Grand Canyon dam proposals
Century Magazine, 15, 55
Chapman, Oscar, 68
Chapple, Steve, 227–28
Chatfield, David, 163, 203
China, at the Stockholm Conference on the Human Environment (1972), 184–85
Chlopak, Robert, 212, 214, 215
Christy, Cicely, 144
Citizens Committee on Natural Resources, 76
Citizens League Against the Sonic Boom, 176, 177
civil disobedience, 168. *See also* direct action
Clair Tappaan Lodge, 1; September 1968 board meeting at, 1–4, 137
Clark, Lewis, 223
Clark, Wilson, 195
climate change and climate activism, 176, 201, 206, 247
Climb to Conquer (Shelton), 37, 38, 48–49
Clinton, Bill, 235–36, 243
Clinton Forest Service, 231, 236
Clyde, Norman, 16, 17
CMC (Concerned Members for Conservation), 143, 145, 148
Coalition Against the SST, 176–78
coal power and development, 127–28, 247
Cohen, Michael, 62, 144
Cohen, Sheldon, 124, 125

Colby, William, 33
Collins, George, 117
Colorado River Compact, 69–70
Colorado River Storage Project, 69–70, 76–77, 78. *See also* Dinosaur National Monument dam proposals; Glen Canyon
Committee for an Active, Bold, Constructive Sierra Club (ABC), 143, 145–46
Concerned Members for Conservation (CMC), 143, 145, 148
Concorde, 176, 177
Condon, Chris, 166–67
The Condor Question: Captive or Forever Free (Phillips, Brower, and Nash, eds.), 194
conferences: Brower's love for, 209–10; Fate of the Earth conferences (1980s), 209–10, 224; Sierra Club's biennial Wilderness Conferences, 61, 62, 84, 86, 87, 209, 233, 256
Conservation Associates, 117
conservation campaigns. *See specific issues and organizations*
Conservation Law Foundation of New England, 114
conservation movement. *See* environmental movement; *specific issues and organizations*
Consolidated Edison: Storm King power plant proposal, 113–14
Corrupt Practices Act, 165
Cosco, Jon, 80
Cosmos Club (Washington, D.C.), 68, 71
Coudert Brothers, 173, 174, 204
Council of Conservationists, 76
Cragmont Rock, 17
Cramer, Helen, 23–24
Cramer, Sterling, 23–24
Cranston, Alan, 212, 215
Cry of the Condor (film), 194
Cumberland Island, Georgia, *154,* 156

dams and dam proposals, 190. *See also* Dinosaur National Monument dam proposals; Glen Canyon; Grand Canyon dam proposals; Hetch Hetchy

environmental impact reporting: NEPA's passage, 168, 179; trans-Alaska oil pipeline EIS, 180–81

Environmentalists against Gore, 236–37

environmental law and litigation: Endangered Species Act, 165, 224–25, 236; FOE as a litigator, 168, 169, 181–83; legal standing of citizens' groups, 113–14, 116, 269n2; legislation of the late 1960s and early 1970s, 165, 168, 179; litigation as a conservation tool, 107, 113–14, 129; Mineral King litigation, 116, 269n2; nonprofit lobbying restrictions, 2–3, 75–76, 124–25; northern spotted owl lawsuit, 224–25; Rainbow Bridge litigation, 181–83; trans-Alaska oil pipeline litigation, 161, 179–80, 225. *See also* Wilderness Act of 1964

environmental movement: broadening of issues of concern, 199, 246; energy industries and, 189, 246–47; mainstreaming of, 152; new organizations of the 1960s–1970s, 160–65, 168; and nonprofit lobbying restrictions, 75–76; significance of the Dinosaur National Monument campaign for, 80. *See also specific issues and organizations*

Environmental Policy Center, 195, 216

Environmental Project on Central America, 221

Environmental Protection Agency, 168, 212, 276n30

Environment Liaison Centre, 205

Equity Party, 235

Erickson, Brad, 221

Eryri: The Mountains of Longing (Lovins), 189

Escalante River, 77, 78, 181

Evans, Brock, 121, 234

Evans, Philip, 188–89

Exhibit Format books (Sierra Club), 2, *92*, 93, 94–102, 195–96; board concerns and criticisms, 98–101, 131, 138–40, 143, 147; effectiveness anad success of, 95–98, 101–2, 245, 246; full list, 253–54; genesis of, 94–96; similar Friends of

the Earth series, 195, 202–3, 256–57. *See also specific titles*

Exxon Valdez oil spill, 178

Fallon, George, 165

Farquhar, Francis, 29, 30, 55, 66

Farquhar, Sam, 38

Fate of the Earth conferences, 209–10, 224

Federal Power Commission (FPC), 113–14

Federation of American Scientists, 177

Felter, Richard, 59, 115

film, 2, 35, 74–75, 116, 263n15. *See also specific titles*

Fire on the Mountain (film), 264n31

Fischer, Michael, 224–25

Fletcher, Colin, 196, 276n33

FOE. *See* Friends of the Earth

Fontaine, Joe, 212

Ford, Daniel, 190

For Earth's Sake: The Life and Times of David Brower (Brower), 225–27, 247

Foreman, Dave, 232, 234

Forsyth, Al, 161, 223

Fort Benning, Georgia, 43–44

fossil fuels development, 247. *See also* coal; oil

Foundation for Deep Ecology, 227

FPC (Federal Power Commission), 113–14

France, FOE activities in, 174–75

Fraser, Charles, 156

Freeman, Mander, and Gossage, 145, 162, 163. *See also* Mander, Jerry; newspaper advertising

Freeman and Gossage, 122–23

"Friend of the Earth" (song), 243, 272n4

Friends of the Earth (FOE): achievements of, 246; Brower's leadership style, 162, 195–97, 246; Brower's retirement and later relations with, 201–6, 214, 215–16, 238; closure of the San Francisco office, 215–16, 221; coalition building by, 177–78, 246; controversy over the title *Not Man Apart,* 210–11, 246; current Bay Area office, 216–17; early board members and staff, 161, 163, 174, 275n20; and *Encounters with the Archdruid,* 160; financial difficulties, 202, 205, 212; founding and early years

Wilderness Act of 1964, 2, 165; background, 57, 62, 83–84; compromises made, 85, 89–90; Forest Service and Park Service opposition, 85; passage of, 89–90; wildlands inventory, 85–86

Wilderness Alps of Stehekin (film), 116

Wilderness and the American Mind (Nash), 62

Wilderness Conferences, 61, 62, 84, 86, 87, 156, 209, 233

"Wilderness Letter" (Stegner), 86

wilderness preservation: Brower's views on, 32, 34, 57–58, 60–62, 248; as the mission of the NPS, 32–33, 56; notable *Sierra Club Bulletin* articles of the 1940s and 1950s, 55–57; the roads vs. wilderness dilemma, 60–62, 86–88; Wise Use views, 48, 58, 264n34. *See also* Wilderness Act of 1964

Wilderness River Trail (film), 74

Wilderness Society, 61, 65, 96; Alderson at, 195; and the anti-SST campaign, 177; and the Dinosaur Natonal Monument dam proposals, 68, 76; and Kings Canyon National Park, 32; San Gorgonio Mountain ski resort opposition, 59; and the trans-Alaska pipeline fight, 180; and the Wilderness Act campaign, 83, 84. *See also* Marshall, Robert; Zahniser, Howard

Wilderness Society et al. v. Hickel, 180

Wildlife Management Institute, 84

Willson, Richard, 184, 190

Wilson, E. O., 234

Wilson, Woodrow, 67

Wingo, Hal, 119

Winnett, Thomas, 227

Winter, Paul, 228–29, 243

Wirth, Conrad, 86–87, 88

Wise Use, 48, 58, 264n34

Wolfe, Tom, 172

Women's Wear Daily, 172–73

Words of the Earth (Wright), 96

Work in Progress (Brower), 227

World War II, 37–49; Anne Brower's War Department job, 45; Brower's Army service, 38, 39–42, 43–49, 53; the Browers' meeting and marriage, 38–39, 42–44; impact on Brower, 49, 191; Japanese bombing and surrender, 48–49, 191; the Sierra Club and the Tenth Mountain Division, 37–38, 48; the Tenth Mountain Division sees action, 46–49, 264n31

Worldwatch Institute, 234

World Wildlife Fund, 186

Worster, Donald, 127–28

Wright, Cedric, 55, 96

Wrubel, Tom, 222

Yellowstone National Park, 56, 57

The Yodeler, 30, 144, 187, 192

Yosemite: Ansel Adams "This is the American Earth" exhibit, 93–94; the Browers' ashes scattered in, 242; Brower's early experiences at, 12–13, 21; Brower's job in, 23–27, *28;* Mount Hoffman funicular proposal, 24; Muir and, 15, 55; protected status for, 15, 31, 55, 56–57, 261n20; the Tioga Pass road, 60–61, 225; *Two Yosemites* film, 75; visitors and activities in the 1930s, 24–25

Yosemite Park & Curry Company, 23, 24–27

"Yosemite: The Story of an Idea" (Huth), 56–57

Your Environment, 184

Zahniser, Ed, 69

Zahniser, Howard, 62, 96, 152; Brower's working relationship with, 62, 68–69, 83, 84, 245; death of, 90; and the Dinosaur National Monument campaign, 68–69, 71, 75; "How Much Wilderness Can We Afford to Lose?," 55, 56; and the Wilderness Act campaign, 83, 84